MEDIA, FEMINISM, CULTURAL STUDIES

The Sacred Cinema of Andrei Tarkovsky
by Jeremy Mark Robinson

Liv Tyler
by Thomas A. Christie

The Cinema of Hayao Miyazaki
Jeremy Mark Robinson

Stepping Forward: Essays, Lectures and Interviews
by Wolfgang Iser

The Christmas Movie Book
by Thomas A. Christie

Wild Zones: Pornography, Art and Feminism
by Kelly Ives

'Cosmo Woman': The World of Women's Magazines
by Oliver Whitehorne

The Cinema of Richard Linklater
by Thomas A. Christie

Andrea Dworkin
by Jeremy Mark Robinson

Cixous, Irigaray, Kristeva: The Jouissance of French Feminism
by Kelly Ives

The Erotic Object: Sexuality in Sculpture From Prehistory to the Present Day
by Susan Quinnell

Women in Pop Music
by Helen Challis

Sex in Art: Pornography and Pleasure in Painting and Sculpture
by Cassidy Hughes

Erotic Art
by Cassidy Hughes

John Hughes
by Thomas A. Christie

FORTHCOMING BOOKS

THE TRILOGY OF LIFE MOVIES

THE TRILOGY
OF LIFE MOVIES

THE DECAMERON
THE CANTERBURY TALES
THE ARABIAN NIGHTS

PIER PAOLO PASOLINI

Jeremy Mark Robinson

CRESCENT MOON

Crescent Moon Publishing
P.O. Box 1312, Maidstone
Kent, ME14 5XU, Great Britain
www.crmoon.com

First published 2022.
© Jeremy Mark Robinson 2022.

Set in Times New Roman 9 on 12pt.
Designed by Radiance Graphics.

British Library Cataloguing in Publication data available for this title.

ISBN-13 9781861718532

CONTENTS

ACKNOWLEDGEMENTS

To the authors and publishers quoted.
To the copyright holders of the illustrations.

ABBREVIATIONS

ES   Enzo Siciliano, *Pier Paolo Pasolini*
PP   *Pasolini On Pasolini*

An ALBERTO GRIMALDI Production

"The DECAMERON"

Based on 'THE DECAMERON' by BOCCACCIO

A Film by PIER PAOLO PASOLINI

with
FRANCO CITTI · NINETTO DAVOLI · M. GABRIELLA FRANKEL · GERHARD EXEL
WOLFGANG HILLINGER · VINCENZO AMATO · JOVAN JOVANOVIC
GIUSEPPE ZIGAINA · Written and Directed by PIER PAOLO PASOLINI
Executive Producer FRANCO ROSSELLINI · A Co-Production PEA / Rome
Les Productions Artistes Associes / Paris – Artemis Film / Berlin · TECHNICOLOR United Artists

UN FILM di PIER PAOLO PASOLINI

IL DECAMERO

con FRANCO CITTI · NINETTO DAVOLI · VINCENZA AMATO · ANGE
GIUSEPPE ZIGAINA diretto da PIER PAOLO PASOLINI prodotto da FRANCO ROSSELLINI per la PEA presenta
TECHNICOLOR distribuzione United Artists Europa Inc.

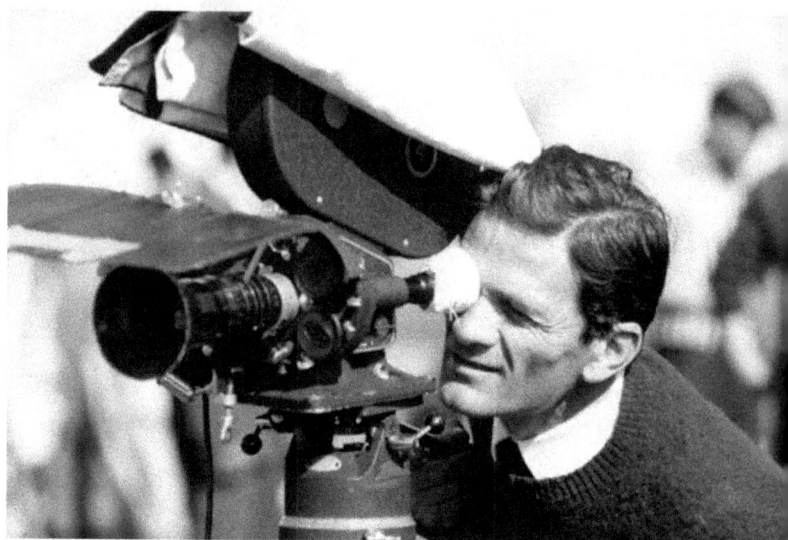

PART ONE
❖
PIER PAOLO PASOLINI

Oso alzare gli occhi
sulle cime secche degli alberi:
non vedo il Signore, ma il suo lume
che brilla sempre immenso.

(Daring to lift my eyes
towards the dry treetops,
I don't see God, but his light
is immensely shining.)

Pier Pasolo Pasolini, 'Mystery' (1945)[1]

1 Trans. A.P. Nicolai, C.U.N.Y., Brooklyn.

1

INTRODUCTION

This study focusses on the 'trilogy of life' films directed by Pier Paolo Pasolini, but it should be remembered that he was also a poet, novelist, essayist and playwright. Indeed, there is still a huge interest in Pasolini as a poet and writer, and there are as many articles and books about Pasolini's writing as there are about his cinema. (For many, it is Pasolini the poet who is more valuable culturally than Pasolini the filmmaker – which's a *very* unusual situation for a film director who's regarded as a major player in Italian and European cinema). But Pasolini is one of those filmmakers, like Orson Welles or Jean-Luc Godard, who is so enormously talented and full of life, they produced major works in a number of areas, not only in cinema.

There are plenty of approaches to the work of Pier Paolo Pasolini – I have focussed on the cinema, and Pasolini as a filmmaker. Another obvious approach is to consider the gay, queer and homosexual elements in Pasolini's work (as I have done so much of this elsewhere, I have left that approach aside).

I began my study of Pasolini's cinema (*Pasolini: Il Cinema di Poesia/ The Cinema of Poetry*) in the early 2000s, and added to it over the years, including in 2011, 2015 and 2017 (when it was nearly complete). It has been difficult to finish – partly because Pasolini is a fascinating filmmaker and artist, and there always seems to be more to say about his work. This book is an off-shoot of my main study of Pasolini, which has been rewritten and expanded numerous times, and has demanded an enormous amount of work to complete.

2

PIER PAOLO PASOLINI: BIOGRAPHY

LIFE.

Pier Paolo Pasolini was born on March 5, 1922, in Bologna, Italy. He died on November 2, 1975, in Ostia, Rome (he was buried in Casarsa, in his beloved Friuli). Italy, by the way, has a population of 57 million (in 1997), and a land mass of 116,341 square miles. The country was re-unified in 1870.

Pier Paolo Pasolini looks like one of the characters in his movies: the suave, chiselled, sometimes gaunt features (beautiful cheekbones!), the short, dark hair, and those beady eyes that don't miss a thing. Pasolini comes across in interviews (and in his films) as an aristocrat – an artist, surely, but debonair, sophisticated and clever. He appears highly educated, intellectual, outspoken, but also mischievous and very individual (people compared him to a priest – and of course he played priests in his movies).

He was a slim, rangy guy, 5' 6" (with those prominent cheekbones and piercing dark eyes, he was often compared to actor Jack Palance: the street kids of Roma called him *Giacche Palànce*).[2] He prided himself on keeping active into middle-age, and being able to

---

[2] Jack Palance in his red Alfa Romeo in *Contempt* (1963) is strikingly reminiscent of Pier Paolo Pasolini.

play soccer.[3]

Later, when he was a film director (starting late, at age 39), Pier Paolo Pasolini was certainly an intimidating presence, with a formidable reputation – like Cecil B. DeMille, Erich von Stroheim or Akira Kurosawa. Very confident, very smart, a great talker and interviewee, a leader on set, with no doubts from anyone about who was the primary creator and author.

It's clear, if you know anything about Pier Paolo Pasolini, that he was a very bright guy from an early age. He doesn't seem to have been afflicted by a lack of self-confidence – certainly with regard to his own work (which affects writers almost as a matter of course). Pasolini happily, in his twenties, takes on any big subject he likes.

Pasolini's background was bourgeois – ironic, considering how passionately he detested the bourgeoisie. His mother, Susanna Colussi, was born in 1891 and died in 1981. His father Carlo Alberto Pasolini (1892-1958) was a lieutenant in the Italian Army[4] (consequently, like many military families, they moved around a good deal). They married in 1921. For Pasolini, his father was 'overbearing, egoistic, egocentric, tyrannical and authoritarian' (PP, 13).

Pier Paolo Pasolini's relationship with his mother Susanna Colussi, and hers with him, has been described as unhealthily eroticized: according to Enzo Siciliano, Susanna invested far too much in her son emotionally: she gave Pasolini what she withheld from her husband Carlo Alberto (ES, 33). The theme of (hints of) incestuous relations between mothers and sons crop up in Pasolini's work (in *Mamma Roma*, obviously; some Pasolini movies, such as *Theorem*, play the incestuous fantasy literally and explicitly).

Pier Paolo Pasolini's brother Guidalberto (b. 1925) died in WWII (in 1945), when he was part of the Resistance. In the war, Pasolini was taken prisoner by

3 Tho', like everybody, he also disliked ageing (the bad teeth, the thinning hair), and dressed younger than his years.
4 His father had once prevented an assassination attempt on Benito Mussolini.

the Germans, but escaped back to Friuli. WWII looms very large over all of Pasolini's work.

Pier Paolo Pasolini described himself as a child as stubborn, capricious, naïve, credulous, easily enthusiastic, and also shy and awkward (ES, 45). As a boy, Pasolini lived in Bologna, Belluno, Conegliano, Casarsa della Delizia (in Friuli), Cremona, Scandiano and Reggio Emilia.[5] From 1950, Pasolini made Rome[6] his home (PP, 19).

Apart from literature[7] (he formed a literature club at high school), Pier Paolo Pasolini enjoyed football. As a child Pasolini studied music (piano and violin) briefly.

Pier Paolo Pasolini worked as a teacher in the late 1940s and early 1950s. Pasolini had a number of teaching posts, and the teacher in him never left – it was always a part of his movies, for instance (indeed, a character such as the talking bird in *The Hawks and the Sparrows* was entirely a teacher figure). And in interviews, Pasolini can't help coming across at times like an instructor.

That Pier Paolo Pasolini was a highly, passionately politicized artist is obvious: his passion for political issues runs throughout his movies and his poetry, his interviews, his essays, and pretty much everything he did or said publicly. Pasolini is always talking about Italian society, Italian culture, about Communism in Italy, about how Italy is becoming modernized, about Italy losing something when it embraces new technologies, etc. If there's an opportunity for ruminating on contemporary, Italian culture and society, Pasolini will take it.

Among the important friends in Pier Paolo Pasolini's life were:

Laura Betti (1927-2004).

---

5 As a youth, Pier Paolo Pasolini said he grew up in Bologna, Parma, Conigilano, Belluno, Sacile, Idria, Cremona and other towns in Northern Italy (PP, 11).
6 Pasolini bought a country retreat at Chai, near Viterbo, which Dante Ferretti had re-modelled for him.
7 Pasolini's early literary idols included Rimbaud, Dostoievsky, Tolstoy, Shakespeare, Novalis and Coleridge.

Alberto Moravia (1907-1990).[8]

Elsa Morante (1912-1985).

Franco Citti (1938-2016).

Sergio Citti (1933-2005).

Susanna Colussi, mother (1891-1981).

Ninetto Davoli (b. 1948).

One of Pier Paolo Pasolini's first lovers was the fourteen year-old Tonuti Spagnol, whom Pasolini had met in Versuta (where he and his mom Susanna Colussi had retreated during the bombings of WW2). Pasolini tended to go for much younger lovers (like Ninetto Davoli later, 26 years younger than him).

Way before Pier Paolo Pasolini began to write for movies and then to direct them, he was deeply into poetry, into writing, and into literature. Way back in the 1940s, when Pasolini was in his twenties (and during WWII), he was already publishing poetry, writing essays,[9] reviews, and memorials (such as for his brother Guido who died in the war at the hands of Communists).

Another of Pier Paolo Pasolini's passions, long before he became enamoured of cinema, was Friuli: Friuli the place, the landscape, and the local people (and, later, the Friulian dialect). Pasolini moved away from Bologna (which he associated with his father) to Friuli.

Pier Paolo Pasolini had grown up around Casarsa, near Pordenone, in the Friuli-Venezia Giulia region, right up in the Northern corner of Italy. Yugoslavia is not far off to the East, with the Alps to the North; Venice isn't too far away (the Venice Film Festival looms large in Pasolinu's career). Friuli is a region that prides itself on being somewhat distanced from Italy. Friuli is known for its peasant culture, which Pasolini revered (tho' it has been disappearing for many decades).

Pier Paolo Pasolini was thus a kid from the sticks, not a city kid at all, not the sophisticated urbanite of Italy's great cities (Milan, Bologna,[10] Venice, Rome, nor

8 The *dolce vita* set included Federico Fellini, Pier Paolo Pasolini, Luchino Visconti, Alberto Moravia *et al.*

9 In his essays and articles for magazines over the years Pier Paolo Pasolini discussed Giuseppe Ungaretti, Umberto Saba, and Gianna Manzaini.

10 Tho' he was born in Bologna.

the Southern country that he later loved – Napoli, Sicily). Rather, it was a world of small towns and villages and the countryside, bicycle rides, flirting with girls, reading books, writing poetry in dialect ('peace and quiet, girls, mental concentration, fields, idleness, drink', Pasolini noted in a letter of 1940, when he was 18).

But it was also the Friulian dialect (*friulano*) that Pier Paolo Pasolini fell in love with, and Friulian culture. Pasolini was a keen connoisseur of dialects; he composed works in dialect (such as his early poetry), and also employed dialects in his cinema.

Pier Paolo Pasolini was a devotee of language like many modern poets and writers. One thinks of Rainer Maria Rilke, André Gide, Lawrence Durrell, Henry Miller, Alain Robbe-Grillet, Samuel Beckett, etc – writers for whom language and communication itself was a mysterious and utterly compelling force in their lives. Language, as French feminist Hélène Cixous remarked, is the key. For Cixous (who is loved and loathed by feminists nearly as energetically as Andrea Dworkin or Princess Diana), writing is absolutely crucial, and central. Writing is oxygen to Cixous, she must write to live. Cixous asserted in "Difficult Joys" that

> writing, writing poetically, treating language as one of the most important things in the world, today sounds mad. Yet for human beings it is the first most important thing.[11]

Pier Paolo Pasolini was one of those filmmakers who, had he been unable to continue to make movies, would've been quite happy writing (Woody Allen and Ingmar Bergman come to mind).[12] Jean-Luc Godard also took that view: for him, filmmaking and writing were part of the same thing anyway. Writing was 'already a

11 "Difficult Joys", in H. Wilcox, 1990, 23.
12 There are, of course, some famous film directors who found writing very difficult to do – Steven Spielberg, David Lean, Stanley Kubrick – filmmakers who couldn't write their own scripts, who had to have collaborators and writers. But of course most directors *do not* write their own scripts at all.

way of making films,' Godard said in 1962 of his time as a film critic, 'for the difference between writing and directing is quantative not qualitative'.[13] Godard often said he wouldn't stop creating if cinema died: he would move into TV, and if that disappeared, he would move into writing again (ibid., 171).

Other areas which Pasolini might've explored had he lived longer would include opera – several of his contemporaries took up directing live opera performances (Luchino Visconti, Ken Russell, Andrei Tarkovsky, Robert Altman – and even Federico Fellini, who disliked opera, came around to it. Fellini claimed that he only liked Nino Rota's music, and didn't like anything else. In the 1980s, however, Fellini decided he liked opera after all).[14]

Another area was pop promos – maybe too capitalist for Pier Paolo Pasolini, but the right pop act and the right deal might've attracted Pasolini to direct some pop videos. (One of the appeals was that they could be done in a single day, often had a decent budget, and were guaranteed an audience).

DVD, Blu-ray and home releases of movies seem an ideal platform for Pier Paolo Pasolini to talk about his works. Some of the most valuable contributions that film directors make are to audio commentaries about their movies (such as Ken Russell, Oliver Stone, Werner Herzog, Mamoru Oshii and Stephen Sommers). Pasolini relating the stories of making *The Gospel According To Matthew* and *The Arabian Nights* would be a treat. (However, some film directors pointedly refuse to talk in audio commentaries about their films, such as Steven Spielberg and Woody Allen. For them, the works speak for themselves).

13 *Godard On Godard*, 171.
14 *And the Ship Sails On* (1983) featured an opera star along with other singers, and many other references to opera, and Fellini planned a documentary about opera in 1987 (there were invitations to direct operas, such as at Covent Garden and in Milan).

PASOLINI AND HIS FATHER

The revolt against the Father, against his own father Carlo Alberto Pasolini, was a violent one for Pier Paolo Pasolini, and it coloured much of his work. 'The public aspect of Pasolini's poetry will take the form of a struggle against all repressive and authoritarian conventions', remarked Enzo Siciliano (ES, 43), and it was his father that inaugurated that rebellion. (It was the loss/ rejection of the father, Siciliano reckoned, that was fatal for Pasolini, a loss and a pain that never left him).

Pier Paolo Pasolini associated his father and the father image with 'all the symbols of authority and order, of fascism, of the bourgeoisie'.[15] Pasolini defined his father as 'a nationalist and a fascist', and con-ventional (PP, 14).

According to his biographer, Pier Paolo Pasolini's father Carlo Alberto was stricken by his son's gay lifestyle:

> he was overwhelmed by the drama of Pier Paolo, by the "scandal," and accepted it with grief. It brought him to a kind of insanity. He drank more and more, and at night cried out that his wife did not love him. (ES, 40)

As Pier Paolo Pasolini put it, he had placed himself 'in a relationship of rivalry and hatred towards my father', which made it easier for him to examine that relationship, compared to that with his mother, which was more latent (PP, 119). For Pasolini, 'everything ideological, voluntary, active and practical in my actions as a writer depends on my struggle with my father' (ibid., 120). Pasolini was thus conscious of using his deep-seated feelings as engines for his creative work (in the way that André Gide said that everything could be material or fuel for a writer. Famously, Gide remarked that as he was living his life he was also considering how it could be exploited in his writing).

According to Sam Rohdie, Pier Paolo Pasolini

15 Quoted in J. Duflot, 22.

associated Northern Italia and Bologna with his father, with the bourgeoisie, with fascism, with technology, with capitalism, and with the Law of the Father. That was not the Italy that Pasolini enshrined, but the one he wanted to move away from. Pasolini's Italy was of the South, of Rome and Napoli and Calabria: the South was alive, it was peasants, it was a link to the past, it was non-technological, it was not capitalist (13). However, Bologna has long been a stronghold for the Italian Communist Party (it has held the city since 1945).

That Pier Paolo Pasolini's cinema exhibits a major father complex is clear to all. The ambiguous, anxious attitude towards fathers, father figures, the Sins of the Fathers, and the older generation, is everywhere. In *Pigsty,* the only words spoken in the 15th century tale are when the chief protagonist (Pierre Clementi) announces just as he's about to die: 'I killed my father, I ate the flesh of humans, I shivered with joy' (or something similar). Killing the father – the atmosphere of *Oedipus Rex* and *Theorem* was still in the air, perhaps (these movies – *Pigsty, Theorem, Medea* and *Oedipus Rex* are perhaps Pasolini's most concentrated attacks on the figure of the father).

POETRY AND LITERATURE

Pier Paolo Pasolini was writing poetry and articles from an early age: it's as if, as with poets such as Emily Dickinson or William Shakespeare, he had always written poetry. It was one of the fundamental creative activities in his life. He became disillusioned with politics, with the cultural life in contemporary Italy, with intellectuals, with the passing of the old world (as he saw it – but it had been decaying for 100s of years), yet his poetry remained central to his existence.

Pier Paolo Pasolini's poetry is in free verse – long,

rambling lines and stanzas in the modernist tradition (recalling poets such as Walt Whitman and D.H. Lawrence, who preferred to write in lengthy, loose lines).

Pier Paolo Pasolini's first artistic efforts in the public arena included publishing a literary magazine (in 1941), and his own poems (*Versi a Casarsa*, 1941). He was editor of *Il Setaccio* (*The Sieve*).

By the late 1940s, Pasolini was writing and publishing regularly: *The Diaries*; *Quaderni Rossi*; the play *Il Cappellano*; and *The Cries*, a poetry book. Pasolini's novels (still in print) include *Ragazzi de Vita* (1955)[16] and *Una Vita Violenta* (1959) (both of which have been filmed).

Pier Paolo Pasolini's novel *Ragazzi di Vita* was 'a succès de scandale, drawing positive reviews, heated sales, hostile editorials, and even legal action for obscenity', remarked Shawn Levy in *Dolce Vita Confidential* (190). *Boys of Life* had a run-in in 1956 with the public prosecution office for being 'obscene'. Among the defenders of *Ragazzi di Vita* were Giuseppe Ungaretti, Carlo Bo, Pietro Bianchi and Livio Garzanti.

Reviewing *Una Vita Violenta*, Mario Montanana (a Communist senator), wondered that

> Pasolini does not like poor people, that he despises in general the inhabitants of the Roman shanty-towns, and despises our party even more. The hero, Tommasino, is in reality a juvenile delinquent of the worst kind: thief, robber, pederast.

Enzo Siciliano called Pier Paolo Pasolini a

> frantically manneristic writer – and of a baroque mannerism, a lover of asymmetry, of tormented versifications of topical matter, who made of his style a shining example of the forbidden, who delighted in a "poetics of regression" in order to break the gilded trappings of twentieth-century academicism. (ES, 398)

---

16 Andrea Di Marco sued Pier Paolo Pasolini for libel in relation to *Ragazzi di Vita* in April, 1962.

An unfinished novel (of 1948), *Amado Mio*, contained autobiographical resonances, coalescing around its central character, Desiderio. In *Amado Mio*, Pasolini secreted 'the meaning of his own obsession,' according to Enzo Sciliano: 'to become father to his boy, so that the latter would mirror, by returning his embrace, all his unsatisfied longings for a son' (114).

The early work, *Amado Mio*, contains a pæan to Rita Hayworth in *Gilda*, as it plays to a cinema of rowdy, young Italians, by moonlight, in the open-air, with the boisterous crowd getting turned on. As the narrator of *Amado Mio* tells it,

> before the image of Gilda something wondrously shared enveloped all the spectators... Rita Hayworth with her huge body, her smile, her breasts of a sister and a prostitute – equivocal and angelic – stupid and mysterious with that nearsighted gaze of hers, cold and tender to the point of languor...

Pasolini was a passionate advocate of Friuli – he was a member of the Friulian Language Academy, the Association for the Autonomy of Friuli, and contributed to the magazine *Stroligùt di cà da l'aga*. Pasolini learnt how to speak Friulian as an adult – it wasn't part of his upbringing: it became part of his poetry – 'I learnt it as a sort of mystic act of love' (PP, 15).

Among Pier Paolo Pasolini's early influences were William Shakespeare (*Macbeth*), whom he discovered at 14,[17] and of course Italy's two giant poets, Francesco Petrarch and Dante Alighieri. Other favourites were André Gide (such as his novel *The Immoralist*[18]), Barbey d'Aurevilly, Niccolò Tommaseo, Johann Wolfgang von

---

17 With *Macbeth* Pasolini entered the world of books, visiting the stalls in the Portici della Morte in Bologna to buy used books.

18 A novel tailor-made for Pasolini, evoking a spiritual journey from Northern Europe to the South, the breakdown of a marriage, the discovery of homosexual encounters in North Africa, and the development of an Existential, outsider persona. Classically, André Gide begins his tale with the anti-hero's father's death, a very Pasolinian device (instantly adding a welter of œdipal associations and an evocation of the Law of the Father). Pasolini didn't need to adapt *The Immoralist* – he lived it (tho' it would have been fascinating to see Pasolini take on Gide).

Goethe, Lautréamont and *Les Chants de Maldoror* (inevitably), Arthur Schopenhauer (his pithy, proto-Existential philosophy is a favourite with many European intellectuals), Villiers de l'Isle-Adam, and Daniell Bartoli (*Uomo al punto*).

As a youth, Pier Paolo Pasolini said he had consumed adventure stories, like many other children, but in his mid-teens discovered Fyodor Dostoievsky, William Shakespeare, Arthur Rimbaud, and authors who were somewhat regarded as rebellious, standing outside of the fascist society of Italy (PP, 17).

There are so many references to the work of Dante Alighieri in Pier Paolo Pasolini's output it's a wonder that he didn't produce a feature film of the *Divina Commedia* (or at least a TV documentary). However, there *are* elements of *The Divine Comedy* in *The Decameron*, in the finale of *The Canterbury Tales,* with its devils, the traveller and his guide (in *The Hawks and the Sparrows* and the 'trilogy of life' films), and of course the *tableaux* from Renaissance art in *La Ricotta* and *The Gospel According To Matthew*.

The significance of Pier Paolo Pasolini's works are often interpreted as a group, and in relation to one another, rather than taken as single pieces to be seen in isolation. Thus, *Accattone* is always related to Pasolini's novels of the rough Roman youth, and the Marxism in *The Gospel According To Matthew* and *Oedipus Rex* is related to Pasolini's political statements. (This interconnectedness was of course encouraged by the maestro himself).

'THE BOURGEOISIE ARE ALWAYS WRONG': MARXISM AND ANTI-BOURGEOIS POLITICS

> I don't think you can make an unpolitical movie.
> Your politics are going to show by permission or
> omission, so that the best you can do is to try and
> focus on them in some way in your movie, organise
> it so that it doesn't happen totally by accident.

Warren Beatty

Only Jean-Luc Godard among comparable filmmakers
has a deeper and more visceral loathing of the
bourgeoisie than Pier Paolo Pasolini. Oh, how Pasolini
hated everything bourgeois! – 'I nourish a visceral,
deep, irreducible hatred for the bourgeoisie, its self-
importance, its vulgarity; it is an ancient hatred, or if
you like, a religious one', Pasolini asserted.[19]

As with Jean-Luc Godard, an ingredient of Pier
Paolo Pasolini's politics is not so much Marxism as
anti-bourgeoisism, anti-capitalism, and anti-
consumerism. It is – again like Godard – partly *against
things* for the sake of it: *against* the bourgeoisie,
against consumerism.[20] And it's a politics that is *for*
revolution, *for* change, for the sake of it, to turn things
upside-down, and to oppose whatever's on offer. (But
how would Pasolini stem the tide of consumerism and
the social decline of his beloved Italy? He doesn't say –
because he can't say – because no one can say. Pasolini
offers nothing to replace contemporary, capitalist
society. His utoptian project is about rewriting or
enshrining the past, or the 'Third World').

Pasolini acknowledged that Marxism was a system
imposed from the top down by an *élite*, like other
political/ philosophical systems. But it gave the
illusion that an individual mattered, or had an effect on
the system. Andrew Sarris reckoned that 'Italian cinema
as a whole – is primarily a Marxist cinema with a deep
sense of doubt' (D. Georgakas, 236).

19 Quoted in J. Duflot, 22.
20 However, Pasolini was happy to drive flashy sports cars, one of the
loudest symbols of consumer-capitalism.

The aim of shocking the bourgeoisie (that childish goal of too many leftist/ Marxist artists), may derive in part from the attempt at reaching a realm where the bourgeoisie and their ideals do not go. That is, to go beyond the limits of what is accepted by bourgeois society, into the crude, the ultra-violent, the bestial.

It's typical that Pier Paolo Pasolini would side with the policemen in the political unrest of 1968, rather than with the student protesters. Why? Because Pasolini thought the students were bourgeois, and the cops were true working class people.

However, that part of the Pasolini Legend isn't the whole story: Pasolini's famous views about the police (expressed in a poem) were modified by his sceptical views of the police as enforcers of the law in Italy, and his sympathies with the political aspects of the counter-culture (Pasolini, the subject of many run-ins with the Italian authorities, held a sceptical view of the *carabineri*).[21] Subsequently, Pasolini's verses were employed by right-leaning groups and commentators., and twisted around, missing the irony and paradox that Pasolini was exploring.

On his Marxism, Pier Paolo Pasolini reminded Oswald Stack that in Italy everybody is a Marxist, and everybody is a Catholic (PP, 22). 'Pasolini's Marxist critique is sadly too narrow in its view of bourgeois neurosis as a symptom of class decadence under advanced capitalism', according to John Orr in *Contemporary Cinema* (1998, 8).

It's ironic for a left-wing and Marxist radical author like Pier Paolo Pasolini that often for his material he took on very traditional, conservative and right-wing texts and authors: the *Bible*, Ancient Greek mythology, Islamic stories, Geoffrey Chaucer and Giovanni Boccaccio. In fact, historical cinema tends to be conservative at the least, and often right-wing, too (this conservatism doesn't only reflect the markets of commercial cinema).

---

21 See an interesting article by Luca Peretti on Pasolini and Communism: "Remembering Pier Paolo Pasolini" (jacobinmag.com).

The decline of the ideological investment in Communism, socialism and Marxism in the 1970s, following the height of the idealism and activism of the late 1960s, was something that many intellectuals and artists had to face. Hayao Miyazaki, Jean-Luc Godard, Milos Forman, and many Eastern European filmmakers, as well as Pier Paolo Pasolini, confronted the fact that in some societies Communism and Marxism were not only not working, they were becoming as damaging as the mythologies and ideologies they opposed to, or were created in opposition to (such as Western capitalism).

The dream was over. Between the heady days of 1968 (manning the barricades, the student/ youth riots, the anti-Vietnam War protests, the civil rights marches), and the mid-1970s, it was a rapid decline.

'Pasolini's interventions were extreme and unflagging, pleasing to practically nobody across the political spectrum, and, uniquely, were intricately inscribed with the fact of his sexual difference', noted Gary Indiana (14).[22] True – left-wingers and Communists found just as much to get irritated by in Pasolini's pronouncements in the political arena as right-wingers and conservatives. (And Pasolini likely secretly enjoyed the fact that his views wound up leftists as well as rightists).

SOUTHERN ITALY

Pier Paolo Pasolini had a very idealized view of Southern Italy, or rural Italy, or pre-industrial Italy, of peasant Italy, of an Italy before television, cars and two World Wars. It was an Italy that never really existed, but which he wanted to exist. It was an Italy that he loved – the Italy of regions, and regional dialects and languages. It was if Pasolini saw himself as born out of his time –

22 For Indiana, Pier Paolo Pasolini was the wrong sort of gay artist – a Marxist who criticized the political system who wasn't like Franco Zeffirelli, a raging queen (and thus harmless).

he might've been happier in the mediæval era, say, or the Renaissance (I think Pasolini would've got along just fine in the Ancient Roman period – and so would Federico Fellini and Walerian Borowczyk!).

A Northern Italian (he was born in Bologna), Pier Paolo Pasolini revered the South, of Naples, of Calabria. Of course he spent most of his adult life in the Eternal City; yet he always maintained the links to the countryside (keeping a Summer house, for instance).

It was no surprise that Pasolini opted to stage his most well-known movie, *The Gospel According To Matthew*, in Southern Italy, using many non-actors who were chosen by the maestro and his casting team for their interesting faces (as with Federico Fellini).

Accattone had inaugurated numerous approaches to cinema which Pier Paolo Pasolini would pursue throughout his career: a cast of unknowns and non-actors, low budgets, filming on location (and adapting existing settings), and employing recorded music, often classical (rather than specially composed scores).

Choosing unknown performers was about achieving some kind of reality, or a non-fictionalized, non-embellished reality: Pier Paolo Pasolini said in 1973:

> I pick actors whose sheer physical presence suffices to convey this sense of reality. I do not pick them at random but in order to offer examples of reality.[23]

Pasolini wanted the real thing, without making it pretty or cute. I can't think of another filmmaker who so loved extras, or who gave more screen time in terms of close-ups to extras – except perhaps Federico Fellini. And Pier Paolo Pasolini was especially fond of anybody who looked odd – terrible teeth, warts on lips, wall eyes, scars, and faces wrinkled by the Southern Italian sunshine.

The casting directors on Pier Paolo Pasolini's movies deserve all the credit coming their way for gathering such an extraordinary collection of actors and

---

23 P. Pasolini, *The Guardian*, Aug 13, 1973.

amateurs (such as Alberto di Stefanis, who cast *The Decameron*). Using non-actors is part of the Neo-realist movie tradition – such as the Roberto Rossellini film *Francesco* (1950), co-written by Fellini. Movies like *Francesco* showed Pasolini how you could adapt a religious subject for the cinema without stars or professional actors.

Pasolini was happy to direct non-professional actors thru scenes, beat-by-beat, in the Italian cinema manner (by coaxing them from beside the *macchina fotografica*). It worked wonders – Enrique Irazoqui as Jesus in *The Gospel According To Matthew*, for instance. But sometimes it failed: Giuseppe Gentile might possess the sportsman's physique to look like the mythical hero Jason in *Medea*, but he sure can't act.

For Sam Rohdie, the extras in the 'trilogy of life' movies didn't need to act, they just needed to 'be', to appear on camera – their appearance was their characterization and their performance. (It's a version of Pasolini's notion of 'realism' – you simply show reality, and show people as people, and the process of cinema does the rest).

'A SEARCH FOR MAGIC': TRAVELS WITH PASOLINI

Pier Paolo Pasolini's is a cinema of journeys and voyages, eternally restless – films as a continuous search for locations (and as what we could term location scouting movies, Pasolini's are some of the finest). But also a search for the sacred, 'a search for magic', a search for mythology. And it's a quest for a place where those things still hold sway. A search for a time, too, an era of magic and the poetic.

Certainly the exotic is a big draw in Pier Paolo Pasolini's cinema, and for the director too. He did not shoot in North America (tho' he enjoyed visiting it), but took his productions to North Africa, the Middle East, India and Nepal (as well as the wildly alien, end-of-the-line wildernesses of dear, old England!).

Always Pier Paolo Pasolini goes South and East – to Africa, the Middle East, India (and Southern Italy), rather than North, to Germany, Scandinavia, Russia... Some have associated the North in Pasolini's æsthetics to his father, and the Law of the Father (i.e., Northern Italy, Bologna, etc).[24] The journey East and South, when taken from Europe, is towards the sun, to heat, to the desert, to the exotic, to the ancient world, to Islam, to old religions, to old mythologies.

As well as India, Pier Paolo Pasolini also visited Africa several times: Kenya in Jan, 1961 and Jan, 1962 (as well as Sudan); Ghana, Guinea and Nigeria in 1963; Africa again in 1970 (for the *Oresteia* film); and Israel and Jordan in 1963 (when he was planning to film *The Gospel According To Matthew* in the Holy Land).

When Pier Paolo Pasolini and his writer chums Alberto Moravia and Elsa Morante visited India in December, 1960, it wasn't for a particular film or book project (tho' a book, *The Scent of India,* duly appeared, as well as a short documentary later, *Notes For a Film In India*, 1969).

PASOLINI THE POET

Was Pier Paolo Pasolini a believer or a non-believer? In what? – in God? Love? Death? Art? Life? Terms like belief, or atheism, or agnosticism, or non-belief, just don't do justice to Pasolini's multi-faceted personality and works. The man and his art were much more complicated than that (also, there are many levels of 'belief', and ways of 'believing').

---

24 Pasolini's beloved Friuli was in the North, of course, but not grouped with the North for Pasolini – it was beyond-the-North.

Pier Paolo Pasolini was a mass of contradictions only to the extent that many (most?) humans are contradictory. Can a Marxist believe in God? What is the relation between Marxism and materialism to religion and the spirit? These and many other questions have been discussed in relation to Pasolini. As he put it in 1966:

> If you know that I am an unbeliever, then you know me better than I do myself. I may be an unbeliever, but I am an unbeliever who has a nostalgia for a belief.

You only have to look at a couple of movies directed by Pier Paolo Pasolini to see there is a wealth of romance, nostalgia, spirituality, desire and yearning. What was Pasolini's 'religion'? What did he 'believe in'?

Poetry.

If there *are* contradictions, that's because Pier Paolo Pasolini was certainly a contradictory personality. Like Orson Welles, Rainer Fassbinder, Jean-Luc Godard and Andrei Tarkovsky (among filmmakers), Pasolini was a complex person – no single view, no one opinion, no philosophy on its own can sum him up, or condense his views into a coherent whole. (Indeed, every single biographical sketch online, in documentaries, books and newspapers always stresses the seemingly contradictory elements of the Pasolini Legend: religion plus Marxism plus homosexuality plus radical cinema, etc etc etc etc etc).

If there's one single word I would use for Pier Paolo Pasolini, it is poetry. He poeticizes life, poeticizes the world and everything in it. 'To make films is to be a poet', he asserted (PP, 154). 'Pasolini's defence of poetry was a political act of complete committment' (S. Rohdie, 89). Poetry and the poet's life sums up many aspects of Pasolini's personality, and also his approach to art, and to cinema, but it doesn't crystallize everything. With Pasolini, you are always aware of depths and levels below the surface. He may talk a lot in interviews, he may appear forthcoming and affable on camera in interviews (or as the interviewer in his own movies, when he won't shut up or let the interviewee get a word in edgeways), but there are whole oceans of things you don't know about, whole continents where acts, thoughts, ideas and gestures are hidden, or will never be found out, and as everybody who knew Pasolini personally eventually dies as the years pass, we won't know.

With Pier Paolo Pasolini, the legend has become enormous, and of course Pasolini fed it no end in his lifetime, as with filmmakers such as Orson Welles, Alfred Hitchcock, Ken Russell, Jean-Luc Godard and Werner Herzog. Those filmmakers liked nothing better than talking about themselves and their work. There should be a sub-category of film directors who luxuriate in their own eccentricities, in rattling out the same stories and anecdotes. The brief moments of self-deprecation (Ingmar Bergman, Woody Allen, Andrei Tarkovsky, Steven Spielberg) don't fool us for a moment.

In Enzo Siciliano's 1978 biography, Pier Paolo Pasolini comes across as a *very* complex individual: he was a mass of contradictions. Nothing could be simple with Pasolini. There were always a number of levels to consider at the same time.

Pier Paolo Pasolini's relationship with his father Carlo Alberto Pasolini was ambiguous, anxious and filled with conflicting emotions. Pasolini spoke of loving his father until his was three years-old; then came a crisis, and he fell out of love, forever. It was during the time that Susanna was pregnant with Pasolini's brother Guido. What exactly happened isn't clear; certainly it is a classic case of oedipal rebellion, with the father as the erotic rival with the boy for the mother's love (it may have been the Freudian primal scene, Enzo Siciliano wondered, of stumbling upon his parents making love in the kitchen). And it is also a (jealous) rivalry with the younger brother.

There's no need to explore the love-hate relation

with the father and the Law of the Father in P.P. Pasolini's art here, because it's plastered all over his films and his poetry. Pasolini's movies are in part a psychoanalytical investigation into the relationship with the father figure. The movies are their own therapy, their own psychoanalytical cases. The depictions of fathers and the Sins of the Fathers is so obvious it doesn't require any gloss here.

Ditto with his mother – there's no need to explore Pier Paolo Pasolini's relation with his beloved mother, Susanna Colussi Pasolini. That Pasolini adored his mom comes over strongly in his poetry and cinema.

> The mark which has dominated all my work is this longing for life, this sense of exclusion, which doesn't lessen but augments this love of life.
> (Interview in a documentary, late 1960s)

PASOLINI AND RELIGION

> I suffer from the nostalgia of a peasant-type religion, and that is why I am on the side of the servant. But I do not believe in a metaphysical god. I am religious because I have a natural identific-ation between reality and God. Reality is divine. That is why my films are never naturalistic. The motivation that unites all of my films is to give back to reality its original sacred significance.
>
> Pier Paolo Pasolini (1968)

Whatever he may have said in interviews or written in essays and poetry, Pier Paolo Pasolini was certainly fascinated by many aspects of religion and Catholicism. The imagery and themes of Catholicism, for instance, run throughout his movies – and not because he was Italian, or because he was brought up amongst Catholicism.

You can think of Pier Paolo Pasolini's 'religion' as being poetry; but even here, the crossovers between religion and poetry are numerous, and have been explored by 1,000s of commentators. Enzo Siciliano called Pasolini 'a profoundly religious man, but in his religion the vocative "God" was absent' (ES, 396).

As commentators have noted, Pier Paolo Pasolini's religious faith wasn't in Catholicism, it was in Communism. For him, Communism was natural, inevitable, essential, a way of looking at the world that explained (and fed) his nostalgia for the peasant world, his dissatisfaction with modern life, his hatred of advanced capitalism, his sympathy with the under-class, and his distrust of authority. And there was a social aspect to Communist politics for Pasolini: it brought him together with intellectuals, of course, but he also 'frequented the dance halls on the "red" outskirts of the city' (as Enzo Siciliano explained [162]). Pasolini continued to vote for the Partito Comunista Italiano (Italian Communist Party) and contribute to its publications (though his relationship with the Partito Comunista Italiano was troubled at times).

Of course, being an intellectual and highly educated observer, Pier Paolo Pasolini was inevitably highly critical of the Church, but he was also intrigued by many issues that the Church was linked to. Social control, and State authority, for instance, or issues such as morality and sexual ethics, or the role that Catholicism had in the political and social formation of young people. (And of course, Pasolini was steeped in Catholic art, to the point where it would have probably been absolutely impossible for him to eradicate all traces of that cultural absorption).

In 1971, he said:

> The Church will probably be able to continue for centuries to come if it creates an ecclesiastic assembly that continually negates and re-creates itself. My criticism is against the Church as power as it is today. I said that when I was a boy I believed, I prayed... but it wasn't anything very

serious. I think there're some facets in my character that have something of a mystifying quality. I'd say this is a part of the trauma that dominates my existence. Nature doesn't seem natural to me, it is a sort of an act between me and the naturalness of nature. (1971)

Whether Pier Paolo Pasolini personally 'believed' or not is not the issue, is not important, and is not even interesting. It's what Pasolini *did* with those beliefs or non-beliefs that's valuable, it's how Pasolini engaged with institutions such as religion, Catholicism, the State, education, Communism, Marxism, and capitalism that's interesting. But even those big issues are not especially compelling on their own, unless, at least for commercial cinema, they are combined with or put into drama, fiction, stories and characters.

'Christianity was part of his moral reasoning, the part that obliged him to interrogate himself (albeit in the guise of a country priest) on the unrelenting demands of the body', Enzo Siciliano noted, *pace Amado Mio* (121).

Pier Paolo Pasolini said he tended to see the world in too reverential, too childlike terms – if he had any religion, he remarked, it would be a vague mystical response to the world (including objects and nature as well as people [PP, 14]).

PASOLINI THE OUTSIDER

The feeling of not fitting in anywhere in the modern world can be found throughout Pier Paolo Pasolini's writings and films (and it makes his work appealing to modern audiences). You can see how Pasolini would be right at home in the Middle Ages (as an assistant to Dante Alighieri or Giotto, say, or in the Ancient Roman world, as a poet rival to, say, Petronius or Ovid) – yet, even here, Pasolini would probably still feel that he didn't fit in, would still have that consuming, near-tragic experience of otherness. Pasolini is an exile in his own life, where his poems and films offer a commentary, a layer, a musing on the discontinuities between his life and his art, his life and his heart, his life and his relationships.

We are all exiles, says French philosopher Julia Kristeva. Her experience of displacement (from her homeland of Bulgaria) was an ingredient in her notion of the 'cosmopolitan' individual, the 'intellectual dissident'. As Kristeva knew, strangeness or otherness (being a foreigner) is fundamental to being human: as Kristeva put it, *étrangers à nous-mêmes* (we are strangers to ourselves).[25]

Some of the forerunners of Pier Paolo Pasolini's lifestyle, which combined outsider status, an eccentric and highly individual cultural trajectory, and a homosexual lifestyle, included Oscar Wilde and André Gide. A touchstone for Pasolini, Gide (1869-1951) was cited by Pasolini as an important influence. Easy to see why: early Gide works such as *The Immoralist* and *Fruits of the Earth* are like early Pasolini movies,[26] with their Existentialist, outsider protagonists, their fashionable (French) avant gardism, their depictions of older, white, European guys falling for young, Arab boys (plus the inevitable guilt and post-coital self-loathing), their Catholic/ post-Catholic *milieu,* their high culture and literary allusions, and their enshrinement of the poetry of being alive.

If you enjoy Pier Paolo Pasolini's movies, you will love André Gide's novels (and vice versa). As Pasolini was a 'filmmaker's filmmaker' (like Orson Welles, F.W. Murnau or Sergei Paradjanov), so Gide was very much a 'writer's writer' (as with Rainer Maria Rilke, Francesco

25 In *Strangers to Ourselves,* Julia Kristeva describes the foreigner as the 'cold orphan', motherless, a 'devotee of solitude', a 'fanatic of absence', alone even in a crowd, arrogant, rejected, yet oddly happy (4-5). The stranger is always in motion, doesn't belong anywhere, to 'any time, any love' (7).
26 *The Immoralist* is ideal for the Pasolinian treatment. Indeed, *Theorem* has the feel of *The Immoralist*.

Petrarch or Samuel Beckett). C.P. Cavafy, the 20th century Greek poet of lyrical, homoerotic nostalgia, is another reference point for Pier Paolo Pasolini (there are numerous affinities between the two).

PASOLINI THE ICONOCLAST

A controversial figure even today, Pier Paolo Pasolini had run-ins with the Italian authorities many times (he was brought to trial on several occasions). His works were condemned for their blasphemy and obscenity. An early encounter with the authorities occurred when he was accused of pædophilia and homosexuality – with the Ramuscello boys in Casarsa. It was this incident that partly encouraged Pasolini to leave Bologna and to live in Rome (see below).

Altho' critics and admirers found some of Pier Paolo Pasolini's writing and movie-making extreme, it wasn't, compared to some authors: William Burroughs, Marco Vassi, Henry Miller, or even Paul Bowles.

There's no doubt that part of Pier Paolo Pasolini enjoyed shocking people, or simply winding them up – he did it in his newspaper articles, in his poetry, in his movies, and in his documentaries. And he succeeded many times: the number of controversies that Pasolini was involved with is very high – compared to most of his contemporaries (either in literature or cinema).

Things seemed to happen to Pasolini.

> Wholly a man of his time [wrote Enzo Siciliano], he chose to live in the enemy camp, launching polemics and accusations, pushing his intolerable personal situation to the point of paradox, and not troubling himself about anything else. (ES, 399-400)

Pier Paolo Pasolini saw himself as something of an

outsider in Italian culture, a 'disturber of the peace', someone whose contributions were unwanted. Yes – but that didn't stop Pasolini pouring out pronouncements and movies and poems and books! Pasolini wasn't going to hurry home, slam the door and vow never to talk to the press or anyone else again for the rest of his life! He was not someone who could keep quiet. (Instead, Pasolini glorified in attention of all kinds: he was one of those filmmakers who revel in the attention – look at his interviews – you see the same enjoyment of adulation in Orson Welles, in Jean-Luc Godard, in Steve Spielberg, in Francis Coppola, etc).

Pier Paolo Pasolini was involved in a brawl in Rome, at nighttime in a rough part of the city (Via di Panico). The case came to trial on Nov 15, 1961 (around the time that *Accattone* opened in cinemas). Pasolini was charged with 'aiding and abetting', but was fully acquitted.[27] Enzo Siciliano speaks of this period as having 'a climate of persecution', when 'hysteria grew around the public figure of Pasolini' (248).

Yet another brush with the law occurred when Pier Paolo Pasolini was accused of holding up a gas station with a gun (!). The accusations came from Bernardino De Santis, a boy working at the garage, who said that Pasolini had used a black pistol to hold up the garage. The trial took place in Latina on July 3, 1962. (Once again, Pasolini's defence used the concept of research – Pasolini often defended himself by saying that he was researching places and people for future projects). Further scandals are noted below.

Few Italian artists in the same era were attacked and criticized more than Pasolini. 'Pasolini remained un-interruptedly in the hand of judges from 1960 to 1975', as Stefano Rodotà put it in *Pasolini: Judicial Report, Persecution, Death* (1977). Magazines and newspapers such as *Il Borghese, Oggi, Gente* and *Lo Specchio* regularly slandered him. Among Pasolini's loudest critics were Maria Predassi (writing as Gianna Preda) and

27 According to Laura Betti in the *Who Says the Truth Shall Die* documentary, Pasolini was accused some 33 times of different crimes but he was always acquitted. Yet the Italian press kept going after him.

Giose Rimanelli (writing as A.G. Solari).

But why? asked Wu Ming in a 2016 article:

> Why such a persecution? Because he was homo-
> sexual? He was certainly not the only one amongst
> artists and writers. Because he was homosexual and
> communist? Yes, but this isn't enough either.
> Because he was homosexual, communist and
> expressed himself openly against the bourgeoisie,
> government, Christian Democracy, fascists, judges
> and police? Yes, this is enough. It would have been
> enough anywhere, let alone in Italy, and in that
> Italy.

PASOLINI AND HOMOSEXUALITY:
THE PERCEPTION OF PASOLINI'S IDENTITY

It's striking how many commentators on the work of
Pier Paolo Pasolini mention his sexual identity (i.e., his
homosexuality). As if they are now professional,
psychoanalytical experts on sexuality and gender
(almost all critics are not). There is something patron-
izing about this, as well as something of the tabloid
journalist's pig's nose for snuffling out sensationalism
(yes, and the bastard was gay, too!). As if to be gay is
automatically to be weird, 'other', or perverted.

Every frigging biographical sketch I've read about
Pier Paolo Pasolini mentions his sexuality. Yes, even
those critics who are supposed to be (1) intellectual, (2)
well-read, and (3) critical/ perceptive. And they often
depict Pasolini's sexual preferences as 'dark', or exotic,
or odd. Were they? And how can anybody know?! Why
is his sexual identity seen as such a big deal? Hell,
maybe Pasolini just liked sex! As Spike Milligan said:
'people like to fuck'.

The issue of homosexuality in relation to
Pasolini's media persona is very minor compared to his

public critiques and attacks on institutions such as the Christian Democrat party in Italy, on the bourgeoisie, on consumer capitalism, etc.

There are so many assumptions and damaging views in the way that the personality of Pier Paolo Pasolini has been discussed. However, it's true that in some respects the media image of Pier Paolo Pasolini conforms to the stereotype of the ageing homosexual who preys upon boys. Many observers have attested to that, how, according to the Pasolini Legend, he would go out night after night in search of rough trade (often in one of his sports cars). Boys that hung around the Termini railroad station in the centre of Roma, or in the *borgate*, or the bathhouses along the River Tiber (such as the Ciriola below Castel Sant' Angelo).28 Boys that wouldn't be brought back home, because home meant his beloved Mamma. (His preference was for *ragazzi* with a roguish smile, curly hair on their foreheads, plenty of vitality, and often a reputation as bad boys, as petty criminals).29

Famous filmmakers who were homosexual include F.W. Murnau, Jean Cocteau, Andy Warhol, Rainer Werner Fassbinder, Kenneth Anger, George Cukor, James Whale, and more recently, James Ivory, Joel Schumacher, and Pasolini's fellow Italians Luchino Visconti and Franco Zeffirelli (also, Visconti and Zeffirelli didn't, as with Pasolini, hide their sexual identity30).

Discussing the idea of the romantic couple in 1970, Pasolini pointed out that societies reject what challenges the norms and the rules – and that includes homosexuality:

Homosexuality is a threat to society. It is incon-

28 Pier Paolo Pasolini was sometimes accompanied by his friend Sandro Penna: they had a joky contest over who could tup the most boys.
29 In Great Britain, in legal history, male homosexuality has been the subject of several laws, including the law on sodomy of 1533 (in Henry VIII's reign), the 1861 and 1885 laws on sodomy and gross indecency; the 1898 Vagrancy Act, the Sexual Offences Act of 1967, and the Criminal Justice Bill of 1991 (however, lesbianism has been largely invisible and unacknowledged).
30 However, Visconti and Zeffirelli didn't loudly criticize the State, the Church and other Italian institutions like Pasolini.

ceivable in any organisms or community, no matter how free. (1970)

Enzo Siciliano in his biography portrays Pier Paolo Pasolini as someone tormented by his passions, his predilections for young, raw boys. 'Pasolini lived in the torment of not being able to give it [his eros] what it demanded of him. And the demand was obscure, indeed dark and nocturnal' (ES, 391).

In 1948, Pier Paolo Pasolini described his homosexuality as something other:

> I was born to be calm, balanced, natural: my
> homosexuality was something added, it lay
> outside, it had nothing to do with me. I've always
> seen it as something beside me like an enemy, I've
> never felt it to be within me.

Pier Paolo Pasolini revered the rugged, working class *ragazzi* of Rome, Calabria and Friuli, but however much he liked to hang around with them (and have sex with them), he was never one of them. Pasolini was always the intellectual, always the poet, always the guy who wrote newspapers columns and directed movies. He was never a street kid, was never one of the tough, poor *ragazzi* that he liked to cruise at night.

For some observers, Pier Paolo Pasolini was the classic predatory homosexual, the older, gay man who takes to exploring the streets of cities and towns at night looking for willing youths to share the momentary pleasures of sex. It was a habit that Pasolini found hard to break: he enjoyed the danger of it, as well as the ecstasy (he would return from his secretive nighttime jaunts battered and bruised sometimes). According to Enzo Siciliano, most times the erotic encounters consisted of fellatio and masturbation.

Sometimes Pier Paolo Pasolini had to be rescued from his nightly adventures, sore and bleeding (producer Alfredo Bini and production manager Eliseo Boschi would respond to telephone calls to go get Pasolini from some nocturnal spree that'd turned sour

– in Africa and the Middle East as well as in Rome). 'I'm leading not a violent but an extremely violent life', Pasolini wrote in a letter of Oct 5, 1959 (ES, 141).

Pier Paolo Pasolini did have heterosexual experiences. One was with a young mother from Viterbo. Another was with a girl at the beach. Another was with Mariella Bauzano in the early 1950s. And as a kid Pasolini had flirted with girls (and referred to them in his letters). However, Enzo Siciliano wondered if some of these 'girls' were in fact boys (ES, 52).

There were also a number of social and criminal scandals, some of which involved under-age youths and sexuality – which were linked to Pasolini's homosexual practices.

When he was 19, Pier Paolo Pasolini was accused by a neighbourhood child's father of pederasty, when he offered the child some ice cream (this occurred in Bologna in 1941). Pasolini insisted that his intentions were innocent.

One of the biggest scandals in Pier Paolo Pasolini's life, and one which changed the course of his life, occurred in 1949 in Casarsa (his home), when Pasolini (then 27) was overheard talking to some 16 year-old lads in Ramuscello (outside of San Vito al Tagliamento). What happened with the boys at Ramuscello ('probably mutual masturbation', Enzo Siciliano reckoned [135]), which Pasolini had enjoyed (he called it an unforgettable evening), became public when complaints were made to the *carabineri*. In December, 1950, the court acquitted Pasolini of the charges of corrupting minors, but he was convicted of committing lewd acts. In April, 1952, the appeals court absolved Pasolini due to insufficient evidence (ES, 135).

Pier Paolo Pasolini trotted out a defence he used again in later scandals a few times: he was conducting research for a novel, he claimed: 'I was trying an erotic and literary experiment, under the influence of a book I had been reading'. Even if he cited a big cultural name like André Gide, it seems a pretty flimsy excuse.

Pier Paolo Pasolini's erotic encounter with the

Ramuscello boys had other repercussions – such as Pasolini's ousting from the Communist Party, which he found very upsetting (he revered Communism). Pasolini lost his teaching job (as well as the financial security it brought).

The scandal tore into Pier Paolo Pasolini's family – his father went ballistic, raging all night about his son, and his mother locked herself in her room ('Yesterday morning my mother almost went out of her mind, my father is in an unbearable state – I heard him weeping and moaning all night', Pasolini wrote to Ferdinando Mautino). To a friend called over for solace, Giuseppe Zigaina, Pasolini confessed he wanted to kill himself (ES, 137). It was the repercussions of this event that precipitated the move to Roma with his mother, where he remained for the rest of his life.

The pattern of this early scandal of 1949 – Pier Paolo Pasolini preying upon young boys, the social intolerance of homosexuality it evoked, and Pasolini's intellectual defence of his actions – would be repeated a few times in his life.

Another incident involving young boys occurred on July 10, 1960, in Anzio, when Pier Paolo Pasolini was thought to have propositioned some boys in the harbour (the parents of the boys filed a complaint). One of the striking aspects about the career of Pier Paolo Pasolini is that he didn't give up in the face of several scandals.

HOMOSEXUALITY IN PASOLINI'S CINEMA

Critics have noted that although he was a gay filmmaker, homosexuality is not often portrayed in Pier Paolo Pasolini's cinema. Well, there are obvious instances, such as the condemned, male homosexuals in the witchhunting sequence in *The Canterbury Tales*, where one of the victims is publicly burnt to death (while an older one buys himself out), and in *Theorem,* homosexual relationships are explored in more depth (but in *Theorem* the homosexuality is with a visitor who is part-god, part-devil – not an 'average' relationship at all!).

But when you look closer, there are further levels of homosexual elements in Pier Paolo Pasolini's cinema. The preponderance of male brotherhoods, for instance, of men being men together, which you can see in *The Canterbury Tales, The Decameron, Accattone* and, yes, in *The Gospel According To Matthew.* The homosocial relationships are right in the foreground from Pasolini's debut (*Accattone*) onwards. Indeed, *Accattone* is a very gay movie from that perspective (even down to the way that women are treated – their maltreatment further bolsters the homosocial bonds of the guys).

And look at the way that Pier Paolo Pasolini includes so many rough and ready youths in his movies (the *ragazzi* of his 1950s novels), and how the camera lingers over them at length. Pasolini is very fond of close-ups of young *ragazzi* smiling into the camera, as part of the conventional shot-reverse-shot editing pattern of cinema, yes, but the amount of screen time given over to close-ups of attractive, macho young men is very striking.

Brotherhoods and male bonding are fundamental to many other filmmakers' work – it's central to Westerns, to the crime and gangster genres, to the war genre, to action cinema, and is a key element in the cinema of Sam Peckinpah, Howard Hawks, John Woo, Ringo Lam, Martin Scorsese, Francis Coppola, etc etc.

I'm reminded of Michelangelo Merisi da Caravaggio,[31] probably *the* painter (at least in Italy), of beautiful, tough, young men. The homosexuality of Caravaggio is another aspect, of course, but in terms of the art itself, Caravaggio's work is certainly a forerunner of this element in Pier Paolo Pasolini's cinema. And the

31 Other writers have noted the affinities between Pier Paolo Pasolini and Caravaggio: Cesare Garboli drew attention to the similarities, with the art historian Roberto Longhi as the intermediary (Longhi had organized an important exhibition of Caravaggio in Milan in 1951).

other artist is of course Michelangelo Buonarroti, the towering genius of the Renaissance, who made the male nude the most sublime, erotic thing you've ever seen (visit the Musée de Louvre to see the *Dying Slave* sculptures, truly orgasmic works of art).

And Pier Paolo Pasolini and his crews did film many men nude. Within the context of heterosexual encounters, that male nudity has a justification. And Pasolini was unusual among many film directors is putting an equal amount of male nudity on screen as female nudity in love scenes (male actors can be more reluctant to disrobe completely – and of course, there are double standards in most cinema, where an actor will stay partially clad, while an actress is fully naked).

As well as nudity,[32] Pier Paolo Pasolini and the camera teams also focussed on the male genitals. In *The Arabian Nights* there are quite a few close-ups of genitals (as well as the usual thrusting butts in sex scenes of heterosexual cinema). *The Arabian Nights* probably contains the most male nudity in Pasolini's cinema, along with *Salò*.

Despite the beauty of Pasolini's imagery, his exaltation of bodies (and men in particular), there isn't much erotic pleasure in some of his works, and sexuality is tied, via his personality, 'to a realm of suffering' which 'inflects his work with melancholy and morbidity', according to Gary Indiana (16).

Pasolini identified with the victim, not the perpetrator, some observed; his masochism was to sympathize with the down-trodden – in Italia, that meant the sub-proletariat (Pasolini invested his social hopes in the sub-proletariat).

Feminists have discussed the male gaze (voyeurism, the look, etc), and wondered if there can be a female gaze in cinema. That there is a homosexual, lesbian, queer and bisexual gaze – or, I would prefer to call it a multi-sexual gaze (why stop at two or three genders?) – is clear from the films of Pier Paolo Pasolini,

---

32 Nobody can miss the fact that Pier Paolo Pasolini's last four films are jammed with nudity and sex. (And also in *Theorem* and *Pigsty*).

Walerian Borowczyk and Ken Russell.

I'm not talking about the sexual preferences of the filmmakers, but of the gaze, the looks, the desire and the structure of their works. For example, although Ken Russell, Francis Coppola, Martin Scorsese, Bernardo Bertolucci and Michael Powell were heterosexual (at least according to their autobiographies and colleagues and wives and girlfriends), some of their works are supremely gay, queer, lesbian and homosexual.

Pier Paolo Pasolini, though, was not particularly interested in foregrounding that aspect of his personality in his cinema. What does come across, though, and very strongly, is the aspect of *desire*. Sexual desire, desire for life. Which's often intensely romantic and poetic, sometimes nostalgic, sometimes ironic, sometimes masochistic, and sometimes vitriolic.

The most unbridled expression of desire in Pier Paolo Pasolini's work is in the three 'life' movies, 1971, 1972 and 1974. But the desire on display is nearly all heterosexual (*Salò* explores desire within an eccentric, S/M environment).

PASOLINI CRITICISM

A huge amount of articles, essays and books have appeared about the works of Pier Paolo Pasolini, focussing on his poetry, his novels, his essays/ statements and his movies. In short, Pasolini has been taken *very* seriously, with critics and journos assuming that he is an important figure with significant things to say. I would imagine that Pasolini himself would be stunned, delighted, and perhaps embarrassed by the number of pieces written about his work, and how he has been placed in the same company as many of his cultural heroes.

I would recommend, as the first point of call, the

amazing biography by Enzo Siciliano (sadly out of print). Among the studies of Pier Paolo Pasolini's films, Sam Rohdie, B. Babington, Pamela Grace, Philip Kolker, John Orr, A. Pavelin, and Gary Indiana are useful.

There are far fewer biographies of Pier Paolo Pasolini in print than one might think. In fact, for years no biographies have been in print in English. The biography by Enzo Siciliano, *Pasolini,* published in 1978 by Rizzoli (in Italian), is among the finest (it was translated in 1982, and published in 1987). Retrospectives of Pasolini's work were mounted at the Museum of Modern Art in 2012 and the British Film Institute in 2013.

Enzo Siciliano concentrates very much on Pier Paolo Pasolini the public figure in Italian cultural life, and on Pasolini's poetry: there is far less in his biography on Pasolini's cinema, for instance, than on Pasolini's poems (Siciliano quotes from the poetry at length). Siciliano also employs the poems in a problematic manner: to illustrate Pasolini's thoughts and even some of his experiences. Assessing and explaining someone's life through their poetry is full of difficulties, filled with assumptions about what poetry is, how it works, how poets write poems, and how poetry relates to the poet's life.

In short, poetry is not autobiography, or documentary, or history. Very often it has no relation to the poet's life whatsoever. Robert Graves called poetry a 'spiritual autobiography', but even that is not always the case.

With Pier Paolo Pasolini, however, some of his poems definitely do reflect upon his experiences, and many poems do express his own views. But it's still a very stylized, literary kind of mirror, reflecting back only what the poet chooses.

Pier Paolo Pasolini has been discussed widely in cinema circles, but when you look into it, there are far fewer really good books about Pasolini's cinema than one might expect (certainly compared to contemporaries such as Jean-Luc Godard or Orson Welles).

And many of the best studies are now out of print (including Enzo Siciliano's essential biography).

In studies of the cinema of Pier Paolo Pasolini's cinema, the context and the references tend to be Neo-realism, and to that select band of Italian filmmakers who have been exported and critically revered: Fellini, Rossellini, Visconti, Antonioni, de Sica, Bertolucci, etc.

Sure – those are the great artists of Italian cinema of the 1950s to 1970s. But they are not really representative of Italian cinema of that era. Rather, cinema in Italy of the 50s through 70s was a thriving industry of remakes, sequels, rip-offs, exploitation movies, *mondo* movies, populist comedies (hugely popular), *James Bond* cash-ins, and endless genre movies (Spaghetti Westerns, *gialli* (horror/ thriller), crime, erotica, and of course the *peplum/* sword & sandal movies), plus the many visiting productions from North America (resulting in the 'Hollywood On the Tiber' cycle). If a movie – from anywhere – was successful, Italian cinema dived in and had a cash-in movie filmed and released within weeks (same with the Hong Kong film business).

We don't think of Pasolini as a director of sequels and franchises, but he *did* sequelize his own movies: *Mamma Roma* follows up *Accattone*, *The Hawks and the Sparrows* led to further collaborations with Totò (in the short films for anthologies, and a feature-length sequel to *The Hawks and the Sparrows* was planned), *Medea* is a follow-up to *Oedipus Rex,* and the 'trilogy of life' pictures can be regarded as a film series.

Pier Paolo Pasolini distanced himself from Neo-realist cinema; while Neo-realism was dead in Italy, it had migrated to England and France, Pasolini noted (PP, 137). He didn't like the British version of the New Wave at all (very few Europeans did!), tho' of course he greatly admired Jean-Luc Godard.

Inevitably, Pasolini would be critical of Neo-realist cinema and distance himself from it (as Federico Fellini and Bernardo Bertolucci did), partly because we know that Pasolini (and Fellini and Bertolucci) didn't like being part of a group, or being pigeon-holed and labelled.

However, Pasolini, like Fellini, certainly employed some of the formal approaches of Neo-realism (even if he denied using them): in her 2005 essay on *Rome: Open City*, Marcia Landy listed some of the styles and subjects of Neo-realist cinema:

> a predominant use of location shooting, deep-focus and long-take photography, non-professional actors, a loose form of narration, and a documentary look, plus in the intermingling of fiction and nonfiction, the privileging of marginal and subaltern groups, and a focus on contemporary situations. (J. Geiger, 404)

The decline of the Neo-realist form of cinema coincided with the changes in Italian society after WWII. As David Cook explained in *A History of Narrative Film*:

> In practice, it was a cinema of poverty and pessimism firmly rooted in the immediate postwar period. When times changed and economic conditions began to improve, neorealism lost first its ideological basis, then its subject matter. (453)

Another factor was the Andreotti Law, instituted in response to the glut of North American movies in Italy in 1949. The Andreotti Law taxed imported films and promoted home-grown products. (Several European nations have attempted to control American cultural imports and promote their national arts).

CRITICS ON PASOLINI

For David A. Cook (in *A History of Narrative Film*), at his best Pier Paolo Pasolini 'succeeded in creating an intellectual cinema in which metaphor, myth, and narrative form all subserved materialist ideology' (1990, 633).

Gary Indiana described Pasolini as:

> Indefatigably productive, ingenious, exasperating, narcisstically didactic, slyly self-promoting, abject, generous, exploitative, devoted to the wretched of the earth with honest fervor and deluded romant-icism…

Pierre Leprohon, in one of the standard books on Italian cinema (1972), was suspicious of the merits of Pier Paolo Pasolini's work: 'originality, violence, controversiality and a taste for (often confused) symbols', Leprohon asserted, with anachronistic music, and it's deliberately, irritatingly mystifying (207).

For David Thomson (an idiosyncratic and not always reliable film critic), Pier Paolo Pasolini's films weren't up to the level of his theories and poetry: there was too much portentousness in Pasolini's imagery, Thomson reckoned, adding:

> His strident compositions were clumsy and mono-tonous, and his appetite for faces often overrode the ability to edit shots together fluently. The style was top-heavy, just as the meanings of his films were too literary, too immediate, and too inconsistent. (1995, 575-6)

Of course I don't agree with any of that. 'Mono-tonous'?! Hardly. And why is being 'too immediate' a problem? But you could agree that some of the imagery and the *mise-en-scène* didn't match up with the grand themes and ideas, that sometimes the imagery is too grandiose for the stories and the characters (or vice versa).

> How would I define myself? It's like asking the
> definition of infinity. There's an interior infinity
> and an exterior infinity. When I think of myself, I
> think of something infinite. It's impossible to
> define myself. For you I'm definable but for me I'm
> infinite. I'm the mirror of exterior infinity, it's
> impossible for me to define myself. I could create...
> some slogans, a few funny things in conversations,
> in salons, perhaps... I could quote something Elsa
> Morante said about me: "I'm a narcissistic
> individual who has a happy love of myself." I must
> add that I have an unhappy love for the world. Or
> maybe, I could say I'm a true devil, not a false devil
> like Sanguineti or the *avant garde* writers.

Pier Paolo Pasolini (1966)

The death of Pier Paolo Pasolini at age 53 has loomed
large in his legend (as with the deaths of figures such as
Marilyn Monroe, Jim Morrison, Jimi Hendrix and Bruce
Lee). The details are still shrouded in mystery and
controversy. No one knows precisely what happened, or
will confess the truth. (It does seem as if some people *do*
know who was responsible, but refuse to say). Anyway,
nobody can agree exactly what went on that fateful night
of November 1-2, 1975.

Some of the events of the night of Nov 1 and Nov 2,
1975 are agreed upon: that Pier Paolo Pasolini picked
up the 17 year-old hustler Giuseppe Pelosi in Rome;
that they ate in a restaurant; and that they drove in
Pasolini's sports car to Ostia (a typical evening for
Pasolini, thus far).

After that, there are many versions of what
happened. That Pasolini was beaten and run over by his
own car seems certain.

Other details of the murder have come to light:

• the green sweater that didn't belong to Pasolini in
the car;

• the bloody handprint on the roof of the car;

• that witnesses claimed they saw at least one

motorbike and possibly a car following Pasolini's vehicle;

• that a skinny kid could not have killed the bigger, athletic Pasolini;

• that Pelosi didn't have any blood on him;

• that the damage sustained by Pasolini was far beyond what Pelosi could have inflicted;

• that, if other people were involved, the murder seems inept;

• that the motives are obscure – for Giuseppe Pelosi, but also for other groups (such as a local gang).

Giuseppe Pelosi confessed to Pier Paolo Pasolini's murder (and was duly imprisoned). Pelosi claimed that Pasolini had proposed things that he didn't want to do (including, preposterously, sodomy with a wooden stake). Pelosi's motives for the murder have never been explained satisfactorily.

In 2005, Giuseppe Pelosi retracted his confession, which he claimed had been made due to threats to his family. Pelosi gave more names in 2008.

Several high profile members of Italian society have asked that the case be re-opened, including former mayors and lawyers, as well as journalists.

When the case was re-opened in 2005, Sergio Citti, Pier Paolo Pasolini's long-time lover and colleague, said that Pasolini had been going to meet someone who had stolen reels of the film *Salò* (with a view to extorting money). Others have also reckoned that film canisters stolen on Aug 27, 1975 from the Technicolor lab in Rome might've been involved (as well as *Salò*, some of the negatives of *Casanova* were taken – 74 cans of film. Some have suggested that the thieves mistook the negatives of *Salò* for those from *Casanova*. Producer Alberto Grimaldi (he was producing both films) refused to pay the thieves the half a billion Lire they demanded).

The extortion scenario doesn't make total sense – not least because it's the producers, the production companies and the studios who control the money in the film industry, not directors. Also, killing someone means you won't get the money you're extorting. That

Pasolini would go to meet some small-time crooks intent on extracting some Lire out of him at night in a lonely spot like Ostia seems unconvincing.

Several theories have been proposed for the death of Pier Paolo Pasolini. That he irritated some groups (and institutions) is well-known – that his views were not welcome in some quarters of Italian society; that he was known as a Marxist and Communist who criticized the social and political status quo; that he wrote articles published in Aug, 1975 which criticized Christian Democrats and other right-wing organizations for the decline of Italian society, etc. But then, many writers and artists have stirred up controversy (and some were louder and more outspoken than even Pasolini). And being a Communist in Italy is common (Pasolini remarked that everyone in Italy was a Catholic, and a Communist).

Anyway, one or more neo-fascist groups have been put forward as possible culprits, plus a local criminal gang (partly because witnesses said several people (perhaps five) murdered Pier Paolo Pasolini, not Giuseppe Pelosi on his own. Laura Betti and others have claimed that a car containing four people followed Pasolini's vehicle). Links have also been suggested between neo-fascist groups and the Italian secret services. (The neo-fascist connection makes sense – it was neo-fascist groups that caused trouble at screenings of Pasolini's films in the early 1960s).

For Bernardo Bertolucci and others, it was a kind of public execution, an over-the-top act of punishment, probably backed by conservative groups in Italy who wanted Pasolini silenced, or to make an example of him. Bertolucci wondered if the perpetrators even knew what they were doing, or if they knew of the real motives behind the murder they were hired to carry out. Certainly, whoever killed Pasolini knew that they could get away with it, that they wouldn't be caught, that they had a scapegoat lined up, and that the Pasolini supporters would not have the means to bring them to justice.

The death of Pier Paolo Pasolini has provided plenty of speculation and gossip-mongering. Inevitably commentators refer to his homosexuality, to his habit of cruising or seeking out rough trade, to his apparent sadomasochism (even with suggestions of a kind of suicide), to the brutality of his last film, *Salò,* and so on. But the sex/ masochism angle, though sensational, isn't the whole story by any means.

With its combination of spectacle, sex and mystery, Pasolini's murder is a 500-word newspaper piece that writes itself. When you add in aspects such as conspiracy, or extortionists, or neo-fascist groups, or political organizations such as Christian Democrats, you have an explosive cocktail that damns segments of Italian society. Pretty much every piece on Pasolini mentions his sensational demise.

Even philosophers such as Julia Kristeva have had their say (in *Tales of Love*):

> Masochism, which, we are told, is essentially and
> originally feminine, is a submissiveness to the
> Phallus that the soulosexual knows well and can
> assume until death in order to become the "true"
> woman – passive, castrated, nonphallic – that his/
> her mother was not. Mishima, mistaking himself for
> Saint Sebastian, and even Pasolini, allowing
> himself to be executed by a hoodlum on an Italian
> beach, carry to the limit the slavish moment of male
> eroticism appended to a deathful veneration of the
> Phallus. (78)

Pasolini on set:
with opera superstar Maria Callas during Medea (above).
And with Enrique Irazoqui during The Gospel (below).

Pasolini and Welles during Curd Cheese (1963).

3

THE WORKS OF
PIER PAOLO PASOLINI

I love life fiercely, desperately... Love of life for me
has become a more tenacious vice than cocaine. I
devour my existence with an insatiable appetite.

Pier Paolo Pasolini[1]

Pier Paolo Pasolini directed thirteen feature films (one is
a documentary), and also many shorter pieces, including
contributions to anthology movies. His feature movies
are:

Beggar (*Accattone,* 1961)

Mother Rome (*Mamma Rome,* 1962)

Love Meetings (a.k.a. *Lessons In Love* = *Comizi
d'Amore*, 1964)

The Gospel According To Matthew (*Il Vangelo
Secondo Matteo*, 1964)

The Hawks and the Sparrows (*Uccellacci e
Uccellini*, 1966)

Oedipus Rex (*Edipo Re*, 1967)

Theorem (*Teorma*, 1968)

Pigsty (*Porcile*, 1969)

---

1 In L. Valentin, "Tête-à-Tête avec Pier Paolo Pasolini", *Lui*, April, 1970.
Andrea Dworkin used that Pasolini quote – 'I love life so fiercely, so
desperately' – in her novels.

Medea (*Medea,* 1969)

The Decameron (*Il Decamerone,* 1971)

The Canterbury Tales (*I Racconti di Canterbury,* 1972)

The Arabian Nights (*Il Fiore Delle Mille e Una Notte,* 1974)

Salò, or The 120 Days of Sodom (*Salò, o le Centoventi Giornate di Sodoma,* 1975)

Pier Paolo Pasolini's contributions to episode or anthology[2] movies are:

The Anger (*La Rabbia,* 1963)

Curd Cheese (*La Ricotta,* episode in *RoGoPaG,* 1963)

The Earth Seen From the Moon (*La Terra Vista Dalla Luna,* episode in *The Witches = Le Streghe,* 1967)

What Are the Clouds? (*Che Cosa Sono le Nuvole?,* episode in *Caprice Italian Style = Capriccio all'Italiana,* 1968)

The Sequence of the Flower Field (*La Sequenza del Fiore di Carta,* episode in *Love and Anger = Vangelo '70/ Amore e Rabbia,* 1969)

Pier Paolo Pasolini's shorter works include:

Location Hunting In Palestine (*Sopralluoghi in Palestina Per Il Vangelo Secondo Matteo,* 1965)

Notes For a Film In India (*Appunti Per un Film Sull'India,* 1969)

Notes For a Garbage Novel (*Appunti Per un romanzo dell'immondizia,* 1970)

Notes Towards an African Oresteia (*Appunti Per un'Orestiade Africana,* 1970)

The Walls of Sana'a (*Le Mura di Sana'a,* 1971)

12 December 1972 (*12 Dicembre 1972,* 1972)

---

2 Advantages for filmmakers with anthology movies included: they didn't have to originate them or raise the cash – the producer did all of that; they could be filmed in one or two weeks; they could dig out unmade ideas; they could write their own scripts or come up with their own ideas; and they often had more freedom than with a feature film.

Pasolini and the Shape of the City (*Pasolini e la forma della città,* 1975)

✲

Pier Paolo Pasolini's 1955 novel *Ragazzi di vita* was adapted into a movie by Jacques-Laurent Bost and Pasolini: *La Notte Brava* (a.k.a. *Bad Girls Don't Cry,* a.k.a. *The Big Night,* Mauro Bolognini, 1959). It was produced by Antonio Cervi and Oreste Jacovini for Ajace Film and Franco-London Film. In the cast were: Rosanna Schiaffino, Laurent Terzieff, Jean-Claude Brialy, Franco Interlenghi, Antonella Lauldi, Mylène Demengeot and Elsa Martinelli.

A chapter from *Ragazzi di vita* was adapted in *La Canta dell Marane* (1960, dir. Cecilia Mangini). It was produced by Giorgio Patara.

Una Vita Violenta (*A Violent Life,* dirs. Paolo Heusch and Brunello Rondi) was adapted by Ennio De Concini, Franco Brusati, Paolo Heusch, Brunello Rondi and Franco Solinas in 1962. *A Violent Life* was produced by Aera Films/ Zebra Film.

✲

Pier Paolo Pasolini worked on about 15 scripts b4 directing his first feature, *Accattone*, in 1961. As a screenwriter, Pasolini contributed to movies (working with many other writers) such as:

• *La Donna del Fiume* (1954, with 5 other writers: Bassani, Franchina, Vancini, Altovitti and Soldati),

• *Il Prigioniero della Montagna* (1955, with Trenker and Bassani),

• *Nights of Cabiria* (1956, alongside 3 other writers: Fellini, Flaiano and Pinnelli),

• *Marisa la Civetta* (1957, with 2 writers: Demby and Bolognini),

• *A Farewell To Arms* (1957, with Ben Hecht and John Huston),

• *Giovani Mariti* (1958, with 5 other writers: Currelli, Martino, Bolognini, Franciosa and Camanile),

• *La Notte Brava* (1959, with Jacques-Laurent Bost),

• *Marte di un Amico* (1960, with 5 other writers: Berto, Biancoli, Rossi, Guerra and Riganti),

- *I Bell'Antonio* (1960, with Brancati, Bolognini and Visentini),
- *La Lunga Notte del '43* (1960, with Bassani, Vancini and Concini),
- *La Giornata Balorda* (1960, with Moravia and Visconti),
- *Il Carro Armato dell'8 Settembre* (1960, with Baratti, Bertolini and Questi),
- *La Ragazza In Vetrina* (1961, with Cassuto, Emmer, Sonego, Martino and Marinucci),
- *The Grim Reaper* (1962, a.k.a. *La Commare Secca*,[3] with Citti and Bertolucci),

He also co-wrote with Sergio Citti the films *Ostia* (1970) and *Storie Scellerate* (1973), both of which Citti directed.

✳

Pier Paolo Pasolini's books of poetry include:
Poesie e Casarsa (1942)
Diarii (1945)
Tal cour di un frut (1953/ 1974)
La Meglio gioventù (1954)
Le Ceneri di Gramsci (1957)
L'Usignolo della chiesa cattolica (1958)
La Religione del mio tempo (1961)
Poesia in forma di rosa (1964)
Trasumanar e organizzar (1971)
La Nuova gioventù (1975)
and *Roman Poems* (1986)
Pier Paolo Pasolini's fiction and narratives include:
Amado Mio - Atti Impuri (1948/ 1982)
Ragazzi di vita (*The Ragazzi*, 1955)
Una Vita Violenta (*A Violent Life*, 1959)
A Dream of Something (1962)
Roman Nights and Other Stories (1965)
Reality (*The Poets' Encyclopedia*, 1979)

3 Pier Paolo Pasolini had conceived *The Grim Reaper* (writing a five-page treatment), but decided to make *Mamma Roma* instead. Producer Antonio Cervi had bought the project from Pasolini, and decided to let Bernardo Bertolucci have a go at directing it, after seeing the script he had commissioned from Bertolucci and Sergio Citti. Bertolucci admitted that his first film as director (he was only 21), *The Grim Reaper*, was made very much in the Pasolinian mold.

Petrolio (1992)

Pier Paolo Pasolini's volumes of essays and writings include: *Passione e ideologia* (1960), *Canzoniere italiano, poesia popolare italiana* (1960), *Empirismo eretico* (1972), *Scritti corsari* (1975), *Lettere luterane* (1976), *Le belle bandiere* (1977), *Descrizioni di descrizioni* (1979), *Il caos* (1979), *La pornografia è noiosa* (1979) and *Lettere (1940–1954)* (*Letters, 1940-54*, 1986).

Pier Paolo Pasolini directed plays. In Turin he directed a version of *Orgia* in November, 1968. The cast included Laura Betti, Luigi Mezzanotte and Nelide Giammarco.

Pier Paolo Pasolini's theatre work includes: *Orgia* (1968), *Porcile* (1968), *Calderón* (1973), *Affabulazione* (1977), *Pilade* (1977), and *Bestia da stile* (1977).

Films/ TV shows/ documentaries have been made after Pier Paolo Pasolini's death from his works (some have quoted from his poems and plays), including:

Laboratorio teatrale di Luca Ronconi (1977)
Mulheres... Mulheres (1981)
Calderon (1981)
Die Leiche murde nie gefunden (1985)
L'altro enigma (1988)
Who Killed Pasolini? (1995)
Complicity (1995)
Il pratone del casilino (1996)
Le bassin de J.W. (1997)
Una disperata vitalità (1999)
Orgia (2002)
Salò: Yesterday and Today (2002)
Pasolini prossimo nostro (2006)
'Na specie de cadavere lunghissimo (2006)
La rabbia di Pasolini (2008)
Pilades (2016)

Of the thirteen features directed by Pier Paolo Pasolini, only one is an acknowledged masterpiece: *The Gospel According to St Matthew* (taking its place alongside meisterwerks such as *8 1/2*, *The Searchers,*

Sunrise, Ran, Rashomon, Ordet, Persona, Vertigo, The Magnificent Ambersons, Citizen Kane and *The Godfather*). Some Pasolini pictures are highly regarded (*Theorem, Salò, Accattone*), some are minor (*Mamma Roma*), some deserve to be much better known (*The Arabian Nights, Medea, Oedipus Rex*), some are almost wilfully obscure (*The Canterbury Tales, Theorem*), some are very patchy (*The Hawks and the Sparrows,* parts of the 'trilogy of life' films), only parts of *Pigsty* are any good,[4] and one is a disaster (*Love Meetings*). But only *The Gospel According To Matthew* has become an out-and-out classic, that can take its place in the top ten lists of the critical academy. *The Gospel According To Matthew* is no. 30 in *Sight & Sound*'s 2012 poll of top movies among directors, and is included in the Vatican's list of important films (which the Pontifical Council For Social Communications produced in 1995, for the 100th anniversary of cinema). Other Italian films on the Vatican's list are *Rome: Open City, Bicycle Thieves, The Road, 8 1/2, The Leopard* and a forerunner of *The Gospel, Francesco.*

And of Pier Paolo Pasolini's short fiction films (for anthology movies), most are disappointing (*The Witches, Capriccio all'Italiana, Love and Anger*), with only two attaining greatness (*Curd Cheese* and *The Anger*).

However, some critics and filmmakers have put *Salò* into their top ten lists, and Bernardo Bertolucci places *Accattone* in there (as have some other critics). Occasionally a film like *The Arabian Nights* or *Oedipus the King* makes it into a critic's top ten. (The Italian movies that regularly crop up in top ten movie lists include *The Leopard, The Road, Bicycle Thieves, La Dolce Vita, The Conformist, Voyage To Italy* and *Rome, Open City*. The single most beloved Italian movie around the world for film critics and film directors is definitely *8 1/2,* the astonishing and enormously

4 Yes, we know that *Pig Fry* is a poetical-political-polemical fable, a savage satire about survival and being human and capitalist consumerism and why aren't there any cafés on Mount Etna where you get a cheeseburger and a decent cup of coffee?

entertaining exploration of a modern film director in crisis helmed by Federico Fellini – closely followed by *La Dolce Vita*).

One should note, too, that directing 13 pictures over 15 years (from 1961-1975) is very productive (plus the anthology pieces and the documentaries). I wish that Pier Paolo Pasolini had started directing earlier (he was 40 when *Accattone* was released), and also that we might have seen the incredible work that Pasolini would no doubt have created from 1975 onwards (his *St Paul*, his *Socrates* – even, maybe, his *Terms of Endearment 3,* his *X-Men 6,* his *Star Trek 9*).

PASOLINI AS EUROPEAN *AUTEUR*

Although Pier Paolo Pasolini is classed with other European *auteurs* as a maker of small-scale art films (as if only North American or internationally-financed pictures could be 'epic' or large scale), in fact many of Pasolini's films as director have an enormous scope (and they were also part-financed by American companies). Sure, some of Pasolini's pictures are intimate and small-scale, but many of them happily contend with hundreds of extras, props, animals, costumes and a huge number of different locations and sets. In many movies directed by Pasolini the frame is teeming with human life – in the mediæval trilogy and in *The Gospel According To Matthew*. Pasolini, in some ways, is the European equivalent of Cecil B. DeMille or D.W. Griffith as a creator of historical epics.

Of course, there have been plenty of European, costume epic films over the years, but Pier Paolo Pasolini's films are very different from those international movies which are usually co-productions between, say, French, Italian, German, Spanish, Swedish or British film companies. Pasolini's films do not have the style, flavour or feel of the typical 'Euro-pudding' with their starry casts, glamour, and self-conscious apeing of Hollywood cinema.[5] Instead, Pasolini goes completely his own way, doesn't pander to creating star parts or scene-stealing cameos, doesn't cast U.S. actors, doesn't have easy-to-follow plots, doesn't shoot in English (or mid-Atlantic), and his cinematic approach is instantly recognizable (and has proved inimitable – very few film directors have the vision, the guts, the energy, the sheer stubbornness or, crucially, the *patience* to pursue that kind of grand, vast filmmaking).

Some of Pier Paolo Pasolini's Italian contemporaries produced large-scale historical films: Federico Fellini, Bernardo Bertolucci and Luchino Visconti, for instance. But Bertolucci's historical epics, from *1900* to *The Last Emperor* and *The Sheltering Sky*, were always commercial, European-American productions (in style and casting, if not in financing). Incredible as many of Bertolucci's later movies were, they were always slickly and glossily turned out, more than half in love with the creation of finely-crafted visuals (what Jean-Luc Godard called the cinema of Max Factor, his comments *pace Schindler's List*. Pasolini thought that Bertolucci had sold out to commercialism with *Last Tango In Paris*). Luchino Visconti's later films also have that eager eye on the international market. (Notice too that Pasolini doesn't do the usual thing of recreating the past accurately of historical movies: no, he preferred to produce characters and settings by analogy. Thus, the *Bible* wouldn't be filmed in Israel or Palestine, but in Calabria and Sicily).

Comparing the cinema of Pier Paolo Pasolini with that of Bernardo Bertolucci,[6] Bruce Kawin and Gerald Mast (in *A Short History of the Movies*) assert that Pasolini's movies are

more abstract, more elliptical, more complexly

5 However, Pasolini's later films were part-financed by American companies.
6 Pier Paolo Pasolini remarked that Bertolucci's 'real master is Godard' (*Pasolini On Pasolini*, 138).

structured, and more ferociously aggressive moral-
political investigations, enlivened and propelled
by dazzling bursts of unforgettable imagery...
(338)

In his history of Italian cinema, Gian Brunetta
remarked that

Of the entire generation of 1960s filmmakers, none
stood out like Pier Paolo Pasolini. He was a postwar
one-man band, capable ot transforming everything
he touched into gold, from painting, poetry, and
narartive to cinematography. Even his life and
death were works of art. (238)

Somehow, Pier Paolo Pasolini's films remained
stubbornly his own, far more idiosyncratic and eccentric
than most of his contemporaries, except filmmakers such
as Federico Fellini (Fellini's films were always highly
self-conscious and comical in their evocations of
history – *Fellini Satyricon*, for example, or *Roma*).
Sometimes reaching for camp eccentricity appears
laboured and clunky in cinema; for Pasolini, as for
Fellini, Walerian Borowczyk and Ken Russell, it seems
almost effortless (indeed, it is their natural habitat;
when people drew attention to the vulgarity, the
eccentricity, the eroticism and the silliness of their
movies, they would reply, eh? I don't know what you
mean. Because for them, it was natural to make movies
like that!).

No doubt Pier Paolo Pasolini was a powerful talent
in cinema, but let's not forget that he was aided by some
of the greatest artists in Italian cinema, some of whom
have been called geniuses: Danilo Donati (costumes),
Dante Ferretti (production designer), Nino Baragli
(editor), Sergio Citti (writer/ director), Giuseppe
Rotunno and Tonino Delli Colli (photographers) and
Ennio Morricone (composer).

There must have been times when Pier Paolo
Pasolini's producers pleaded with the *auteur* to at least
include some big names in some cameos, or to cast one

or two star actors. But no, Pasolini simply didn't. However, he and his casting directors did put some well-known faces into his movies, include Silvana Mangano, Anna Magnani, Terence Stamp, Orson Welles, Totò, Hugh Griffith, Jean-Pierre Léaud, and Maria Callas. (And of course Pasolini helped to make Franco Citti a star, at least in Italy).

But I'm sure some of Pier Paolo Pasolini's producers wished he'd used plenty more stars, or used them in the conventional way (that would be the instinct of Italian producers such as Dino de Laurentiis and Carlo Ponti). There would be all sorts of factors involved here, not least money – the budgets of some of Pasolini's movies were small, compared to big, international co-productions, and to Hollywood A-pictures. Also, I would guess that some film stars wouldn't want to appear in the kind of movies that Pasolini was making (and also, they wouldn't do some of the things that the movies required, such as nudity. Sure, Marlon Brando might bugger Maria Schneider in *Last Tango In Paris*, but he did it fully clothed!).

It's intriguing to note that Pier Paolo Pasolini made three ancient world movies: *The Gospel According To Matthew*, *Medea* and *Oedipus Rex*, and three Middle Ages movies: *The Arabian Nights*, *The Decameron* and *The Canterbury Tales*. He was very happy in distant history (most filmmakers, if they film historical periods, go back to the mid or early 20th century (often their early years, or that of their parents), or to the 19th century[7] at most). Indeed, the last significant work that Pasolini produced that was set in the contemporary period in feature movies was one half of *Porcile* (the other half was set in the 15th century). His next four films after 1969 were historical pieces.

You can easily discern the influence of the cinema of Pier Paolo Pasolini on filmmakers such as Sergei Paradjanov (a huge admirer of Pasolini), Federico

---

7 Pier Paolo Pasolini's works are steeped in Victoriana – the hysterical melodrama, the Gothicism and Romanticism, the early Industrial Revolution, the emerging metropolises, the industrialization of desire in mass prostitution, early capitalism, etc.

Fellini, Francis Coppola, Oliver Stone, Terry Gilliam (and the Monty Python team),[8] Derek Jarman, Peter Greenaway, Bernardo Bertolucci, Martin Scorsese, Jeunet and Caro, Guillermo del Toro and Abel Ferrara. In 2003 Gian Brunetta noted Pasolini's continuing impact on Italian filmmakers such as Mario Martone, Luigi Faccini, Nico d'Alessandria, Aurelio Grimaldi, Pappi Corsicato, Daniele Ciprí and Franco Maresco (239).

> Pasolini's life's work and his cinema continue to speak to us thanks to his cultural nomadism, his ability to mix and hybridize all codes, his asystematic working method, and his ability to tap into the pulse and capture the soul of minorities and regional identity. (239)

FIRST WORKS IN CINEMA

In Bologna, Pier Paolo Pasolini saw some of the classics for the first time: Charlie Chaplin, Jean Renoir, René Clair, etc. 'That's where my great love for the cinema started' (PP, 30). Films like *Rome, Open City* and *Bicycle Thieves*[9] made a big impact on the young Pasolini (ibid.).

Pier Paolo Pasolini had written his first film script in 1945 (aged 23), called *I calzon* or *Lied*. When he arrived in Roma (in 1950), he began writing movie scripts professionally. Some of the early screenplays were co-written (such as *La Donna del Fiume*, with Giorgio Bassani).

In the mid-1950s, Pier Paolo Pasolini was working

8 One can see the influence of Pier Pasolini Pasolini in the Ancient Greek sequence in *Time Bandits* (Terry Gilliam, 1981), or in Monty Python's *Life of Brian* (the desert sequences in both films also allowed the two Terrys (Jones and Gilliam) to recreate Pasolini, whom they loved, as well as a bit of the Biblical epics – *Ben-Hur* and *The Ten Commandments*).
9 He went to Udine (from Casarsa) specially to see *Bicycle Thieves.* He wasn't so young, tho' – *Bicycle Thieves* was released in 1948, when Pasolini was 26.

in movies as a scriptwriter. He published his key works in this period – such as *Ragazzi di vita* and his poetry book *La Meglio gioventù.*

When Pier Paolo Pasolini was dating Sergio Citti in the mid-1950s, he became friendly with many of the *ragazzi* of the *borgate*, the real-life street kids who would become non-professional actors in his first movies, from *Accattone* onwards.

Pier Paolo Pasolini was most productive in the years prior to his entry into film production, according to his biographer Enzo Siciliano: from 1953 to 1961. This was the period when he published novels (*Ragazzi di Vita, Una Vita Violenta*), poetry (*La Ceneri di Gramsci, La Religione del mio tempo*), 13 film scripts, translations (*Oresteia*), and magazine articles (such as for *Officina*).

SCRIPTS

All of the movies that Pier Paolo Pasolini wrote before taking up directing with *Accattone* were *co*-written: Pasolini was *not* the sole screenwriter on *La Donna del Fiume, Il Prigioniero della Montagna, Le Notti di Cabiria, Marisa La Civetta*, etc. Instead, he was part of writing teams which included Basilio Franchina, Florestano Vancini, Antonio Altovitti and Mario Soldati (*La Donna del Fiume*), Luis Trenker, and Giorgio Bassani (*Il Prigioniero della Montagna*), Federico Fellini, Ennio Flaiano and Tullio Pinelli (*Nights of Cabiria*), etc. Other films Pasolini contributed to were: *The Big Night, La Giornata balorda, Giovani mariti, Morte di un amico, Il Carro armato dell '8 settembre, La Ragazza in vetrina* and *La Cantata delle marane.* Pasolini worked with Bassani (1916-2000) on several films, including *Una Notte del' 43.* Bassani dubbed Orson Welles in *Curd Cheese,* and he wrote the novel *Il*

Giardino dei Finzi-Contini (later filmed by Vittorio de Sica).

It's also worth noting that before he started to direct with *Accattone*, Pier Paolo Pasolini had already had some of his works made into movies – though he didn't direct them. A chapter of the important Pasolini novel *Ragazzi di Vita* was adapted in *La Canta dell Marane* (1960, dir. Cecilia Mangini), and *Ragazzi di Vita* was made into a movie in 1959, as *La Notte Brava* (= *The Big Night*, dir. Mauro Bolognini), and *Una Vita Violenta* (= *A Violent Life*) was filmed by Ennio De Concini, Franco Brusati, Paolo Heusch, Brunello Rondi and Franco Solinas in 1962 (*Una Vita Violenta*, dir. Paolo Heusch and Brunello Rondi).

✼

Only a very few filmmakers write and direct their movies. I don't mean co-write, I mean who are the sole writers of their films. And even fewer filmmakers write and direct *from their own ideas* (i.e., they come up with the fundamental concept). Because most movies are adapted from existing material, whether it's comic-books, plays, books, computer games, TV shows, musicals, newspaper articles, or even theme park rides (plus remakes, sequels, reboots, etc).

And Pier Paolo Pasolini is no different: although we think of him as an *auteur*, writing and directing his movies (each one with the possessive credit: '*un film scritto e diretto da*'), in fact maybe half of his movies are based on existing material. They do not come from ideas and stories that Pasolini has conceived himself. Instead, they are adaptations – usually of classic literature: mediæval literature in three movies (the 'trilogy of life' series), three ancient world sources (*The Gospel According To Matthew*, *Medea* and *Oedipus Rex*), and the Marquis de Sade (*Salò*). So Pasolini didn't invent the concepts, the characters, the stories, the situations, the themes, the settings, the interactions, the relationships or many other elements of those adaptations.

The movies that are based on Pier Paolo Pasolini's

own ideas and stories include: *The Hawks and the Sparrows, Accattone, Mamma Roma, Theorem, Curd Cheese, The Earth Seen From the Moon* and *Pigsty*. Also, Pasolini did *not* write everything himself: he co-authored his scripts with writers such as Dacia Maraini, Pupi Avati, Giorgio Bassani, and Sergio Citti.

Pier Paolo Pasolini didn't take up pot-boilers, sleazy novels, airport fiction, computer games, theme park rides, TV comedies, sit-coms, radio shows, comicbooks or the backs of cereal packets to adapt into movies: he took up the very greatest literature, heavy-weight authors like Sophocles, Euripides, Aeschylus, the *Bible*, Giovanni Boccaccio, Geoffrey Chaucer, the Marquis de Sade and *The Thousand and One Nights*. Well, that's a *very* impressive list! Nobody can doubt the high ambition or the seriousness of the master's approach!

For Jean-Luc Godard, all of the work in making a film is *already done* before the cameras started rolling. The real work of making the film was the scriptwriting and the preparation. 'Most people think they work only when the camera is rolling, but that's not it. When the camera rolls, everything is done already'.[10] That certainly applies to Pasolini – it's all about the conception and the writing.

FLAWS IN PASOLINI'S CINEMA

I am writing about the movies directed by Pier Paolo Pasolini primarily as movies, as movie experiences, in a deliberately simple and direct manner. But of course there are *thematic* and *narrative* and *political* and *psychological* and *theoretical* perspectives to these films which are rich and inspiring.

However, there are times in watching a Pasolini

10 *Interviews*, 1998, 174.

movie when you think:

This is twaddle.[11]

I don't care if he's a major poet and political rebel and cultural iconoclast! It's as if Dante Alighieri directed *Deep Throat*!

Observers of the Legend and Cult of Pasolini in the early 1970s might've looked at the 'trilogy of life' movies with exasperation and dismay: when is Pasolini, they might've thought, going to stop bothering with these silly saucy frolics and get back to something worthy of his immense talents, like *Medea* or *Oedipus Rex*? (Well, Pasolini *did* come back to something very serious after the three Middle Ages romps, but it was *Salò, or The 120 Days of Sodom*! – a film that was so far in the other direction, it wasn't what audiences were expecting, and probably not what the Pasolini admirers wanted).

Unfortunately, with the less-than-successful movies in the Pier Paolo Pasolini canon – such as *Love Meetings, The Hawks and the Sparrows, Pigsty* and *The Canterbury Tales* – it becomes more difficult to sustain the hi-falutin' theoretical approach. I mean, if you didn't know that Pasolini directed *The Canterbury Tales,* would we even be discussing it today? Wouldn't it have been relegated to the marginal critical discourses of cult movies or *mondo* cinema? An entertaining, weird, over-the-top slice of 1970s kitsch, but ultimately small potatoes?

Not *everything* by a great filmmaker has to be 'great' (or can be 'great'), does it?[12] Orson Welles completed twelve features (a comparable number with Pier Paolo Pasolini's thirteen features): seven are masterpieces, by my reckoning – *Kane, Ambersons, Othello, Touch, Macbeth, F For Fake* and *Shanghai* –

---

11 This thought – am I watching piffle? – occurs with many directors who are highly critically acclaimed – Steven Spielberg, Sergio Leone, Billy Wilder, Martin Scorsese, John Woo, Vincente Minnelli, even Alfred Hitchcock, John Ford and D.W. Griffith.
12 Like many filmmakers (such as Woody Allen, Tim Burton and Hayao Miyazaki), Pier Paolo Pasolini said he never went to see his own films (PP, 108). Sometimes he saw them at film festivals, but he'd never dared to go see one of his movies in a public theatre.

but his 1955 movie *Mr Arkadin* (a.k.a. *Confidential Report*) was, by his own admission, a failure (whichever you look at, in whichever botched, public domain version you get to see it, *Mr Arkadin* is incredibly disappointing). *Mr Arkadin* was an important personal project for Welles, but the post-production had been unhappy (a recurring motif in Welles' film career), and the film had been re-cut by the producer (Louis Dolivet).

Or take Francis Coppola: an all-round filmmaker with few peers and a truly colossal talent, Coppola has directed at least three masterpieces (*The Godfathers 1* and *2* and *Apocalypse Now*, though some would include *The Conversation*, and I would include more), but many critics found *Jack* (1996) perplexingly lightweight, and Coppola's two early movies – *Finian's Rainbow* (1968) and *You're a Big Boy Now* (1966) – are uneven (some would say mis-conceived and very dissatisfying – certainly *Finian's Rainbow*, as a Fred Astaire musical, is under-whelming).

To a degree, Pier Paolo Pasolini suffered like Orson Welles and Francis Coppola from a similar problem, seen in conventional critical terms: they were very successful early in their careers. Everything Welles did after *Citizen Kane* was compared with *Citizen Kane*, and his films never escaped that blinkered view from critics.[13] And Coppola is routinely satirized by critics as the man who directed *The Godfather* but went into artistic 'decline' in the 1980s with *The Cotton Club* and *One From the Heart.*

Rubbish, of course, but persistent rubbish.

Pier Paolo Pasolini, meanwhile, launched a filmmaking career with a minor masterwork, *Accattone*, and produced the staggering, 100% classic *The Gospel According To Matthew* three years later. As with Orson Welles and Francis Coppola and other filmmakers, early successes mean other movies can get made, but the stigma of early triumphs can colour the critical reception of later works. And in the case of Welles and

---

13 Which is also applied all the time to Woody Allen, where audiences prefer his early, funny films.

Coppola, critics' emphasis on the early triumphs becomes obsessive (both Coppola and Welles became completely exasperated by everybody harking on about those early works, even while they appreciated that at least people were talking about them!).

I'm sure that the later films of Pier Paolo Pasolini tried the patience and devotion of even his most ardent admirers (as with the later work of Jean-Luc Godard, Walerian Borowczyk, Ken Russell and Terry Gilliam). You can imagine Pasolini-worshippers turning up to theatres to see *Pigsty* in 1969 or *The Canterbury Tales* in 1972, and wondering if their Freudo-Marxo-Poetico God was losing his marbles. Jean-Pierre Léaud getting freaky with pigs in a film about cannibalism? Eh?! Hugh Griffith humping on top of Charlie Chaplin's daughter in a movie stuffed with spotty, greasy, British non-actors?

✳

When you watch the films of Pier Paolo Pasolini again and again, some of the technical aspects and the flaws do rankle: the shaky, handheld camera,[14] the patchy sound, the endless shots of people walking, and too much Ninetto Davoli.

There is a *lot* of filler in Pier Paolo Pasolini's later films. Filler meaning, for example, shots of people walking in landscapes and towns. Now, the Pasolini sympathizers can point out the atmospherics, the mood, the Existential loneliness, the exquisitely-poised, onto-logical *ennui*, etc, of a shot of a guy walking across a volcano (*Pigsty*) or thru an anonymous, Middle Eastern town (*The Arabian Nights*). But Pasolini detractors can rightly criticize such images as pointless, redundant, or dramatically, poetically empty – the characters have already been established, the story is already in progress, the chief locales have been explored, so four shots of a guy getting from A to B are not necessary, and even harm the narrative flow.

---

14 Pier Paolo Pasolini operated the *macchina* himself sometimes. Unfortunately, he's no Stanley Kubrick, Ridley Scott or Ken Russell. He can't
hold a camera. (One of the reasons for his terrible camerawork might be
that he's yelling instructions at his actors at the same time!)

Take a movie everybody has seen – *Jaws* (1975): do we need to watch Police Chief Brody driving for 15 minutes down to the dock where he joins the crew of the *Orca* boat? No – we cut straight to it. Do we need to see all fifteen hours of the connecting flights from the U.S.A. to the island off the coast of Costa Rica in *Jurassic Park* (1993) – plus four hours waiting in the terminal at Panama? No – we cut straight to the island. (An Ancient Greek text might say, 'And then he went to Thebes'. But that doesn't mean we need to see five lengthy shots of a guy walking to Thebes!).

Endless shots of people walking are a sure sign that a filmmaker is out of ideas. Yes, even a hyper-super-mega-genius like Pasolini. There's no juice in such shots (even isolated, Existential, metaphysical, onto-logical, outsider-ish juice). The filmmaker has admitted to the audience: *I have no idea how to dramatize the script or the story.* (This occurs even in *The Gospel According To Matthew*).

ANTI-CINEMA

When you consider all of the films of Pier Paolo Pasolini, sometimes it seems as if these movies *don't* want to be liked, or enjoyed (at least in the usual manner). As if, as with Carl-Theodor Dreyer, Robert Bresson and Andrei Tarkovsky, Pasolini wasn't going to make it easy for the viewer. And sometimes it can appear as if Pasolini's movies are being deliberately off-putting. Not 'offensive' or 'obscene', just plain difficult or obscure. A kind of anti-cinema, where expectations are wilfully, stubbornly scuppered. (Yes, there is definitely in Pasolini a delight in being difficult for the sake of it, as with Jean-Luc Godard).

For example, how would a Pier Paolo Pasolini movie play in a big cinema multiplex today? Reactions might run from laughter, scorn and ridicule to dismay and walk-outs. These are not movies that're going to preview well! They would die a death in the preview process, where unreleased movies are shown to invited audiences from the general public, getting a near-zero rating from the score cards. (Pasolini's personality, his financial contracts – and his reputation – would mean his films would be exempted from the preview process. Is a Pasolini movie going to be screened before an audience culled from shopping malls in San Diego who're then going to 'judge' his movie? I don't think so!).

They are not funny when they're meant to be funny, they are not scary when they're meant to be scary, they are not thrilling when they're meant to be thrilling, they are not dramatic when you expect/ hope them to be dramatic, they are not romantic when you think they might be romantic. They don't do what audiences would expect them to do. The technical aspects let Pier Paolo Pasolini's movies down, from the sound (the crude voice dubbing, the lack of sound effects (or 'immersion'), and the poor sound mixes),[15] to the picture (the too-shaky camerawork, and the sometimes indifferent staging).

There's an impossible-to-miss self-analysis in Pier Paolo Pasolini's cinema, a love-hate relationship with the material: as with the movies of Jean-Luc Godard, you can feel Pasolini's films arguing with themselves, simultaneously loving as well as distrusting the material, the themes, even individual shots. Like all artists, Pasolini wants to have it all ways: to evoke a scene of, say, extras in exotic costumes in a dusty, Mediterranean setting, but also to critique the subject and the very idea of making a movie in the first place.

This restlessness and dissatisfaction permeates not

15 Oh, how I wish that Alfredo Bini or Franco Rossellini or Alberto Grimaldi, the principal producers of Pier Paolo Pasolini's movies, had said, OK, we will use some of the budget to buy some decent sound equipment. This time it's live sound for us! Direct sound! Sound recorded on the set! *Si, si*, no more crappy dubbing at Cinecittà for us! (But the maestro of course preferred to deal with the sound in post-production).

only Pier Paolo Pasolini's cinema but also his poetry, and his whole work. And his personality, too, as those who knew him attest. Pasolini, everybody agrees, was a very complicated person.

✳

The cinema of Pier Paolo Pasolini does not do other things that audiences expect from movies. They do not employ conventional dramaturgy, for example. They avoid the conventions of rising action and cause and effect. So the flow of the drama and the narrative from scene-to-scene of your average movie is negated. Pasolini's movies do not build and build with suspense or tension or drama. Many scenes are self-enclosed, with little relation to scenes before or after.

And when you couple that avoidance of conventional dramaturgy with the intense stylizations of Pier Paolo Pasolini's cinematic approach – the flattened, static, *tableau* approach, for instance, or the paucity of dialogue or exposition – it creates a cinema that can be tough-going for some viewers. You can't slide thru a Pasolini movie easily, quickly and cheaply (with no investment): you have to *work*. It's not easy-to-digest television, like *C.S.I.* or *Friends*.

Pier Paolo Pasolini wasn't interested in action, either, or staging impressive spectacles (the 1st A.D.s would organize a vast array of extras, animals and props, which would then be filmed with a single, wobbly, handheld shot from a single viewpoint).[16] Like Jean-Luc Godard, Pasolini was indifferent to action (Godard famously filmed action as quickly as possible; he just couldn't be bothered with it). Pasolini wasn't interested in the glamour of cinema, or in making people look gorgeous, like the Hollywood Dream Factory (tho' he would insist on very extravagant costumes and hats. Which would then be filmed somewhat casually – unlike Walerian Borowczyk, who has probably the most acute and sensual feeling for clothes in all cinema).

---

16 No multiple cameras, either, or additional takes for safety, to make sure that a scene had been captured.

DOCUMENTARIES

Sam Rohdie noted that 'Pasolini's documentaries were feigned. His past was not real, but a fragment framed, cut out. Reality was mutilated to make it all the more beautiful' (1995, 109). Pasolini realized that his essay/ documentary pieces were for a minority, intellectual audience (PP, 140).

Pier Paolo Pasolini's documentaries are niche, certainly, and they are let down by misguided concepts, some dubious ideology, and poor technical aspects. But with the right producer, or maybe the right commissions from television companies, I reckon that Pasolini might've been amongst the finest documentary filmmakers in cinema. He possessed all of the skills required to deliver some great material, except for the discipline and rigour to really make the material fly. Plus, with a major TV company behind him, he could have drawn on the resources necessary to complete the ambitious projects he wanted to make. (But he would also need a very strong TV producer who could say 'no' to his face).

Take the documentary made in Africa and Italy about staging an African version of Aeschylus' *Oresteia* – *Notes Towards an African Oresteia* (1970). The concept is full of ideological holes, and the execution is scrappy at best, and downright dreadful at worst.

So dump all of that material, and start again with a decent team of filmmakers and decent resources, and put the director himself in the picture (it's silly to squander a striking and well-known personality on camera like Pasolini, and have him hide behind a microphone back in Roma. Put Pasolini front and centre. And let's also see Pasolini directing his cast of amateurs in Africa).

Compare Pier Paolo Pasolini's documentaries with two geniuses of the medium in the same Euro-art arena: Werner Herzog and Jean-Luc Godard. Herzog has produced a striking and lively set of documentaries and film essays, often about exotic subjects in far-flung places (the Amazon, Africa, caves, etc). Like Pasolini,

Herzog often appears in his documentaries, exploring places and interviewing people. He is a far more sympathetic interviewer than Pasolini, who tended to dominate his interviewees, and to ask them rhetorical questions (as if he'd already decided what he wanted his documentary to say). Herzog's documentaries are quirky and very distinctive (Herzog's German-accented voiceovers identified them as thoroughly Herzogian).

Jean-Luc Godard, meanwhile, is a master of the film essay form – half of his fiction movies, for example, might be characterized as film essays. Godard produced several fascinating film essays about his feature films, which he called notes for films (and Godard can talk about cinema as few people can, including Pasolini. Godard is a formidable intellectual talent). And with *Histoire(s) du Cinéma,* Godard created an epic history of cinema (between 1989 and 1998). *Histories of Cinema* was a major work, and has generated a good deal of critical comment. As well as being a history of cinema, it was also a history of the age – and a history of Godard himself.

DOCUMENTARIES ABOUT PASOLINI

Pier Paolo Pasolini has fascinated TV documentary producers – there was a documentary of 1970 (filmed with Pasolini's co-operation), and *Who Says the Truth Shall Die* (Phil Bregstein, 1981). Several documentaries have appeared on *Salò – Fade To Black* (2001), *Salò: Yesterday and Today* (2002), *Enfants de Salò* (2006, French), *Pasolini Prossimo Nostro* (2006, Italian) and *The End of Salò* (2008). Pasolini's murder was explored in *Who Killed Pasolini?* (1995). A ficionalized account of Pasolini was released in 2014 (with Willem Dafoe as the great man).

PASOLINI.

Pasolini (Abel Ferrara, 2014) was a biographical portrait of the last days of Pier Paolo Pasolini. Starring Willem Dafoe, Maria de Medeiros, Ninetto Davoli, Adrianna Asti and Riccardo Scamarcio, produced by Thierry Lounas and Fabio Massimo Cacciatori for the production companies Urania Pictures/ Dublin Films/ Belgacom/ Canal Plus, and scripted by Maurizio Braucci, *Pasolini* was a curiously flat and unengaging take on an incendiary filmmaker and poet. For Pasolinians, there was not only nothing new here, and the opportunities for depicting a complex and compelling artist were squandered. *Pasolini* took a de-dramatized approach, flattening the aspects of this passionate artist into a series of boring images and boring dialogues.

We see: Pasolini working on the post-production of *Salò;* a snippet of Pasolini's home life (with his mother Susanna prominent (played by Pasolini regular Adriana Asti – she was Amore in *Accattone*)); an interview with a journalist; a visit from an effervescent actress;[17] and extracts from a novel that Pasolini was working on.

Pasolini was one of those works in which nothing much happens – either visually, narratively, dramatic-ally, psychologically or philosophically. More like notes for a possible movie about Pier Paolo Pasolini (in the Godardian manner). It's scrappy. Bitty.

Time passes… *Pasolini* ends… a pointless group of images and sounds. Cinema at its worst.

Pasolini came alive a tad when Ninetto Davoli entered the frame – sort of playing himself (and shadowed by his former self, played by Riccardo Scamarcio), in an illustration of an unmade film idea from Pasolini about a spiritual journey/ religious skits, which included a visit to a gay and lesbian Sodom and Gomorrah (a festival where couples tup and the audience around them jeers and cheers. Presumably this is meant to be the 1973 unmade film project *Porno-Teo-Kolossal*). Not a patch on what Pasolini himself

17 Is that meant to be Laura Betti? (Played by Maria de Medeiros).

would've done with a modern-day Sodom and Gomorrah scenario, of course.

Pasolini recreated the night in November, 1975, when the director was murdered after picking up a youth. This played out as expected, but without the political/ ideological/ blackmailing motives (instead, the three youths who round on Pasolini attack him partly for homophobic reasons, yelling insults as they kick him. That fudged the issue, avoiding an opportunity to explore the more controversial issues surrounding Pasolini's demise).

4

ASPECTS OF
PASOLINI'S CINEMA

PIER PAOLO PASOLINI AND ITALIAN CINEMA

Pier Paolo Pasolini made his thirteen feature movies as a film director between 1961 and 1975, the years of a boom in the Italian film business, and of the European New Wave (but he had been working on co-written scripts thru the Fifties). This period of Italian cinema was marked by the regeneration of production after WW2, with movements such as the development of Neo-realism (embodied in productions such as *Rome: Open City,* Roberto Rossellini, 1945 and *Bicycle Thieves,* Vittorio de Sica, 1948). However, Neo-realist cinema was not popular in Italy itself, but overseas (especially North America). The significant filmmakers of this period were, with Rossellini and de Sica, Luchino Visconti and Alberto Lattuada. North American companies increasingly used Italian studios (such as Cinecittà): they followed the money, which couldn't be repatriated. When M.G.M. made *Quo Vadis* in Italy in 1950, other U.S. studios followed (and the Yanks visited Italy throughout the 1960s).

Actually, how 'Italian' is Italian cinema? Pasolini's and Fellini's later films, for example, were backed by North American companies (such as United Artists). It was the same with Visconti and Antonioni, as director Glauber Rocha of Brazil's New Cinema pointed out in the mid-1960s: 'Italy does not really have a national film industry, a truly Italian cinema, anymore' (in D. Georgakas, 17).

In the 1960s, Federico Fellini, Michelangelo Antonioni, Bernardo Bertolucci, Marco Bellocchio, Sergei Leone and the Tavianis were among the key film directors in Italy, as well as Pier Paolo Pasolini. The film stars included Marcello Mastroianni, Monica Vitti, Anna Magnani, Gina Lollobrigida, Sophia Loren, Vittorio Gassman, Totò and Silvana Mangano (Pasolini used Totò and Mangano the most). Among film producers of the period, such as Alberto Grimaldi and Alfredo Bini (who produced Pasolillni's films), two stand out in the Italian industry: Carlo Ponti[18] (married to Loren) and Dino de Laurentiis (married to Mangano); Pasolini worked with all of them).

The 1960s, according to Gian Brunetta,

> would prove to be the years of the greatest experimentation, freedom, and expressive riches. Not everything in the cauldron was made of gold, but the average qualitative level was the highest of all time. (171)

The Italian film industry reacted swiftly to any big hit movie, hurrying copies and sequels into production. Thus, successful movies such as *Spartacus* (1960), *Cleopatra* (1963), *Ben-Hur* (1959), and *Hercules* (1958) led to instant cash-ins. As Howard Hughes noted in *Cinema Italiano*:

> The story of Italian cinema is essentially a series of creative explosions, interspersed with fallow periods of audience exhaustion. If a film was popular, literally dozens of imitations would be made to cash-in at the domestic and international

18 Carlo Ponti (1912-2007) is one of the legends of the Italian film industry. Ponti produced some 140 movies, including many film classics, such as *La Strada, Boccaccio '70, Doctor Zhivago, War and Peace, Closely Watched Trains, Cléo From 5 To 7,* and three Michelangelo Antonioni flicks, *The Passenger, Blow-Up* and *Zabriskie Point.*

box office. This intense technique often resulted in each fad enjoying rather limited longevity, as the glut quickly satisfied audience interest. (ix-xi)

Thus, there was a craze of muscleman movies with mythological or ancient world settings, inaugurated by *Hercules*[19] (1958),[20] which lasted from 1958 to 1964. The Spaghetti Western fad, sparked by the *Dollars* films starring Clint Eastwood, ran from 1965 to 1970 (but continued into the 1970s). The *James Bond*-inspired spy cycle ran from 1963 to 1967. Gothic horror flicks were popular from 1960 to 1965 (and again in the 1970s with the *gialli*). 1960 was a triumphant year for Italian cinema, with *Rocco and His Brothers* and *La Dolce Vita* becoming big critical and commercial successes. Pasolini's cinema had its own cash-ins (the 'trilogy of life' movies were obvious candidates for rip-offs, which were released rapidly following the success of *The Decameron*. Producers saw that they could deliver sex romps much cheaper, by leaving out the elaborate set-pieces with extras and animals).

Along with Germany, Spain, Holland and of course France, Italy has been one of the most significant film production territories in Europe. The number of productions made each year and the number of tickets sold (i.e., punters going to the cinema) is among the highest in Europe.

Pier Paolo Pasolini benefited from the boom years of Italian film production, when it was making more movies per year than Hollywood: 242 films were produced in 1962, for example, compared to 174 in North America. 245 films in Italy in 1966, compared to

19 The Italian 1958 *Hercules* (the first one), starring Steve Reeves (Mr Universe) and helmed by Pietro Francisci, was so successful it inaugurated a series of Italian 'muscle-men', sword-and-sandal epics – some 180 films. *Hercules* cost $120,000 and made $20 million, and was released in 1959 thru Warners (producer Joe Levine had paid $120,000 for the rights). Its budget was less than 1% of that of Hollywood's *Ben-Hur* or *The Ten Commandments*, yet it made somewhere between 1/8th and 1/3rd as much (a producer's dream!). Levine launched *Hercules* with $1.1 million of advertizing, including on television ('the most aggressive campaign any film ever had', as William Goldman put it). 20 The couple in *A Violent Life* go to see a *Hercules* movie at the cinema.

168 in the U.S.A. 237 productions in 1974, compared to 156 in America (the recession hit Hollywood badly in the early 1970s).

In the 1960s and the 1970s, the period when Pier Paolo Pasolini was active as a film director, Italy made more movies than any other European country, including France (which since then has become the premier country for production *and* consumption), and more people went to the cinema in Italy than in any other nation (this's if you exclude Russia from Europe – which most people did in the Cold War era).

So film culture is immensely significant in Italy (even though de-regulated, hyper-capitalist television in the Silvio Berlusconi era has over-shadowed it). And the star filmmakers, like Federico Fellini, Luchino Visconti, Bernardo Bertolucci, Michelangelo Antonioni and Pier Paolo Pasolini, have become well-known outside film circles. And Dino de Laurentiis is a legendary mogul whose movies (and those produced by his daughter Raffaella) have generated billions.[21]

Dino de Laurentiis (1919-2010) was probably the most well-known Italian producer of recent times, a formidable mogul who moved from Italian movies (*Il Bandito, Bitter Rice, Anna, Europa '51, La Lupa, La Strada*), to North American co-productions (*War and Peace, Ulysses*), to international movies (*Barabbas, Bandits In Rome, Serpico, Barbarella, Three Days of the Condor* and *The Valachi Papers*), and epics (*The Bible, Waterloo, The Bounty* and *Dune*). De Laurentiis produced all-out commercial ventures (such as *King Kong, Death Wish, Hurricane, Orca the Killer Whale, Flash Gordon, Conan the Barbarian, Year of the Dragon, Body of Evidence* and *Hannibal*), but also movies by art maestros like Ingmar Bergman, Federico Fellini, Luchino Visconti, Michael Cimino, Milos Forman, David Lynch, Vittorio de Sica and Robert

21 Jean-Luc Godard sent up Italian producers such as Carlo Ponti and Dino de Laurentiis (whom he's worked with), in his film *Passion* (1982), who always turn up with a beautiful woman on their arm. The producer in *Passion* yells: 'where's my money?', 'what have you done with my money?' It's one of the recurring phrases in the film business (usually yelled out, of course it should be).

Altman (such as *Buffalo Bill, Desperate Hours, Face To Face, Lo Straniero,* and *Blue Velvet*). In North America in the 1980s, de Laurentiis founded D.E.G. (De Laurentiis Entertainment Group) in North Carolina, which flourished until it ended in 1988 (with, some said, debts of $200 million).

Dino de Laurentiis' career is truly remarkable – and long-running (he began producing during the German Occupation of Italy). He formed Real Cine in 1941 (when he was 23), produced *Il Bandito* (Alberto Lattuada, 1946), when he was 28, and married actress Silvana Mangano (who appeared in Pier Paolo Pasolini's *Theorem, The Decameron, The Witches* and *Oedipus Rex,* among others). With Carlo Ponti, de Laurentiis formed Ponti-De Laurentiis in 1950 (they owned the Farnesina Studios in Rome). De Laurentiis created Dinocittà outside Rome, where *The Bible, The Great War* and *Barabbas* were based. (Dinocittà has since become a movie theme park).

PASOLINI AND FELLINI

In the late 1950s, Pier Paolo Pasolini became part of Federico Fellini's court.[22] They had met at the Canova (Franco Rossi had brought them together). They took to wandering around Roma at night, with Pasolini introducing Fellini to some of the locations he drew inspiration from: Idroscalo, Tiburtino Terzo, Pietralata and Guidonia. The maestro had brought in Pasolini (and his partner, Sergio Citti) to help with some of his scripts (such as advising on the dialect in *Nights of Cabiria*[23] – dialect being one of Pasolini's passions). Pasolini wrote

22 Totò parodied *La Dolce Vita* in *Totò, Peppino and La Dolce Vita* (1960).
23 The settings of *Nights of Cabiria* – the outskirts of Roma, the scrubland and the caves – were employed several times in Pasolini's early films.

about 40 pages of the screenplay, according to Moraldo Rossi, but Fellini hardly used any of it.[24]

Federico Fellini later invited P.P. Pasolini to sit in on auditions at Cinecittà for projects such as *La Dolce Vita* (1960). Although some in the Fellini camp resented the maestro becoming so close to Pasolini, it was not a long-lasting friendship.[25] Fellini's wife Giulietta took 'an immediate dislike to the homosexual Pier Paolo as a corruptor of innocent young souls'),[26] and Fellini's regular screenwriter, Ennio Flaiano, refused to work with Pasolini on *La Dolce Vita*. Flaiano (known as a cynical, spiky writer) wrote a skit about it – *"La Dolce Vita* According To Pasolini"* (which Fellini begged him not to publish).

Pier Paolo Pasolini had hoped that Federico Fellini (and his new company, Federiz, formed with the publisher Angelo Rizzoli), would back his first movie as director, *Accattone*[27] (Fellini and Rizzoli were also planning movies by Vittorio De Seta, Ermanno Olmi, Marco Ferreri and of course Fellini. But in the end, Fellini wasn't bothered about becoming a movie mogul – he only wanted to make his own films).

Tests for *Accattone* were shot (in September, 1960),[28] including two scenes: at via Fanfulla da Lodi, in the pine woods, and outside Castel Sant'Angelo. Pasolini later recalled meeting with Fellini to discuss them (after hearing nothing from the maestro): but it

24 Quoted in *Fellini On Fellini* 1995, 50.

25 It was a lively friendship, tho', according to Enzo Siciliano, 'a deep human attachment' (ES, 223).

26 Quoted in T. Kezich, 178.

27 *Accattone* announces its quirkiness from the outset: after those Renaissance-elegant opening titles, and the breezy, rarefied tones of J.S. Bach, what is the first shot of the movie? A pretty aerial view of the Eternal City? Oh no, this is not going to be a film featuring dignified professional actors spouting Shakespeare or Petrarch! Instead, it's a close-up of the ugly mug of Fulvio, joshing with the lads in their customary position: sitting outside the café in the side street. The final shot of *Accattone* is of Balilla, crossing himself as he looks down at the dying Accattone.

28 This was Pier Paolo Pasolini's first experience of being a film director, at least with his own material. His model was the 'absolutely simplicity of expression' in *The Passion of Joan of Arc*, directed by Carl-Theodor Dreyer. Another influential film for Pasolini was the 1950 *Francesco*, the portrait of St Francis and his followers directed by Roberto Rossellini using all non-professional actors (except for Aldo Fabrizi).

became apparent that Fellini and Rizzoli were not going to get behind *Accattone* (which in the event was produced by Alfredo Bini[29] – it was Bini who persuaded Pasolini to make *Accattone*).[30] According to Moraldo Rossi, Pasolini 'had staked everything on Fellini, but Fellini had dropped him'.[31] And from that point, Fellini and Pasolini fell out, sniping at each other's projects in the press.

PIER PAOLO PASOLINI'S COLLEAGUES

Critics typically talk about Pier Paolo Pasolini's movies in awed, auteurist terms, as if the director did *everything* in his movies. He didn't, though: he directed them, sometimes appeared in them in cameos, and wrote or co-wrote most of them (Pasolini did, however, believe in the *auteur* theory, unlike almost every filmmaker).[32] Thus, his films usually have the credit:

> *scritto e diretto da*
> or: *un film scritto e diretto da*

But one must always remember that Pier Paolo Pasolini was surrounded by some legends in Italian cinema – such as designers Dante Ferretti and Danilo Donati, DPs Giuseppe Rotunno and Tonino Delli Colli, producers Alfredo Bini and Alberto Grimaldi, and composer Ennio Morricone. And numerous others: by the 1960s, when Pasolini started to direct features, the Italian film industry boasted some of the finest, most

29 Mauro Bolognini saw photographs of the tests, and suggested the project to Bini.
30 E. Siciliano, 227.
31 Quoted in C. Constantin, 1995, 50.
32 Pasolini insisted that he 'always thought of a film as the work of an author, not only the script and the direction, but the choice of sets and locations, the characters, even the clothes. I choose everything – not to mention the music' (PP,32).

imaginative and skilled technicians and talents in the world. (Italian cinema was on a high, an up, a boom in this period).

The *auteur* credit, the 'un film de' credit, is dishonest and dumb. Who drew up all of the contracts (sometimes thousands for big movies)? Who oversaw the insurance, taxes, and liabilities? Who bought the cloth for the costumes? Who built the sets? Who booked the hotels? Who carried the lights up ten flights of stairs?[33] Who drove the actors to the locations? Who created the opticals for the titles? Who logged all of the rushes and takes? Who rented the vehicles? Who processed the exposed celluloid?[34] And who does 100s of other jobs in movie production?

Not the director.

This is a simplistic argument of who does what in movies, but *auteur* theory has also been disparaged on ideological, political, social, philosophical and cultural grounds.

The producers of Pier Paolo Pasolini's movies included Alfredo Bini, Alberto Grimaldi, Franco Rossellini (brother of Roberto Rossellini), Carlo Lizzani, Dino de Laurentiis, and Gian Vittorio Baldi. Bini produced the early works, Rossellini the middle period pictures (late 1960s), and Grimaldi the later ones.[35]

ALFREDO BINI (Dec 12, 1926-Oct 16, 2010)[36] is a hugely important figure[37] in the cinema of Pier Paolo Pasolini.[38] That he not only produced Pasolini's movies (and took a chance on him with his first film as director), but also supported the movies and stood behind them (when they attracted controversy), is also not to be

33 No elevators in some of those old buildings.
34 I could go on!
35 The only problems he had with producers, Pasolini said, were *Pigsty* and *Medea*, which were flops.
36 Pasolini was four years older than Bini.
37 Occasionally you see snipes at Bini – but that goes with the territory of being a film producer. It doesn't detract from Bini's significance in Pasolini's film career.
38 'My contemporary from Gorizia | red-haired, hands in his pockets, | heavy as a paratrooper after mess-hall', as Pasolini characterized Bini in a poem in *Il padre salvaggio.*

under-estimated. Producing Pasolini's films wasn't the easiest gig in town, I would imagine, adding all sorts of unforeseen challenges that went beyond your run-of-the-mill producing duties. I bet you had to be on top of your game to keep up with Pasolini.

> Bini had confidence in me at a time when that was extremely hard: I knew nothing about the cinema, and he gave me *carte blanche* and let me work in peace. (PP, 138)

Alfredo Bini formed Arco Film in 1960, and the companies Finarco and Gerico Sound. Bini produced most of Pier Paolo Pasolini's earlier movies (such as *RoGoPaG*, *The Gospel According to St Matthew*, *Mamma Roma* and *Accattone* and, later, *Oedipus Rex*). Bini's other producer credits included films helmed by Mauro Bolognini (*The Mandrake,* 1965), *El Greco* (1966), a rival version of *Satyricon* to the Federico Fellini film (1969), *Simon Bolivar* (1969), *Gli Eroi* (*The Horse*, 1973), *Lancelot du Lac* (Robert Bresson, 1974), and adaptations of theatrical plays aimed at the video market. He was married to actress Rosanna Schiaffino.

ALBERTO GRIMALDI (Mch 28, 1925-Jan 23, 2021, born in Naples) produced Pasolini's last four films, from *Il Decamerone* to *Salò*. Grimaldi was a lawyer from Naples; he had formed Produzioni Europee Associate S.p.A. in Roma in 1961. He had made plenty of $$$$ by producing the *Fistful of Dollars* Spaghetti Westerns starring Clint Eastwood. Grimaldi went on to become a big cheese in the Italian film industry – producing several Federico Fellini films, for instance, plus *Last Tango In Paris, 1900, Burn!, Trastevere, Man of La Mancha* and *Bawdy Tales*. One of Grimaldi's last producing jobs was *Gangs of New York* (2002). Grimaldi had a distribution deal with United Artists (hence, the films were released thru U.A. in North America, including the Pasolini productions).

United Artists was investing, like other North American studios in the 1960s, in European productions (brokering deals with Dino de Laurentiis as well as Alberto Grimaldi and other Italian producers). United Artists wanted prestige pictures – 'more complex, larger-scale pictures' than Spaghetti Westerns (see below).

The films produced by Alberto Grimaldi often had erotic content – in the 1970s alone, there was *Last Tango In Paris*, the 'trilogy of life' films, *Salò, Novecento* and *Casanova* (dir. Federico Fellini, 1976). But that also reflects the era, when eroticism meant box office.

Many of Pasolini's later films were backed by Les Productions Artistes Associées along with Alberto Grimaldi's Produzioni Europee Associate (so they were Italian and French co-productions). Les Productions Artistes Associées had been founded in 1963 in Paris. Their movies included *Last Tango In Paris, Le Cage aux Folles, The Night Porter, 1900, Man of the East, The Story of Adele H., Roma, The Train, Burn!,* and *Moonraker* (the *James Bond* film).

UNITED ARTISTS. In the early Seventies, United Artists was known as one of the more adventurous of the Hollywood studios, and backed some of the more eccentric or left-of-centre productions. (U.A. was instrumental in forging the 'New Hollywood' cinema, for instance). From its early days, United Artists was known as a filmmaker-friendly studio, on the side of the filmmaker-as-artist. It was set up by Mary Pickford, Charlie Chaplin, Douglas Fairbanks and D.W. Griffith in 1919, where it was known as a company that would control marketing and distribution of the artists' products, rather than a conventional film studio (it didn't have sound stages and production facilities, didn't own cinemas, and didn't have a roster of stars).

By the 1960s, among United Artists' successes were the *Pink Panther* franchise (led by Blake Edwards and Peter Sellers), the Beatles films (*A Hard Day's Night* and *Help!*), and the ever-reliable *James Bond* franchise. (There were flops in the 1960s, however, such as the very costly picture *The Greatest Story Ever Told* (1965) – $20 million, and disappointments such as *Chitty Chitty*

Bang Bang (1968, cost: $10m), *Battle of Britain* (1969, cost: $12m) and *The Private Life of Sherlock Holmes* (1970, cost: $10m). These productions were part of the over-spending cycle of the late Sixties.)

In the 1970s, *Rocky* was an important franchise for U.A. – the Chartoff-Winkler movies were sequelized several times. Chartoff and Winkler made a *ton* of money from United Artists' *Rocky* series (the first *Rocky* movie cost $1.5 million and took $55.9 million in North American rentals alone – equivalent to $487m in 2005 dollars). Among Chartoff and Winkler's productions was the controversial movie *The Last Temptation of Christ* (1988), which they had set up with Paramount in the early 1980s.

And let's not forget editor NINO BARAGLI (1925-2013), who cut nearly all of Pier Paolo Pasolini's features. Thus, Baragli (three years younger than the maestro), is one of the most important figures in Pasolini's cinema, and in Italian cinema of recent times (yet some film critics don't even mention him). Baragli worked with all of the major Italian filmmakers, including Federico Fellini, Luchino Visconti, Sergio Leone, Bernardo Bertolucci, Damiano Damiani, Mauro Bolognini, Massimo Troisi, Alberto Lattuada, Tinto Brass and Roberto Benigni, and directors such as Gabriele Salvatores and Margarethe von Trotta (for many of those directors, Baragli worked on many of their projects).

Editing is always underrated by film critics, even critics you'd think would know better (partly because critics don't really know what editing is. I think film critics should spend a day or so with a film editor, to learn exactly what the job entails). Among Baragli's credits were important collaborations with Sergio Leone (the *Fistful* Spaghetti Westerns and *Once Upon a Time In America*), *Ginger and Fred* and *The Voice of the Moon* (Federico Fellini), and *Mediterraneo*.

Editing a Pier Paolo Pasolini production, though, meant working with intuitive, spontaneously-shot material, where eyelines didn't match, where inserts and close-ups were often not filmed (plus all of the other 'coverage' of a scene of a typical movie), where non-naturalistic and discontinuous images had to be welded together. Pasolini didn't arrive on set with a regular shot list, and didn't approach scenes in a conventional manner. Editing a Pasolini film would be a challenge, with different requirements from your average film or TV show. Luckily, Nino Baragli was a master editor – some critics have called him a genius.

As for costumes, in DANILO DONATI (1926-2001), Pier Paolo Pasolini had one of the great costume designers (and set designers) of recent times: Donati's feeling for costume is simply astonishing.[39] Solely in the realm of *hats* and *headgear*, Donati has few peers. If you want to study the history of costume in cinema, you have to include lengthy research into Danilo Donati, or the cinema of Federico Fellini and Luchino Visconti. (In many ways, in Pasolini's cinema, as with Vincente Minnelli, Walerian Borowczyk and Ken Russell, it's all about the clothes).

For Pier Paolo Pasolini, Danilo Donati designed *RoGoPaG, The Gospel According To Matthew, The Hawks and the Sparrows, Oedipus Rex, Pigsty, Salò* and the 'trilogy of life' movies. For Federico Fellini, Donati designed *Satyricon* (1969), *The Clowns* (1971), *Roma* (1972), *Armarcord* (1973), *Casanova* (1976), *Ginger and Fred* (1986) and *Intervista* (1987). As well as working for Visconti, Fellini and Pasolini, Donati also provided costumes for films such as *The Taming of the Shrew* (1967), *Romeo and Juiliet* (1968), *Bawdy Tales* (1973), *Caligula* (1979), *Flash Gordon* (1980), *Red Sonja* (1985), *Nostromo* (1996), *Life Is Beautiful* (1997) and *Pinocchio* (2002).

On a Pier Paolo Pasolini production, costume designers were often encouraged to go all-out, and not hold back from outrageous designs. A huge challenge were the ancient world and mediæval movies – especially the ones set in archaic societies. Not least

---

39 Pier Paolo Pasolini praised Donati's genius with costume – 'he does all that, extremely well, with excellent taste and zest' (PP, 32).

among the challenges would be getting all of the costumes to those remote locations in Africa or Turkey (or even Southern Italia). No doubt quite a few costumes were manufactured near the set, using local workers (which would require a whole new way of working). For some of the historical productions, the wardrobe dept also had to clothe huge numbers of extras – and on budgets that were a fraction of their Hollywood equivalents. Yet each Pasolini movie has a look in costume design that's unique: a single frame, or a single still photograph from a Pasolini movie is instantly recognizable as coming from Danilo Donati. If there was a touring exhibition of costumes from Pasolini's movies, I would be first in line. (You can see some of Donati's costumes today at Cinecittà).

DANTE FERRETTI (b. 1943) is one of the superstars of production design in recent cinema. His list of credits is extraordinary by any standards. Ferretti worked with Pier Paolo Pasolini as production designer on *Medea, The Arabian Nights, The Decameron, The Canterbury Tales* and *Salò* (and as an assistant on earlier pictures, such as *The Gospel According To Matthew*). Ferretti also designed for Federico Fellini – *City of Women, And the Ship Sails On, The Voice of the Moon* and *Ginger and Fred,* and films such as *The Night Porter, Tales of Ordinary Madness, The Name of the Rose, Hamlet, Titus, The Adventures of Baron von Munchausen, Bram Stoker's Dracula, Sweeney Todd* and *Interview With a Vampire*; Ferretti worked with Martin Scorsese on *The Age of Innocence, The Aviator, Kundun, Bringing Out the Dead* and *Casino,* and with directors such as Tim Burton, Francis Coppola, Terry Gilliam, Jean-Jacques Annaud and Marco Ferreri.

Pier Paolo Pasolini would research the designs for his films from paintings, Ferretti said. Ferretti recalled that he was

> always a little intimidated by Pasolini. He was like a poet or a priest, and his approach to filmmaking was architectural: his shots were always like

geometrical *tableaux*, with the camera dead centre.
(P. Ettedgui, 49)

TONINO DELLI COLLI (1923-2005) began, with *Accattone,* a long-running collaboration with Pier Paolo Pasolini that must rank as one of the finest in recent cinema – alongside Federico Fellini and Giuseppe Rotunno, Bernardo Bertolucci and Vittorio Storaro or Jean-Luc Godard and Raoul Coutard. Delli Colli (a year younger than Pasolini) was the cinematographer on eleven out of the maestro's thirteen feature films[40] (plus the episodes for anthology films). He was also DP for Federico Fellini, Roman Polanski, Jean-Jacques Annaud, Claude Chabrol and Sergio Leone (you can see Delli Colli at work with Fellini in *Interview*, 1987).[41] Delli Colli was known for subsuming his style into the material, and what the director wanted. He didn't impose his style on the movie, he served the movie. (He was described by Enzo Siciliano as short, Roman, nervous and given to uncontrollable rages, but was gentle with Pasolini.[42] From Delli Colli Pasolini learnt much of the art and practice of cinema).

> Come on, Tonino, come on,
> set it at fifty, don't be afraid
> of the light sinking – let's take
> this unnatural shot![43]

Tonino Delli Colli recalled: 'Our relations were perfect. [Pasolini] was an incredibly sweet and kind person, and he had respect for everyone on the set.' In terms of camera movement and style, Pier Paolo Pasolini preferred a simple visual approach: Pasolini was not interested in tricks, gimmicks or the 'magic' of cinema (even the greatest of filmmakers are full of tricks and gimmicks: Orson Welles, D.W. Griffith, F.W. Murnau, Jean Cocteau, Akira Kurosawa, Ingmar Bergman and

---

40 And Tonino Delli Colli would've shot the other movies if it weren't for scheduling conflicts.
41 He filmed the famous Spaghetti Westerns, for instance.
42 Delli Colli was described by Gideon Bachmann as a 'small, wiry man'.
43 Pasolini, *La Poesie*, 337.

Jean-Luc Godard. And Federico Fellini, of course, used every trick available).[44] Pasolini liked the 50 mil lens, Delli Colli said,[45] which gave a slightly compressed, squashed image, but approximated to the field of vision of the naked human eye.

GIUSEPPE ROTUNNO (1923-2021) is one of the great cinematographers of Italian cinema: he was DP on many classics, including the incredible *The Leopard* (1963), and worked for Federico Fellini (as his chief cameraman, from the late 1960s to the end of Fellini's life), Luchino Visconti,[46] Terry Gilliam (*Baron Munch-ausen*), Bob Fosse (*All That Jazz*) and John Huston (*The Bible*). Rotunno also lit films such as *Candy, The Secret of Santa Vittoria, Carnal Knowledge, Popeye, Red Sonja* and *Five Days One Summer.* Solely for his work for three Italian maestros – Fellini, Pasolini and Visconti – Rotunno should be regarded as one of the greats among photographers.

SERGIO CITTI (1933-2005) was a very important collaborator in the cinema of Pier Paolo Pasolini – he worked on the scripts, on the dialogue, and was an assistant director (as well as having a relationship with the maestro). Born in Rome, Citti was one of the longest-serving members of the Pasolini Movie Circus, following the master everywhere.

In 1970, Sergio Citti stepped up to become a film director: Pier Paolo Pasolini co-wrote Citti's first two films as director: *Ostia* (1970) and *Bawdy Tales* (1973). If anyone could step in to direct in Pasolini's absence, it would be Citti.

Sergio Citti's subsequent films included: *Beach House* (1977), *Happy Hobos* (1979), *Il Minestrone* (1981), *Mortacci* (1989, *We Free Kings* (1996), *Cartoni Animati* (1997), *Vipera* (2001) and *Fratella e Sorello* (2005). *Sogni e Bisogni* (1985) was a TV mini-series.

---

44 Sergio Citti, in the 1970 documentary on Pier Paolo Pasolini, insists that *he* didn't use zooms or dollies or other trickery on his movies, as Pasolini did.
45 Delli Colli said that Pasolini liked to use either long lenses or wide angle lenses.
46 Rotunno started out on Visconti productions such as *Senso* and *White Nights*.

SILVANA MANGANO. One of Pier Paolo Pasolini's favourite actresses was Dino de Laurentiis' wife Silvana Mangano (1930-89): she appeared in *Theorem, The Decameron, The Earth Seen From the Moon* (the episode in *The Witches*), and *Oedipus Rex*. As well as films helmed by Pasolini, she was in *Ulysses, Barabbas, Black Magic, Mambo, Tempest, Il Processo di Verona, Gold of Naples, Five Branded Women, Conversation Piece, Dune* and *Death In Venice* (many of those movies were produced by de Laurentiis). Like Sophia Loren, Gina Lollobrigida, Anna Magnani and Alida Valli, Mangano was an icon of Italian cinema; her face, which could melt the camera, was instantly recognizable (she was a hit aged nineteen in *Bitter Rice* (1949), walking in rice fields with her skirt up around her thighs).

LAURA BETTI (1927-2004) was another of Pier Paolo Pasolini's special actresses, appearing in many of his films (and providing the voice in others). Betti was one of his most important friends. The bond between Betti and Pasolini could be fiery, however – she would yell at him, hurling insults, and Elsa Morante, listening, would interject: 'If you two want to make love, stop doing it in words' (ES, 261). Betti was possessive over her friendship with Pasolini, pushing away anyone who threatened it (such as Maria Callas).

ALBERTO MORAVIA (1907-1990, born in Rome) was a favourite author with Italian filmmakers – most of his fiction was adapted into movies (including *The Conformist, La Romana, Agostino, Gli Indifferenti*, etc). Moravia also wrote films.

Novelist ELSA MORANTE (1912-85) was an valued advisor and encourager for Pier Paolo Pasolini, and influenced several of his film projects (such as advising on the music for *The Gospel According To Matthew* and others). Morante's husband, author Alberto Moravia, was a fellow colleague and traveller (he appeared in *Love Meetings* and went on trips with Morante and Pasolini, such as to India in 1960).

FRANCO CITTI

Apart from six Pier Paolo Pasolini movies, Franco Citti (1938-2016) has also appeared in mainly Italian movies – by Bernardo Bertolucci (*La Luna*), Sergio Citti, Sergio Pastore, Elio Petri, Franco Rossi, Antonio Bido, Antonio Avati, and two *Godfather* movies.

While Nino Davoli represented the lighter side of Pasolini's art, the Charlie Chaplin aspects which mocked existence, Franco Citti, from *Accattone* onwards, embodied the murky, egotistic, and degenerate sides of the Pasolini persona, with its tendency towards self-loathing, violence and depression. Citti played Pasolini's grandiose but doomed hero Oedipus (his finest role for the maestro, along with Accattone), a ruthless crook (in *The Decameron*), a fellow cannibal (in *Pigsty*), the Devil in *The Canterbury Tales,* an enigmatic demon (in *The Arabian Nights*), and an arrogant pimp (in *Mamma Roma*).

Franco Citti's characters operate on the wrong side of the law, are introspective and difficult, and see themselves as Existential rebels (who feel that the whole world is against them). They want an easy life (they think they deserve it), and they can't understand why everybody isn't falling over themselves to do their bidding. They are charismatic and independent (which makes them initially attractive), but they implode under pressure (and arrogance).

NINETTO DAVOLI

While actors such as Franco Citti might be associated with Pier Paolo Pasolini's cinema in its arty, handsome, dramatic mode, just as significant were actors such as Ninetto Davoli (b. 1948, Calabria).[47] With his toothy

47 Davoli's parents were Calabrian peasants.

grin and frizzy hair, Davoli is terrific as hapless, lusty, rather dim youths on the make. Energetic, naïve, indefatigable, cowardly, Davoli is an unlikely leading man: he can never be the romantic lead, he is always the ordinary guy looking for the easiest way out.

Enzo Siciliano portrays Davoli as having a

> slight and skinny build, pimples on his face, kinky hair, and incredibly "merry" eyes... His voice was raucous, his physicality pliant and emaciated. His histrionics had a melancholy tinge and conveyed from the depths an inexpressible emotional anxiety. (284-5)

Ninetto Davoli was also Pier Paolo Pasolini's lover (from 1963, when Davoli was 15) – and they lived together for years after they'd ceased being lovers. So Davoli plays a special role in Pasolini's cinema on many levels[48] (he is also, like Franco Citti, a manifestation of the street kid from the Roman shanty towns, the kind of youth that Pasolini liked to hang out with).

Enzo Siciliano characterized the relationship of Pier Paolo Pasolini and Ninetto Davoli after the eroticism had gone as a male friendship of near-equals (tho' Pasolini was 26 years older). Pasolini wasn't a father figure to Davoli, Siciliano reckoned, and they were not dependent on each other. But Pasolini was in despair when Davoli wed (in January, 1973).

In the midst of filming *The Canterbury Tales* Ninetto Davoli told Pier Paolo Pasolini that he was getting married (during shooting in Bath in the West Country). According to Enzo Siciliano, Pasolini was distraught: 'Pier Paolo's despair was uncontainable. He wanted to die' (ES, 338). The high emotion behind the camera may have coloured the movie (Pasolini composed many poems about his relationship with Davoli).

In a 1965 poem, Pier Paolo Pasolini wrote:

---

48 'Pasolini deserves credit for foregrounding his relationship... with Davoli, who was not from the class in which the director's chic friends thought he should look for a boyfriend, and for his public frankness about this infatuation', commented Gary Indiana (91).

Ninetto is a herald
and overcoming (with a sweet laugh
that blazes from his whole being
as in a Muslim or a Hindu)

And that's exactly how Pasolini cast him in some films: in *Theorem*, he's the angelic messenger who visits the morose Milanese family; in *Oedipus the King*, he's the herald who guides Oedipus to the Sphinx.

However, altho' Pier Paolo Pasolini became infatuated with Ninetto Davoli and put him in quite a few films following *The Hawks and the Sparrows*,[49] he is a somewhat limited actor in terms of range (Davoli on screen tries the patience of even the most committed Pasolinian devotees). But Pasolini was quite enamoured of Davoli – especially when Davoli was teamed up with Totò (after *The Hawks and the Sparrows*, Pasolini cast Davoli in a series of films alongside Totò, including the episodes in *The Witches* and *Love and Anger*).

MAKING A FILM WITH PASOLINI

I imagine that Pier Paolo Pasolini, though a perfectionist in some areas of filmmaking, would not push his actors to numerous takes.[50] It seems as if Pasolini and the team are searching for the spontaneity of performances that *haven't* been rehearsed and blocked at length. There must be times when Pasolini would ask for many takes, but I bet in general he would shoot one or two takes then move on.

'I always shoot very short takes' (PP, 132). Pier Paolo Pasolini's cinema is constructed from short pieces of film – not for him lengthy takes where the camera and

49 And a brief cameo in *The Gospel.*
50 Sometimes Pasolini would ask for retakes with the camera still running – asking his actors to do the scene repeatedly without cutting.

the actors're hitting many marks, and seven minute takes run thru numerous beats. 'I never use the long take (or virtually never). I hate naturalness. I reconstruct everything' (ibid.). And he didn't shoot a single master shot to cover a scene – 'I never do a whole all in one take' (ibid.). However, there *are* many examples of lengthy takes in Pasolini's films (or lengthy by the standards of today's cinema).

Sometimes Pasolini would shoot a scene with both actors in shot, and ask them not to get too close, so that he wouldn't have to film a reverse angle. That way, a scene could be covered with a single shot (Pasolini like to move fast, and get shots done quickly).

Like George Lucas in the age of digital filmmaking (and the *Star Wars* prequels), Pier Paolo Pasolini spoke of shooting as 'collecting material': he was gathering content that he would shape later into a movie (in the editing room). Thus, there were opportunities for spontaneity and improvization from the non-professional actors, and later in post-production the best bits from the takes would be selected and put together.

While crews complain about being cold and wet on locations, I wonder if Pier Paolo Pasolini's crews moaned about the heat (Pasolini and co. filmed in hot, dry climes far more than in rainy, chilly regions). I bet a Pasolini shoot moved fast, too – I bet the crew didn't sit around on the grass, drinking and chatting and dancing to Euro-pop as depicted in *La Ricotta*, either. Instead, I bet it was one or two takes for each set up, then swiftly on to the next set up.

Filming a Pier Paolo Pasolini movie would provide many opportunities for cinematographic challenges for DPs – candlelight, firelight, magic hour, sunrise, sunset, plus lighting all sorts of existing locations, some of which would probably be miles from the nearest town, and with no power nearby (thus, many of the African and distant European locations in Pasolini's movies were filmed during daytime, using available light augmented by lamps. Because filming at night in remote locations is tough – and expensive).

Camera operators on a Pier Paolo Pasolini movie would need to be physically fit, too – there would be much clambering over rocks in hot sun to reach that perfect spot under an over-hanging cliff, or climbing Mount Etna[51] yet again in gales or heat. And Pasolini often preferred to have the cameras handheld, so the operators would be shouldering heavy cameras all day.[52] (On the plus side, most scenes would be filmed in one or two takes – no going to 12,457 takes like Jackie Chan or Michael Cimino for Pasolini!).

Pasolini was fond of staging scenes as *tableaux*. Carl-Theodor Dreyer often used the frontal, *tableau* style – in *Ordet* (1955), for instance.[53] Walerian Borowczyk used it in all of his films. Theo Angelopoulos took it up in films like *Ulysses' Gaze* (1995). Sergei Paradjanov was a master of the form (in *The Color of Pomegranates*, 1969). Werner Herzog exploited the *tableau* approach in movies such as *Aguirre, Wrath of God* (1972)[54] and *Heart of Glass* (1976 – in which he also hypnotized the cast!).

For the first features, Pier Paolo Pasolini and his DP Tonino Delli Colli filmed in black-and-white (Delli Colli, like many cinematographers, spoke nostalgically of b/w, and preferred it in many respects to colour film). By the Sixties, tho', colour film stock was cheaper, and distributors and television wanted colour (everybody wants colour except for filmmakers). Pasolini stuck with monochrome longer than necessary, perhaps (as did filmmakers like Federico Fellini and Ingmar Bergman), tho' the pressure of the marketplace prevailed, and from around 1966 onwards, his movies were in colour.

51 A favourite Pasolini location.
52 Thus, tripod shots were dispensed with – no need to carry a tripod if the shot's going to be handheld anyway.
53 Many of the compositions in *Ordet* are flattened, with the performers arranged in a tight, flat space at right angles to the camera. It's a frontal, *tableau* approach to composition that Carl-Theodor Dreyer favoured in other movies. You might say that action is staged this way in *Ordet* because it derives from a theatrical play, and the film set is a replica of a stage. No. That has nothing to do with it: this is how some filmmakers like to block their actors (Walerian Borowczyk was the same, and so was Sergei Paradjanov).
54 *Aguirre* employed stylized *tableaux*, scenes which were consciously staged as paintings or portraits.

Colour was more complicated for Pier Paolo Pasolini, and it took more planning. Pasolini's approach to colour films was to take out all of the colours he didn't want: there are too many colours in real life, Pasolini remarked. He said he chose to shoot *Oedipus Rex* in Morocco[55] 'because there are only a few main colours there – ochre, rose, brown, green, the blue of the sky' (PP, 63). That's one reason why some filmmakers preferred to film in the studio, where the settings could be controlled entirely.

The running times of Pier Paolo Pasolini's films as director tend to be in the 80-110 minute range (with *Accattone* and *The Gospel According To Matthew* and others going over slightly). One wonders what sort of movies Pasolini might've made in the era of the 1990s, 2000s and after, when movies (and not only prestige productions), ran to 140 and 150 minutes. We might've seen longer, perhaps more rambling pictures (Pasolini was headed that way, though, with the 'trilogy of life' movies).

Compared with his contemporaries, it's striking how much of Pier Paolo Pasolini's output is comical: his first three fiction features were dead serious, but for his fourth feature, *The Hawks and the Sparrows,* Pasolini and the team attempted a comedy (with mixed results). Short films of the period, such as in the anthologies *RoGoPaG* and *The Witches*, were also comedies. And large parts of the 'trilogy of life' pictures were humorous (or they tried to be). A good reason for making the 'trilogy of life' series was to tackle something upbeat and positive after the gloom and seriousness of *Pigsty, Medea* and *Theorem.*

However, contemporaries of Pasolini's such as Federico Fellini and Jacques Tati were far more skilled with comedy, and Pasolini's attempts at humour are often badly conceived and badly executed (excellent editing is absolutely foundational for screen comedy, and Pasolini's films really do lack that, even with

---

55 *Edipo Re* was shot in Italy and Morocco (including San Petronio, Bologna).

cutting by the great editor Nino Baragli). Pasolini is also *way* too indulgent with his performers (with Totò and Ninetto Davoli in particular. Totò is a great screen clown, but you can see even him struggling with the material and the situations. Davoli, meanwhile, relies too much on charm, energy and enthusiasm. Pasolini's comedies hope to get by on Marx Brothers-type clowning around, but it doesn't work. Mel Brooks and the Zucker-Abrahams-Zucker team insisted that the performers or the director shouldn't try to be funny – it was the script, the situations and the characters that were funny. And that was what Pasolini's comedies lacked – amusing characters and situations).

Indeed, it's curious that Pier Paolo Pasolini persisted in attempting to direct (and write or co-write) movies in a comical mode, when they clearly were not working. Surely people in Pasolini's entourage pointed out to him that his so-called comedies were not funny – and worse, they might damage Pasolini's reputation as a world-class director? (Or did no one dare to voice their opinion to the director? Would *you* have the guts to tell Pasolini to his face that his comedies stank?[56]).

Well, anyway, the maestro kept going, from *The Hawks and the Sparrows* and the anthology movies of the mid-Sixties onwards, to the mediæval trilogy. (It's possible that nobody dared to suggest to the maestro that the comedies weren't amusing. And anyway, *The Decameron* had been a big hit in Italia in 1971, encouraging the production of further historical comedies).

One of the chief reasons why the comedy of the 'trilogy of life' films and others can seem laboured, or haphazard, or incomprehensible is due to that issue that irks so many TV broadcasters and film distributors: cultural translation. Humour is often difficult to translate not only into different languages but different cultures and societies. Thus, comedy stars can be huge in Asia (Stephen Chow Sing-chi, for example), but almost unknown in the Western world (Stephen Chow is

---

56 Not if you wanted to keep all of your fingers! Just kidding.

very funny – as a performer, writer and director – *Royal Tramp, Fight Back To School, Shaolin Soccer, The Mad Monk*, and the later *Journey To the West* adaptations, etc – but nobody knows who Chow is in the West, and he's rarely celebrated).

Some of the producers of
the films directed by
Pier Paolo Pasolini.
Alberto Grimaldi (left).
Franco Rossellini (below),
and Alfredo Bini (bottom).

Pasolini with Totò during The Hawks and the Sparrows (top).
And with Anna Magnani during Mamma Roma (above).

ACTORS AND ACTING

Like Tim Burton, Woody Allen and Ken Russell, Pier Paolo Pasolini preferred actors who just 'got it' straight away, without needing lots of discussion, coddling, encouragement, and analysis. No lengthy sessions of questions and answers between actors, producers and directors, and no arguments about the characterizations. 'I choose people for what they are and not for what they pretend to be', Pasolini remarked (PP, 49).

> In general, I choose actors because of what they are as human beings, not because of what they can do. Terence Stamp was offended by this because I never asked him to demonstrate his acting ability. It was like stealing from him, using his reality. I had a similar experience with Anna Magnani on 'Mamma Roma.' She also felt I was stealing from her. (1968)

Actors were given the screenplay, but Pasolini preferred to talk them through their roles. As with many directors (such as Ken Russell), it was in the chats before filming that Pasolini really did much of his directing. The scripts might be adjusted slightly during shooting, usually in response to what an actor was doing.

The trouble with the non-acting, Robert Bressonian approach to film performance is that it can too easily come over as wooden, uninspired or just plain *boring*. There are instances in the cinema of Pier Paolo Pasolini, as well as Robert Bresson, Michelangelo Antonioni and Carl-Theodor Dreyer (four of the key exponents of the non-performance performance style), where any heat/ juice/ drama/ tension/ suspense in a scene is deflated or negated. Yes, that may be one of the goals of Bresson, Antonioni, Dreyer and Pasolini, but there are trade-offs with every performance style. (More recent proponents of po-faced non-acting include Mamoru Oshii and Theo Angelopoulos).

❋

You have to admit that Pier Paolo Pasolini's appearances in his own movies were, like those of many other film directors, not especially special (quite a few film directors are convinced they can act). He was no Orson Welles or John Huston. But at least he didn't deliberately send his movies up, like Jean-Luc Godard did in his cameos in his own films.[1] And Pasolini is a significant presence in his documentaries, too – he had no problem appearing before the camera, interviewing people (or simply talk-talk-talking), or providing voiceovers (which sometimes sound like he is making it up on the spot).

SAINTS, SINNERS AND STRANGERS (OUTSIDERS)

Filmed like mediæval saints[2] (or martyrs) in the modern world, Pier Paolo Pasolini's characters – Accattone, Stracci, Zumurrud, Ninetto – were ancient souls, who didn't fit into contemporary society, as Sam Rohdie explained in his book on the *maître*: they were outsiders, eternally at odds with their society; they are useless in terms of economy and capitalist production; they are innocents in a corrupt land; they are otherworldly, and as such were revolutionary: 'their otherworldliness, essentially their uselessness, made of them revolutionary in *this* world' (123), but not because they existed within this world, but because they refused it, they didn't compromise with it.

And yet the Pasolinian sanctification of these subproletarian characters was æsthetic and artistic, not practical or even social: that is, it was a sacralization of the subproletariat that could only take place in cinema

1 Jean-Luc Godard's best cameo is in *First Name: Carmen*, where he plays a director who commits himself to hospital because he can't – or won't – make movies anymore. And Godard's worst cameo is in *King Lear*, in which he sports a wig of electrical cables and plugs, chomps on a cigar permanently, and speaks out the side of his mouth like a would-be wise guy. It's *so* bad!
2 In *Accattone*, they refer to themselves as saints. What they really mean is martyrs.

and poetry and similar arts. As Sam Rohdie commented, Pier Paolo Pasolini gave his characters

> a sacred halo, as if they were sanctified angels. He made them into Masaccio saints, Caravaggio apostles, a Mantegna Christ, a Piero della Francesca Madonna, the Christs of Pontormo and Rosso Fiorentino. (123-4)

THE POETRY OF CINEMA

> The cinema should always be the discovery of something. I believe that the cinema should be essentially poetic.

Orson Welles[3]

Pier Paolo Pasolini was a poet: his aim was to be 'purely poetical and natural'.[4] Pasolini remarked that he was 'the least Catholic of all the Italians I know' and that his religion was 'probably only a form of psychological aberration with a tendency towards mysticism'. Pasolini said he saw the world in childlike, reverential ways (PP, 14).

Poetry was an early love of Pier Paolo Pasolini's – he started to write poems in the Friulan dialect, poems of the hermetic, Symbolist kind (he cited Stéphane Mallarmé, Giuseppe Ungaretti, Eugenio Montale and Rainer Maria Rilke as influences [1969, 15]). He began publishing his books of poetry in the mid-1940s (with *Poesie e Casarsa* in 1942 and *Poesie* in 1945).

Instead of one recognizable style, as with Robert Bresson or Orson Welles, underneath Pasolini's cinema was his own recognizable tone. 'You can always feel underneath my love for Dreyer, Mizoguchi and Chaplin – and some of Tati, etc, etc' (PP, 28). Of Dreyer,

---

3 O. Welles, interview, in A. Sarris,1969.
4 In A. Pavelin, 33.

Mizoguchi and Chaplin,[5] Pasolini said: 'all three see things from a point of view which is absolute, essential and in a certain way holy, reverential' (PP, 43). (Notice that Pasolini cites big, serious names in cinema, not commercial, exploitation directors such as Roger Corman or William Castle.) You can't cheat in style, Pasolini maintained, but you could cheat with the content (PP, 83).

'One sees, often, an *idea* of sensuality instead of sensuality, a *concept* of comedy', Gary Indiana commented (20). Pier Paolo Pasolini's films come across as essays or notes for movies that might be made. They are films of ideas, of possibilities for future projects. The comedies aren't funny, but they contain seeds that might be explored in further works.

Pier Paolo Pasolini defends himself in this respect by insisting that his films are not finished works: rather, they are questions. 'My films are not supposed to have a finished sense, they always end with a question. I always intend them to remain suspended' (PP, 56-57).

> I've never wanted to make a conclusive statement.
> I've always posed various problems and left them
> open to consideration. (1971)

'I don't want to be paternalistic, or pedagogical, or engage in propaganda, or be an apostle', Pasolini insisted in 1970 (yet part of his personality couldn't help being a teacher).

Jean-Luc Godard was greatly admired by Pier Paolo Pasolini – to the point where some of Pasolini's films are infused with the spirit of Godard (such as *Pigsty, Theorem* and *Salò, or The 120 Days of Sodom*). Most committed filmmakers in the 1960s in Europa were inspired by Godard's films: Godard's 1960s movies remain one of the most extraordinary groups of works in cinema history.

---

5 Charlie Chaplin and silent movie comedy was a touchstone for Pasolini, according to Sam Rohdie; Chaplin is *hommaged* in many Pasolini movies. But what did Chaplin himself think of the often very strange tributes to him in Pasolini's films?

And so many filmmakers have tried to put some Jean-Luc Godard on the screen as well as Pier Paolo Pasolini: Francis Coppola, George Lucas, Oliver Stone, Martin Scorsese, Luc Besson, Jean-Jacques Beineix, Bernardo Bertolucci, Terence Malick, Donald Cammell, Abel Ferrara, Rainer Werner Fassbinder, Wim Wenders, Peter Greenaway, and Robert Altman. But not even cinema giants like Coppola or Pasolini have managed it as successfully as the maestro himself. As they say, Godard is still the Man.

Pier Paolo Pasolini said he wasn't much fond of North American cinema (PP, 136), and the American films he did like were directed by Europeans who had moved to the U.S.A. (such as Fritz Lang and Ernest Lubitsch). Among American directors Pasolini has cited John Ford and Orson Welles.

Though he regarded himself as 'born from the Resistance' and a Marxist, Pier Paolo Pasolini was inevitably drawn to what he called 'irrational' and 'decadent' literature.

Pier Paolo Pasolini's form of cinema was (like that of Andrei Tarkovsky or Walerian Borowczyk) the 'cinema of the image', one of André Bazin's two definitions of cinema (the other was the 'cinema of reality').[6] Pasolini had more in common with Soviet silent cinema than with Italian Neo-realism, with Dziga Vertov and Sergei Eisenstein rather than Roberto Rossellini.[7]

Pier Paolo Pasolini used the formal aspects of cinema (quotation, pastiche, parody, analogy, repetition, rhyme) to foreground its construction, its writing, to make the viewer aware of the process of fictionality. Terence Stamp (*Theorem*) said Pasolini made films in a particular way which could be called 'using the camera to write poetry'.[8]

> To watch Pasolini's films [commented Sam Rohdie] is to watch a parable, a type of non-fictional fiction,

6 A. Bazin, 1960, 9f, 23f.

7 S. Rohdie, 1995, 3.

8 M. Cousins, *Scene By Scene*, Laurence King, 2002, 83.

evidently made up and false, yet whose falsity is there to express a truth. (1995, 3)

Orson Welles made the same distinction: like Pier Paolo Pasolini, Welles advocated a theatrical, abstract, expressive kind of cinema. Welles' take on the realism vs. artificiality debate was simple: his films might be 'unreal', might be 'theatrical' and 'baroque', but they were 'truthful'.[9] Welles' goal was to make something that wasn't necessarily 'real', but was 'true'. It could be unreal, stylized and theatrical, but it had to be true to life.

'Cinema represents reality with reality; it is metonymic and not metaphoric' (PP, 38). Yes but exactly what 'reality' is, and what 'reality' is in cinema, is difficult to define, Pier Paolo Pasolini admitted. The first question to ask when people use terms like 'reality' or 'realism' is: *whose reality? Whose realism?*

Alain Robbe-Grillet's comments (made at the time of 1962's *Last Year At Marienbad*) summarize the position of Pier Paolo Pasolini neatly:

> I don't think either the cinema or the novel is for explaining the world. Some people believe there's a certain definite reality and all that a work of art has to do is pursue it and try to describe it... I don't think believe a work of art has reference to anything outside itself. In a film there's no reality except that of the film, no time except that of the film... The only reality is the film's, and as for the criterion of that reality, for the author it's his vision, what he feels. For the spectator, the only test is whether he accepts.[10]

For Pier Paolo Pasolini, cinema was not an image but 'an audio-visual technique in which the word and the sound have the same importance as the image' (PP, 146). Pasolini said that it was easy to see, by looking at a page, if a text was in poetry or prose, but in cinema it was more difficult. A cinema of poetry could be

9 'In my case, everything has to be real', Pier Paolo Pasolini insisted, 'even if only by analogy' (PP, 90).
10 A. Robbe-Grillet, *The Observer*, Nov 18, 1962.

produced by particular techniques. For Pasolini, certain sounds could get closer quicker to the mystery of reality than written poetry.

> Even a sound image, say thunder booming in a clouded sky, is somehow infinitely more mysterious than even the most poetic description a writer could give of it. A writer has to find oniricity through a highly refined linguistic operation, while the cinema is much nearer to sounds physically, it doesn't need any elaboration. All it needs is to produce a clouded sky with thunder and straight away you are close to the mystery and ambiguity of reality. (PP, 150)

For Pier Paolo Pasolini, cinema was 'substantially and naturally poetic', because it was dream-like,[11] and because things in themselves were 'profoundly poetic':

> a tree photographed is poetic, a human face photographed is poetic because physicity is poetic in itself, because it is an apparition, because it is full of mystery, because it is full of ambiguity, because it is full of polyvalent meaning, because even a tree is a sign of a linguistic system. But who talks through a tree? God, or reality itself. Therefore the tree as a sign puts us in communication with a mysterious speaker. (PP, 153)

Even the most banal films could contain the poetry of cinema, Pier Paolo Pasolini said, but the cinema of poetry proper was a cinema 'which adopts a particular technique just as a poet adopts a particular technique when he writes verse' (PP, 153). In short: 'to make a film is to be a poet'.

Pier Paolo Pasolini believed in the notion of the author of a film. He said he was the author not only of the script[12] and the direction, but of everything else (such as the choice of sets, locations, characters and

---

11 'Cinema is already a dream' (PP, 150)

12 Many of Pasolini's scripts didn't alter much during production. And the filmmakers shot pretty much what was in the script. For *The Hawks and the Sparrows*, a sequence was filmed but cut (for running time). For *Accattone*, a scene was cut because the film was too long.

costumes [PP, 32]). True, Pasolini's stamp is all over his movies, but he could not have made them without a large group of collaborators, such as regular actors like Ninetto Davoli, Silvana Mangano, Laura Betti, and Franco Citti, and production crew such as Nino Baragli (editor), Tonio Delli Colli (DP), Umberto Angelucci (assistant director), Ennio Morricone (music), Dante Ferretti (production designer), Alfredo Bini, Franco Rossellini, and Alberto Grimaldi (producers).

Once again, let's not forget the actors: no matter how well a script is written, or the concept of the film is conceived, it is actors on set who have to express it all. So Pasolini *did not* do everything himself! (But his reputation persists even today in overshadowing everybody else).

In Pier Paolo Pasolini's poetics of cinema, reality and cinema commingle, as a system of signs.

> The cinema is a language which expresses reality with reality. So the question is: what is the difference between the cinema and reality? Practically none.

(Though in postmodern theory, the difference is practically everything). To express people, Pier Paolo Pasolini used people; to express trees, Pasolini used real trees, as he found them in reality. In a interview in the *New York Times* (1968), Pasolini stated:

> the cinema forced me to remain always at the level of reality, right inside reality: When I make a film I'm always in reality, among the trees and among the people; there's no symbolic or conventional filter between me and reality as there is in literature. The cinema is an explosion of my love for reality. I have never conceived of making a film that would be a work of a group, I've always thought of a film as a work of an author, not only the script and the direction but the choices of sets and locations, the characters, even the clothes. I choose everything, not to mention the music. (PP, 29)

No veils or no distantiation between the filmmaker and reality – and no metaphors either.

> Reality doesn't need metaphors to express itself...
> In the cinema it is as though reality expressed itself
> with itself, without metaphors, and without any-
> thing insipid and conventional and symbolic. (ib.,
> 38)

However, despite Pier Paolo Pasolini's penchant for realistic, non-metaphorical or non-symbolic cinema, he did not like naturalism. He aimed for realism, not naturalism. 'I believe deeply in reality, in realism, but I can't stand naturalism', he asserted (PP, 39).

Pier Paolo Pasolini repositioned himself *vis-à-vis* the Neo-realism tradition (in Italian cinema) and the films of Roberto Rossellini, saying that the naturalistic, credulous and crepuscular everyday reality of Neo-realist cinema was not his style. The detachment, warmth and irony of Neo-realism were 'characteristics which I do not have', commented Pasolini (PP, 109). Maybe – but Pasolini's cinema, and not only his early works, exhibit many of the elements of Neo-realist cinema. In the late 1960s, Pasolini said he did not go to the cinema anymore for entertainment, unless he could be sure the film was going to be worth seeing (PP, 136).

PASOLINI AND PAINTING

Pier Paolo Pasolini is known as a Mannerist (the same accusations have been made of Bernardo Bertolucci, Walerian Borowczyk and Peter Greenaway). Sometimes critics also use the term 'Baroque' (yes, even film critics, God bless them!, don't know their art history as well as they should). Yet altho' the Mannerist artists – Pontormo, Michelangelo, Rosso, Mantegna – were cited often by the maestro, he also revered the Early Renaissance artists (Giotto, Duccio, Piero, Masaccio, Angelico, etc).

Pier Paolo Pasolini was something of a 'Renaissance' man, in the sense of being happy to work in a number of disciplines: poetry, painting, criticism/ essays, short stories, novels, films, reportage and theatre. He was 'Renaissance' in another sense, taking much of his inspiration from (mainly Italian) Renaissance art (in the deployment of religious imagery in *The Gospel According To Matthew*, for example).

The two favoured periods of painting in Pier Paolo Pasolini's cinema were the Early Renaissance (Giotto di Bondone, Duccio Buoninsegna, Masaccio and Piero della Francesca), and the High Renaissance, Mannerism and Baroque (Michelangelo Buonarroti, Jacopo Pontormo, Sebastiano del Piombo, Giovanni Battista Rosso and Andrea del Sarto). Pasolini spoke of being deeply influenced by the Early Renaissance masters like Giotto and Masaccio – to the point where, in cinema, he automatically composed shots using their visual techniques (where 'man stands at the center of every perspective', as Pasolini put it). Even moving shots were like the lens was moving over a painting. 'I always conceive the background of a painting, like a stage set, and for this reason I always attack it frontally' (and even tho' he sometimes fought against the Renaissance pictorial approach, he could never lose it completely, because it was so deeply embedded in his psyche). Books of art were used on the set to help with setting up shots.

STYLE

One can cheat in everything except style.

Pier Paolo Pasolini

Pier Paolo Pasolini said he didn't have a cinematic style of his own, like Charlie Chaplin or Jean-Luc Godard: his style was made up of many influences and inspirations; he was a *pasticheur*, he said (among the filmmakers that Pasolini cited were Jacques Tati, Carl Theodor Dreyer, Kenji Mizoguchi, Chaplin and Godard). The dream in *Wild Strawberries* (1957) was admired by Pasolini – 'remarkable, it comes very close to what dreams are really like' (PP, 150). Anyway, what counts, Pasolini insisted, wasn't the form or even the content, but the violence and intensity of the work, 'the passion I put into things' (PP, 28). Tsui Hark, a dragon emperor among film directors, said a similar thing: sometimes, it's not the characters, or the stories, or the themes that interest a filmmaker, but the *attitude* of the piece. In 2011, Tsui said (in *Twitch*):

> The best thing actually to do is write according to what you feel. If you feel your heart would take you to the point where you would want to express something to do with the story or the film. Sometimes it's not the story; sometimes it's the way you tell the story. Sometimes it's the attitude you have with the story. The attitude is something you build and you accumulate for a long time for no reason and no logic, it's there. When you write that way, you might want to make it that way.

Pier Paolo Pasolini's cinema is full of conventional and clichéd elements. Some are so obvious that they're seldom remarked upon, as if Pasolini is somehow exempt from being treated like any other filmmaker, as if he soars above narrative conventions (in the legend that is Pasolini the Poet, Pasolini the Saint). He doesn't: the motif of the death of the hero is a good example: films like *Accattone, Mamma Roma, Pigsty, Theorem* as well as the tragedies close with the demise of the main characters.

✳

Not known as a technically brilliant filmmaker, or rather, a filmmaker for whom technique was an end in itself, or something that had to be got absolutely right, as with F.W. Murnau, Andrei Tarkovsky or Alfred Hitchcock, Pier Paolo Pasolini could nevertheless orchestrate the technical arsenal of cinema to do anything he wanted. But Pasolini is the opposite of a technical film director, the polar opposite of someone like Jackie Chan or Stanley Kubrick, who would shoot take after take until they got what they were looking for.[13] But for directors like Pasolini and Jean-Luc Godard, that approach to filmmaking would be ridiculous, wasteful, and pointless (Godard, like Werner Herzog, preferred to shoot one or two takes. No more were necessary).

Pier Paolo Pasolini did share one thing with perfectionists like Jackie Chan, Michael Cimino, Fritz Lang and George Lucas of course: total control. I bet there was no question as to who was the top guy on set in a Pasolini movie. Pasolini regarded cinema as the work of one man, an author. Terry Gilliam commented that in Italy the director is treated like a maestro (à la Luchino Visconti and Federico Fellini). Consequently, when Gilliam was shooting The Adventures of Baron Munchausen in Roma in 1988, one of the things he couldn't get used to was that production crew were reluctant to offer suggestions, and Gilliam preferred to work as a team.

---

13 The final shot of The Shining, the slow tracking shot towards the hotel wall and the 1920s photograph, took ages to film. Stanley Kubrick wanted it to be as fluid as possible. The camera crew tried changing the dolly cart; they put it on a track; they took it off the track; they loaded it with more weight; they put more people on it (in V. LoBrutto, 1997, 444).

The idea of re-shooting that tracking shot again and again, until it was as smooth and perfect as possible, just wouldn't occur on a Pier Paolo Pasolini set! (Or a Jean-Luc Godard set!). Forget it!

Consider the works of Pier Paolo Pasolini in print, theatre, TV or cinema (and in numerous interviews), and a host of concerns and themes will pop out time after time:

• Politics is part of pretty much everything that Pasolini did or said in the public arena.

• Communism – Pasolini was in constant dialogue with Communism, and with the Partito Comunista Italiano (which he voted for and was once a member[14]).

• Pasolini celebrated peasants, the under-class, and never lost his reverence for them.

• Southern Italy and its peasants were very important for Pasolini (he linked the area and its inhabitants to the Third World).

• The love of the Friulian dialect is part of Pasolini's exaltation of all things sub-proletarian and working class.

• The progress of Italy towards being a modern, capitalist nation was a recurring concern for Pasolini (in particular how modern technology would affect his beloved peasant class).

• For Pasolini, consumerism[15] was nothing less than 'a real anthropological cataclysm', and 'pure degradation'.

• Pasolini venerated his mother, and had a very ambiguous relationship with his father.

• Pasolini had a vision/ theory of cinema as poetry, as a means of mythicizing life.

• Pasolini was searching for the epic and the mythological in everyday life (and said he saw it everywhere).

• Sexuality – altho' many commentators always draw attention to Pasolini's homosexuality, it actually plays a much smaller role in his works than the Pasolini Legend would suggest.

※

14 He had been thrown out of the Communist Party following the sex scandal in 1949.
15 Pasolini said he detested consumerism 'in a complete physical sense'.

Nothing is resolved to a point of bliss or unity in the cinema of Pier Paolo Pasolini: his art is one of eternal strife and dissatisfaction. There is a conflict between opposites, and the oppositions are instantly familiar:

Male	Female
Men	Women
Masculine	Feminine
Father	Mother
Present	Past
Youth	Age
Realism	Fantasy
Reality	Poetry
Heterosexuality	Homosexuality
North (Europe/ Italy)	South (Europe/ Italy)
Bologna	Rome
Italy	Third World
Europe	Asia/ Africa
Christianity	Communism
Capitalism	Marxism
Wealth	Poverty
Bourgeoisie	Proletariat

PRE-MODERN, PRE-INDUSTRIAL, PRE-CAPITALIST

Pier Paolo Pasolini enshrined pre-industrial Italy, the Italy of his youth, which he reckoned was being eroded in the modern era, with its advanced (North American/ Western) capitalism, its technology, its science. By the 1960s, much of the world that Pasolini yearned for was rapidly disappearing underneath concrete and tenements (it was a similar story of suburbanization all over the developed world).[16] Pasolini neglects to recognize that young people in the Western world embraced all things

16 Yet if you visit Italy today it can still feel archaic.

American with incredible fervour. They *wanted* America, even more than America or the Americans did! (As director Elio Petri remarked, America had already been colonizing Italy culturally from the 1930s – via Hollywood cinema).

In short: after the war, *teenagers in Europe* <u>*wanted all things American.*</u>

They *yearned* for the U.S.A. following World War Two. The choice was: America or Europe? Dreary, war-torn, impoverished Europe or glitzy, out-size America? Pop acts in Britain such as the Beatles and the Rolling Stones opted for the Great American Dream. The coolest youth culture was American. The clothes. The music. The movies. The cars. The places. The language…

As Paul McCartney put it, Route 66 and the American South in the blues music that he and John Lennon loved sounded so much more glamourous than dear, old England:

> We know about the Cast-Iron Shore and the East Lancs Motorway but they never sounded as good to us, because we were in awe of the Americans. Even their Birmingham, Alabama, sounded better than our Birmingham.[17]

Anyway, these yearnings of Pier Paolo Pasolini's for earlier times which were thought to be better (even if they actually weren't), occur in many artists. Fifty years before Pier Paolo Pasolini, for instance, D.H. Lawrence (1885-1930) had spoken with incredible fury of the ugly, industrial Midlands, and how his England ('England, My England') was being destroyed by modern social and industrial forces (the Midlands is far worse today than in Lorenzo's time). And before Lawrence, Thomas Hardy had decried the advances of the modern era and the Industrial Revolution.

And so it goes, back and back, so that artists and writers can never reach that Eden, that Paradise, when all was better, richer, deeper, purer, juicier. No it wasn't. This is age talking, this is growing up to become an

17 B. Miles. *Paul McCartney*, Secker & Warburg, London, 1997, 201.

adult talking. Because if you are an eighteen year-old today, in the 21st century, I bet you could be having a *fantastic time*! But in thirty years, you'd look back and think, darn, things were cooler thirty years ago!

You can't win, because you can't turn back time. You can't be 17 again. What? Did Pier Paolo Pasolini want to return to the 1920s, the decade of his birth? Or – why hold back? – why not go back to the 1810s (pre-industrialization)? Or the 1580s, the height of Pasolini's beloved Renaissance era? Or, hell, why not go back to the Roman Empire?!

Truth is, Pier Paolo Pasolini's comparisons of then and now, of the 1930s with the 1960s, are simply more of his dualistic worldview, his penchant for oppositions, for automatically and violently slamming two eras, two political views, two artforms, two whatevers together. That's how Pasolini made art, by setting something up he could kick against (whether it was capitalism, or consumerism, or technology, or fascism, or old age, or poverty, or concrete jungles). With Pasolini, it's always 'us and them', 'me and that', 'I and those'.

Pier Paolo Pasolini knew that his mythical, ancient past didn't exist, and probably had never existed. But, as with God, or belief, or religion, an Eden was necessary for his existence.[18] He needed to believe that primitive cultures were more in touch with nature, or more 'authentic', or more substantial as communities, even if they weren't, even if nothing like his idealized, utopian communities ever existed.

The *idea* of the ancient world – and the Third World – is thus vital to Pier Paolo Pasolini's project: it might never have had any 'reality', outside of essays, and discussions, and films, and poems (the past as cultural imaginary), but that didn't matter. Because it was useful for Pasolini to have an invented, mythical past with which to accuse the present day (for falling short of his ideals, his utopia). The utopian, idealized past was also a

18 One of the recurring motifs in the 'trilogy of life' movies (and in other Pasolini movies) is the notion of miracles. Many times characters are speaking in awed tones of a *miracolo*. And in Fellini's cinema.

realm, as Sam Rohdie pointed out (1995, 110), in which Pasolini could play and explore, and in which he was in control.

Pier Paolo Pasolini's utopias were not to be found in the real, contemporary world, which was too capitalist, too bourgeois, too consumerist and too superficial for him. Instead, he looked to exotic climes (to Southern Italia), to the Third World (particularly to Africa, the Middle East and India), and to the distant past (of the ancient world). The notion of *ancestors*, then, is crucial – Pasolini explored the idea of people living today who had ancestors going back to the ancient world.

The exaltation of peasant, primitive societies in Pier Paolo Pasolini's philosophy has a right-wing, regressive and racist component, as Sam Rohdie noted: this nostalgia for archaic, pre-modern societies (communities which Pasolini claimed to have found in Africa and the Middle East), chimes with the writings of Claude Lévi-Strauss, with D.H. Lawrence and Gustave Flaubert, with Marguerite Duras' novels of the Orient, and, most problematically with racist and Nazi theorists such as Ernest Renan and Arthur de Gobineau.

Pier Paolo Pasolini might've known what was wrong with contemporary society in the West, but he didn't know how to put it right, or how to make his utopian visions come to fruition. Of course. It's much easier to attack, to identify targets and hit them, than it is to build a whole new world. (No artist of recent times has come up with a complete, complex, and convincing vision of how a utopia/ paradise/ new world would work).

Artists complain about modern society, and in TV and films super-villains are always destroying the world (or trying to). But *no one* has any idea at all what to put in its place. (We could get into a really fascinating topic here – the formation of alternative communities or societies in the modern era. For example, communities that have been developed along women-only, or feminist and lesbian lines (several female communes/

communities have been founded in the U.S.A.). Many would-be utopias tend to be very small, and often last only as long as the lifetimes of the original founders. When the creators die, or leave, alternative communities often go into decline and break up).

PASOLINI AND AMERICA

Pier Paolo Pasolini remained a European film director, and didn't leave for North America like some of his contemporaries. Nor did he venture into co-productions with North American companies. And he tended to cast from European (mainly Italian) actors, and didn't use North American actors, like many of his contemporaries. He also didn't take up North American subjects: his movies stay in Italy, or they venture into the Middle East, Africa, Britain or India (whereas a filmmaker such as Jean-Luc Godard has explored probably the most passionate love-hate relationship with the U.S.A. in all of cinema). Pasolini's films are Italian, made by and for Italians, even when their subjects are Ancient Greek or Arabian. However, thru producer Alberto Grimaldi and his distribution deals with United Artists, Pasolini was linked to the North American movie business (and some of his movies were financed with U.$. dollars; this occurred throughout the Italian film industry).

Pier Paolo Pasolini visited Gotham in October, 1966, for a retrospective of his cinema organized by Richard Roud, an important showcase for Pasolini's work in the New World. Pasolini loved N.Y.C. (it was his first trip to the U.S.A.).

> I'm in love with New York. I have a passion beyond words for it. Like Romeo and Juliet – love at first sight. It is the most beautiful city in the world. I

love the huge mingling of enormous amounts of
people, races. The mixture of cruelty and innocence.
New York is a piece of mythical reality, as beautiful
as the Sahara Desert.

ON EROTICISM AND VOYEURISM

A significant ingredient in the cinema of Pier Paolo
Pasolini is the emphasis on voyeurism: every movie
contains sequences of people looking and being looked
at. And, like the cinema of Tsui Hark, Alfred Hitchcock
or Orson Welles, Pasolini is a master at orchestrating the
network of looks and camera angles: consider the angles
and the viewpoints that Pasolini and the DPs select, for
instance, or how editor Nino Baragli cuts those shots
together.

It's not only the erotic aspect of voyeurism and
scopophilia that Pier Paolo Pasolini's cinema activates
– power and the relationship of power between the
observer and the object are more to the point than sex.
'Desire' is a better term than sex or eroticism – 'desire'
with all its philosophical associations with the Lacanian
lack, with loss, with distance, with Kristevan abjection,
with Foucauldian power. Yes – *distance* – the looking
and looked-at-ness in Pasolini's cinema emphasizes the
sadness and loss evoked by the distance between
people. Looking is not pleasurable in Pasolini's work –
the observers are not getting off on looking: rather,
looking reminds them of their own loneliness, their
separateness from everything. Pasolini made a remark
about sex in cinema that resonates here, how seeing sex
emphasizes sadness and distance.

As for sex, titillation, nudity – well, Pier Paolo
Pasolini didn't use *those* particular ingredients the same
way anyone else did, either. Sex and nudity are some of
the tried and tested and above all *cheap* means of

getting an audience's attention (maintaining it is something else). Hence so much of exploitation cinema, *mondo* cinema, cult cinema, and European (art) cinema, has used the genres of horror, fantasy and thriller (all cheap genres to produce), and included plenty of naked bodies. Or any scenario where characters can disrobe and get freaky. Sex and nudity are simply easier to market than, say, abstract concepts like Ludwig Wittgenstein's philosophy of language or the notion of pessimism in the philosophy of Arthur Schopenhauer.

So if Pier Paolo Pasolini wasn't going (to be persuaded) to use stars in his movies, a producer might think, at least we'll have some T. and A. to be able to market the picture – something for the film poster and the trailers (in the way that producers Joe Levine and Carlo Ponti asked Jean-Luc Godard to shoot some nude scenes featuring Brigitte Bardot in *Contempt*. [19] As Levine told Godard, the 1963 movie 'didn't have enough ass in it'. So Godard, Raoul Coutard and co. duly filmed B.B. naked [20]).

But Pier Paolo Pasolini wouldn't do that! Yes, there *would* be naked bodies and people Doing The Deed in his movies, but the sex would be either desperate or off-the-wall, or the bodies wouldn't be slinky, European vixens and handsome, buff men.

---

[19] Joe Levine and Carlo Ponti, wanted Brigitte Bardot to be seen nude in *Le Mépris*. Levine demanded reshoots of Bardot nude, and Godard drew up a budget which he thought Levine might not pay, being twice what it should be. But Levine OK-ed it and the scenes were filmed: Bardot nude with Michel Piccoli, Bardot nude on different coloured rugs, Bardot running by a lake, and Bardot with Jack Palance (dressing after sex, tho' this wasn't used).

[20] That must've been a tough day of filming: 'OK, Brigitte, now you take your clothes off, *bien*?'

Sometimes, the over-use of handheld camera can be irritating in the films of Pier Paolo Pasolini. So much effort has clearly gone into the production design, the costume design, the props, the art direction, the casting, the hair and make-up, the lighting and the visuals of Pasolini's films, it seems wasteful or irresponsible (at first) that all that hard work should be captured with a shaky camera (a *very* shaky camera at times – there are many ways of doing a handheld shot!). But the viewer soon gets used to it, and the handheld camera becomes a cinematic device that Pasolini and the camera operators employed repeatedly to achieve a sense of poetic immediacy and urgency to their narratives.[21] The handheld camera becomes a tool of someone totally confident about capturing the action in front of the lens. (One can't imagine studio executives in a Hollywood studio being satisfied with that kind of loose, improvized camerawork if they had been financing Pasolini's films. Of course, self-consciously shaky camerawork has become fashionable in TV and movies since the 1990s, but it's fake, simulating *cinéma verité*, and is never as haphazard as the handheld camerawork in Pasolini's movies).[22] (You can see Pasolini at work filming *Salò*, where it seems that he operated the *macchina* himself sometimes, and you can see that he is wobbling the camera at times).

Other *auteurs* employed handheld camerawork far more than usual – Walerian Borowczyk comes to mind, and also Ken Russell (which Russell often operated himself – his camerawork is instantly recognizable). In their movies, the handheld camera isn't used to evoke a 'documentary' approach, or to emulate an actor's

21 Enzo Siciliano has rationalized the shaky camerawork by saying that it expresses 'the sign of his hand, the visual possibility of his retina. Style tries to be life, life in its entirety' (240).
22 The actors are always in focus and framed nicely and well-lit, for a start. The framing is traditional, even if the camerawork seems shaky. And the self-conscious, wobbly camerawork is always integrated into familiar editing patterns and dramatic structures. Not so with Pasolini's cinema.

movement or viewpoint, it is a whole stylistic manner bound entirely to the material and the drama.[23]

SOUND

One reason given for the tradition of dubbing in Italian cinema is the lack of decent equipment following WWII (and the absence of it during the war). Yes, true, you could use that excuse at the start of the 1960s, but not by the end of the 1960s, when so many hit movies had been filmed in Italy. And movies that shot in Cinecittà, such as 1963's *Cleopatra,* used direct sound (when Italy was the biggest film production centre in Europa). Besides, the cost of a Nagra tape recorder, a couple of mics, a boom and some electrical cables isn't really *that* much (even provincial film schools have them).

There are other reasons, however: one is that Italian sound stages could be noisy (and were not constructed to the same sound-proofed standards of state-of-the-art studios. Cinecittà, for instance, might possess the largest stage in Europe, but it had only had one indoor restroom). Another reason is that the casts of Italian movies often comprised actors who spoke different languages. A key reason is probably the cinema distributors and exhibitors, who wouldn't want to pay the extra costs for sound editing and mixing (with looping, actors can sit in a studio and dub their lines in a few hours). Also, apparently, Benito Mussolini (a big influence on Italian cinema) didn't want to hear foreign languages in movies, so they were dubbed in Italian.

For overseas versions of his films, Pier Paolo Pasolini said he preferred subtitles rather than dubbing (PP, 40). Jean-Luc Godard preferred dubbing to sub-titling for foreign prints – he thought it was more

---

23 And also for speed – Borowczyk liked to use the handheld camera to start shooting quickly once everything was ready.

honest. As Godard noted in *Histoire(s) du Cinéma*,[24] postwar Italian cinema was filmed without sound – instead, the great Italian poetry (Ovid, Dante) replaced the sound.

And not only is the sound added afterwards in all Italian cinema after WWII, it's often a completely new cast. As in any industry which relies on voices, like radio, or TV commercials, or feature animation, producers and directors will have their favourite voice actors (often they're also the actors who dub Hollywood movies for Italian distributors). Pasolini would have likely certain voice actors in mind when he was casting their screen counterparts, for example.

Pier Paolo Pasolini followed the example of Federico Fellini in the use of sound. For Fellini, direct sound wasn't a big deal, and he didn't think highly of the fetishization of it in North American movies. In short, Fellini much preferred to add the sound on after shooting. It was also because Fellini liked to talk to his actors during takes (or, as U.S. director Elia Kazan observed on a visit to a Fellini set: he 'yelled at the actors'). So a take on a Fellini film often had the maestro telling his actors what to do. Famously, Fellini had his performers simply recite numbers if they didn't know the text.

The point is, when you are replacing the entire soundtrack to a movie, and not using any live sound recorded on set at all, there is an enormous *potential* for exploring some really interesting things in sound and music and dialogue. Unfortunately, the films directed by Pier Paolo Pasolini don't often take advantage of that (compared to the king of post-synchronized sound-tracks, Orson Welles. And even when some of Welles' experiments were spoilt by technical faults, as in *Othello* or *Macbeth*, and interference from studios or producers, the results are still fascinating). The truth is, Pasolini as a film director is far less compelling in the realms of sound compared to some other filmmakers

24 Pier Paolo Pasolini appears in *Histoire(s) du Cinéma*, with Jean-Luc Godard intercutting a photograph of the maestro with a painting by Piero della Francesca (from *The Legend of the True Cross*).

(even tho' he thought of cinema not as simply an image, but as an audio-visual experience). Part of this is attributable to the poor technical facilities in sound in Italian cinema.

Pier Paolo Pasolini preferred to dub voices on later: he reckoned that dubbing 'while altering a character, also makes it more mysterious; it enlarges and enriches it. I'm against filming in sync' (PP, 39). It was part of Pasolini's penchant for pastiche and anti-naturalism: 'I believe deeply in reality, in realism, but I can't stand naturalism' (ibid.).

It was also because many of the actors in Pier Paolo Pasolini's films were non-professionals, and weren't used to the rigours of acting, such as remembering cues and dialogue (so their voices were replaced by professional actors back in Roma). And Pasolini also liked to direct actors during takes (like Federico Fellini), from behind the camera (again, this is also partly due to using non-professionals, who needed more guidance than professional actors).

Often even the professional actors in a Pier Paolo Pasolini movie didn't dub their own voices.[25] Pasolini liked this – and he liked to have two non-professional actors create a character: one to perform it on set, and one in the dubbing theatre.[26] In fact, Pasolini would travel to parts of Italy to hire actors who weren't Roman or part of the film business, because he was after unaffected, untrained, working class voices, or a particular regional accent. (Thus, the performances in Italian cinema are actually a double act: the actor *and* the voice actor).

25 The voice dubbing actors in *The Gospel* include Enrico Maria Salerno, Cesare Barnetti, Gianni Bonagura, Pino Locchi and Emanuela Rossi.
26 Pier Paolo Pasolini also said that he wasn't interested in actors who depended on their voices (PP, 40).

MUSIC

Too many film critics had (and still have) little idea about the music that Pier Paolo Pasolini included in his movies – particularly what is now known as 'world music'. After several decades of 'world music' circulating in the media and popular culture, we can spot particular sounds and musics, we are used to hearing those sounds – but critical accounts of the 1960s tended to flounder (but musical appreciation is often way down the list for film critics, and they also don't have the intellectual capabilities to assess it. Also music can be fiendishly challenging to *really* describe (try describing the physical sound of a piano). Hence, critics talk about everything else – the musicians, the singers, the lyrics, the celebrities, the fashions, the concerts; anything but the actual music).

Notice that the classical music composers that Pasolini liked to use in his films tended to be German/Austrian – Bach, Mozart, Webern, Orff, etc – rather than Italian. Pasolini did employ Antonio Vivaldi, but often neglected the big names of Italy, such as Verdi, Rossini, Puccini, Monteverdi, etc.

Sometimes the music in a Pier Paolo Pasolini-directed movie is allowed to burble along, without editing, punctuation or dramatic significance: altho' Pasolini is often described as a genius with putting music in movies, occasionally the underscore meanders thru scenes at a low volume for too long (this usually occurs with existing recordings). And his films do that with genius composers such as Vivaldi, Bach and Mozart (for musos, this is sacrilege, demeaning, a crime against music, turning music into muzak).

Also, the music is often mixed far too low – this may be due to the unsatisfying sound mixes on the home entertainment releases of movies. (Sometimes movies are remixed for DVD and video releases, but often they're not: the sound mixes of the films directed by Pier Paolo Pasolini, stemming from 1961-1975, will probably all be the original mono mixes).

There are times in Pasolini's movies when you wish that some effort had been undertaken during pre-production (1) to select the *final* pieces of music for a film, and (2) to clear the rights to use the music. Adding the music later often doesn't work in sections featuring singing and dancing. There are wonderful scenes captured in the historical movies (*Medea, Oedipus Rex, The Arabian Nights*, etc) of players playing and singers singing which have completely different music dubbed over them.

PASOLINI, BOROWCZYK AND JARMAN

The cinema of Walerian Borowczyk (1923-2006) has many affinities with that of Pier Paolo Pasolini: both come from the same highly intellectual, highly educated, European backgrounds which valorize *avant garde* art, philosophy (Existentialism), Surrealism, de Sade, etc. Both were mavericks, who worked on the fringes of commercial cinema. Both produced contro-versial, Euro-art movies which included plenty of eroticism and nudity as well as politically provocative subject matter. Borowczyk's debut feature, *Goto: Island of Love*, was seen as an allegory about a Communist state, echoing Borowczyk's own experience of growing up in Poland. It amused Borowczyk, for example, that *Goto: Island of Love* was banned in fascist Spain as well as Eastern Bloc nations. In the truly remarkable *Immoral Tales* (1974), Borowczyk attacked European fascism in the 20th century, with his take on the 'Countess Dracula' myth – in which Countess Báthory collects and slays a group of virgins in order to bathe in their blood (*Erzsébet Báthory* was set in Eastern Europe in 1610, and starred Pablo Picasso's daughter Paloma in her only film role). With its scenes of mass degradation and nudity, of naked victims being herded and controlled like concentration camp inmates, *Immoral Tales* chimes closely with *Salò*.

Derek Jarman (1942-1994) was one of a number of filmmakers who cited Pier Paolo Pasolini as an inspiration. Jarman worked with Ken Russell in the early 1970s (on *The Devils* and *Savage Messiah*). Jarman came to critics' attention with the gay film *Sebastiane* (1976), a totally Pasolinian piece. Jarman wanted the film to be like Pasolini, but it turned out (or was sold or consumed) as gay soft porn (though it wasn't). Jarman spoke of a 'romance in the camera' that he saw 'all over the Pasolini films – something vulnerable, an archaic smile. I see it in our films, nowhere else. This is all I really want to film' (1991, 143).

Attempting a film in the manner of Pier Paolo Pasolini on one's first feature was very ambitious (Derek Jarman had already made many short Super-8 films by 1976). But Pasolini is by far the greater artist than Jarman in every respect. None of Jarman's films come close to even Pasolini's middling efforts. There is simply a welter more life, more humour, more emotion, more imagination and more invention in Pasolini's cinema than in Jarman's cinema. Take the use of non-actors, which both directors liked to do a lot: Pasolini could compose a poetry of unusual faces and characters from the simplest means, while in Jarman's pictures the non-actors drift about aimlessly. Pasolini had a genius for choosing fascinating people and orchestrating them within sequences, and putting them in amongst his professional actors which's pretty much unique in cinema. Absolutely no other filmmaker employs extras like Pasolini. By contrast, too often the non-professional actors in Jarman's movies are dull people doing dull things.

Pasolini making documentaries in Africa (top) and India (above).

Filming The Arabian Nights
in Isafahan (left).
Filming Salò (below).

Pasolini's books and films on display in Rome's biggest bookstore

PART TWO
✤
THE TRILOGY OF LIFE MOVIES

There is nothing else
beside nature – in which moreover only the charm

of death is spread – nothing
of this human world I love.
Everything is painful to me...

Pier Paolo Pasolini, from 'The Religion of My
Time' (1957-59)

1

THE TRILOGY OF LIFE MOVIES

INTRO.

Ah, the early Seventies! What wonderfully liberal, free, experimental times they were! The 'trilogy of life'/ 'trilogia di vita'/ 'mediæval trilogy' movies of 1971/ 1972/ 1974 and *Salò* were produced at a very particular time in film history: they were part of a group of European art movies of the early-to-mid-1970s which explored the boundaries of 'taste', 'decency', morality and film classification: *Last Tango in Paris, Ai No Corrida, I Am Curious, Yellow, The Music Lovers, Blow Out* and films directed by Walerian Borowcyzk – *The Beast* and *Immoral Tales* (and related porn films, such as *Deep Throat* and *Emmanuelle*). This was also the period of the 'New Hollywood' cinema, for some the finest moment in recent North American film history.

The era of the late 1960s to the mid-1970s was a time when movies with graphic sexual content, including porn flicks, entered the mainstream, or at least were widely distributed, and became chic. It was a time of *Deep Throat*, when relaxed censorship regulations, the new permissiveness, the sexual liberation, audiences demanding more liberal films, and other factors, enabled filmmakers to depict more sex and nudity in their movies.

As well as porn manufacturers, 'serious' filmmakers began to include 'X' rated or 'adult' material. So you have Bernardo Bertolucci and co. showing sodomy in *Last Tango In Paris*, Walerian Borowczyk depicting fellatio and bestiality in *Immoral Tales* and *La Bête,* Nagima Oshima revealing penetration in *In the Realm of the Senses*, and Pier Paolo Pasolini including erections in his 'Trilogy of Life' films, and so on.

It was the relaxing of censorship/ film classification laws that enabled Pier Paolo Pasolini's later films, with their graphic sexual content and nudity, as well as softcore porn like the *Emmanuelle* series, to receive wide releases. It was the golden age of the X-rated movie (really kicking in during 1974), with 167 porn flicks being released in La France in 1978. At this time, porn films accounted for more than a quarter of all film production in France. The French government passed a law in 1976 aimed at limiting the production and release of porn films. The government wanted sex movies to go back to their marginal status, as the Minister of Culture, Michel Gay, explained, of 10% of the market.

The later, graphic productions of Pier Paolo Pasolini and co. have to be understood in this historical and cultural context, when X-rated movies, or films with sex, nudity and similar material, took up a large amount of the market, and a significant proportion of film production. Ten years later or ten years earlier, and Pasolini's movies probably wouldn't contain so much sex and nudity (though no doubt some. We know that Pasolini tended to react *against* his previous productions, and move in a different direction in the next one: but altho' *Salò o Le 120 Giornate di Sodoma* was made in opposition, so to speak, to the 'trilogy of life' movies, it still contained plenty of nudity and sex). In the wake of the AIDS epidemic, one can't imagine Pasolini delivering the same sort of sexual content in his movies (the emergence of AIDS ironically coincided with an explosion of porn on video).

Inevitably, each of the 'trilogy of life' movies kicked up controversy upon their releases. In Italia, *The Canterbury Tales* was confiscated (in 10.7.1972), then released (1.9.1973), then confiscated again (3.19.1973), then released again (4.2.1973), then confiscated two days later. A complaint was raised against *The Arabian Nights* (6.27.1974), then annulled (8.5.1974). As for *The Decameron*, over 30 complaints were filed against it in Sept-Nov, 1971. It was confiscated in Ancona and Sulmona.

STYLE.

Although these are chameleon movies, which shift and transform with each viewing, plummeting from genius to garbage, there is something hypnotic about them, something that draws you in. Texturally, they are beautiful: even the muddy cinematography in dull, cloudy England (in *The Canterbury Tales*) has a loveliness about it. As *costume* movies, they are simply insane (for instance, the decision by Danilo Donati in *The Decameron* to put the guys in pants that leave the genitals pouched in leather, or the incredible gold and scarlet armour and helmets in *The Arabian Nights*. Donati was not a shy, retiring costume designer! Nothing was too loud or too colourful for him).

Stylistically, the wardrobe and production teams on the 'Middle Ages' trilogy have gone thru tons of research (as everyone does on historical movies), but they have filtered the look of the movies thru the history of painting. Interiors have the look of Dutch interiors from the 1600s and 1700s, with shafts of sunlight in amongst shadowy, dusty zones. The costumes, meanwhile, are fantasies of mediæval life culled from Italian Renaissance art but also Northern European Renaissance art (from the Early Netherlandish masters). The costumes might've stepped out of paintings by Rogier van der Weyden or Petrus Christus. (Add to that some 19th century art, some Symbolist art and Decadent art).

But only when Pier Paolo Pasolini and the teams are consciously referring to the history of painting – as in their stunning recreation of the Madonna enthroned at the end of *The Decameron* – do these art historical sources reveal themselves. Although he sometimes decried the reliance on painting in cinema, in general Pasolini managed to subsume painting to cinema. He wants to have it all ways, of course (what filmmaker doesn't?): to send up painting but also to celebrate it; to simulate painting but also to surpass it; to modernize it but also to keep it pure and untainted.

At times the costumes in the 'trilogy of life' flicks are delightfully artificial – the aristocrats in *The Decameron* wear anachronistic, pastel-hued garments (yellow, pale blue, pink), with silver and gold braiding which look as if they were taken off the rails and hangers just before each shot, so they appear completely *un-lived*-in and fake (compared to the contemporary tendency among costume designers to carefully stress, age and dirty garments to suit the characters). The colour design resembles mediaeval illuminated books, and stained glass.

And in *The Canterbury Tales*, Danilo Donati created gloriously over-the-top robes for the merchants and aristos, with scarlet as the favoured hue. And *The Arabian Nights* is a riot of Oriental fantasy clothing, with acres of blue, crimson and yellow cotton billowing about, chunky gold jewellery, and astonishing head-dresses (like the King's in the final tales).

There are many curious æsthetic decisions in the 'mediæval trilogy': one is that altho' many scenes occur at night (much of the trilogy is about what people get up to at night, after all), there are very few attempts at recreating nighttime. There are several solutions to filming at night: the costliest one is to hire truckloads of lights and film at night. Another is to shoot day-for-night (which occurred in *The Gospel According To Matthew*). Another is to shoot in the studio with appropriate lighting and settings. In the 'trilogy of life' films, those solutions are seldom used: instead, the movies were filmed in real locations (in the main), but not lit for night. It's as if night in these fantastical tales is as golden as late afternoon.

THE PRODUCTION.

How did movies like *The Decameron* or *The Canterbury Tales* get made in the first place? To a degree, the chief elements from a financing point-of-view are the material (which's out of copyright, of course) – Giovanni Boccaccio or Geoffrey Chaucer, and the director. Because these movies do not contain big stars: they feature Franco Citti, yes, and Ninetto Davoli, yes, and occasionally one or two other known faces (such as Hugh Griffith and Laura Betti), but not big European or American stars.

What about the actual stories and parables that Pier Paolo Pasolini and the team are relating in the three 'life' movies? Well, they are wholly conservative, tame, reactionary, and traditional. They are also heterosexual in the main (tho' with several allusions to male homosexuality),[1] and, aside from *The Arabian Nights*, white and European. Put the class issue to one side for the moment (the usual Pasolinian celebration of the peasant and working class – yes, but there're also plenty of evocations of ruling classes, of aristocrats, priests, kings, queens, merchants, etc), and you see stories that are archaic and utterly conventional: older men lusting after younger women, simple-minded husbands being cuckolded, young lovers meeting in secret on balconies, husbands and wives who don't love each other anymore, etc.

The 'trilogy of life' movies present a totally traditional evocation of sexuality, lust, jealousy, betrayal, crime, anger... and they feature a wholly conventional portrayal of social institutions such as family, marriage, government, religion, and the Church.

So there is little in front of the camera that is revolutionary or radical. In fact, nothing. We've seen these stories a million times before: well, *of course*, because they are drawn from three classics of mediæval literature: two European, and one heavily Europeanized,

---

[1] There is more homosexuality in *The Arabian Nights.*

the *Thousand and One Nights*.²

And behind the camera, there is not much radical, experimental, or unusual about the 'trilogy of life' movies. Take away the flashes of nudity, and they might have been made in the 1920s or the 1930s. In the 'trilogy of life' movies, the filmmakers delivered very conventional products: unusual from the extensive use of unknown actors and extras, yes (though this is a staple of European art cinema), but as for what the movies embody, what they say, what themes they explore, it's very traditional material.

So why did Pier Paolo Pasolini decide to make *The Decameron*, *The Canterbury Tales* and *The Arabian Nights*? These are movies depicting archaic, mediæval worlds, full of social repression and psychological regression, with very few obviously 'political' or 'ideological' moves either in front of or behind the camera.

Thus, for Pasolini-supporters, and for trendy intellectuals and counter-cultural æsthetes, who enshrine the radical, revolutionary aspects of Pasolini as a filmmaker, the 'trilogy of life' films are very problematic. These are not Marxist, polemical statements, but indulgent, old-fashioned stories about lovers, fools, jesters, kings, queens, layabouts, priests and thieves.

You can see why Pier Paolo Pasolini made *Medea* or *Oedipus Rex*, with their ascetic, anthropological (and autobiographical) elements, or how he was burning with fire and really had something to say with *Accattone* and *The Gospel According To Matthew*.

But with the 'trilogy of life' pictures, what was he thinking? Did Pier Paolo Pasolini fancy taking on some of the great works of the Middle Ages? Yes, Pasolini was a poet and intellectual who clearly exalted great works of literature, so it's easy to see why Pasolini would be attracted to Giovanni Boccaccio, *1001 Nights* and Geoffrey Chaucer. • Did Pasolini and co. want to try a

2 Among the famous *The Thousand and One Nights* movies are: *The Thief of Baghdad* (1924 and 1940), *Arabesques* (1988), *Aladdin* (1992 and 1994), and numerous *Sinbad* flicks (those overseen by Ray Harryhausen being among the most well-known).

new angle on material that'd already been filmed 100s of times before? (adding, for instance, a more explicit emphasis on sex, nudity and violence). • Did Pasolini hanker after filming in exotic locales like Nepal, India, Ethiopia and, err, England? (filmmaking as a working vacation). • Did he want to take up the ancient, mediæval worlds and the 'Third World' yet again, but with more upbeat, life-affirming stories than the Ancient Greek tragedies like *Oedipus Rex* and *Medea*?, and to leave aside the Marxist/ Freudian critique and satire of *Pigsty* and *Theorem*?

For Colin MacCabe, Pasolini's project with the 'trilogy of life' films was not simply a return to the past, but a way or exploring alternatives to the crushing consumerism which was ruining his beloved Italy:

> His obsession with finding a world outside of all the commodifications of capitalism, including, prominently, the bodily. By grafting the marginal modern (the Italian lumpen poor, the third world) onto medieval texts, Pasolini hoped to fashion an alternative to a present that he found ever more repellent. (2012)
> ✦

I guess I'm saying that the 'trilogia di vita' movies had the right ingredients (at least on paper) to become much better known movies – at the time, and since then (outside of Italia, that is – because *The Decameron* was a hit for the home audience, with over 11 million tickets sold, making it the biggest hit of Pasolini's career). They had comedy, romance, beauty, drama, sex, action, etc. But they haven't reached the larger audience today, where they seem confined to the margins.

Consider Bernardo Bertolucci: even today, *The Conformist* is revered by Western filmmakers and critics, with Hollywood filmmakers often citing it as a key influence.[3] And of course, Bertolucci hit the big time internationally with *Last Tango In Paris* (true, he also had one of the biggest North American stars of the period, hot after *The Godfather*. And no matter what you thought of the state of Marlon Brando's career (usually dubbed as being in the doldrums prior to *The Godfather*), everyone had heard of Brando). Although Bertolucci's career slid thru a wayward patch in the late 1970s and early 1980s (*La Luna* and *The Tragedy of the Ridiculous Man*), *The Last Emperor*, Bertolucci's biggest hit, was much celebrated in the West (including at the Oscars).

One can only imagine what Pier Paolo Pasolini would've thought of his friend's success in the 1980s and 1990s: but judging by his turn against his own 'trilogy of life' movies, one imagines that Pasolini would've viewed *The Last Emperor* and other Americanized or mid-Atlantic movies directed by Bertolucci (*The Sheltering Sky, Little Buddha*) sceptically. Pasolini reckoned that Bertolucci had sold out to commercialism with *Last Tango In Paris*. (Indeed, the movie towards the East in Bertolucci's 'Oriental' trilogy – *The Last Emperor, The Sheltering Sky* and *Little Buddha* – certainly mirrors Pasolini's own 'trilogy of life' cycle. And *Little Buddha* has some of the fantastical elements of the Orient (including naïvety and special effects) which Pasolini depicted in *The Arabian Nights*.

In short, Bernardo Bertolucci – and Federico Fellini – have both had far bigger financial successes – and recognition – than Pier Paolo Pasolini, among North American and European audiences (they both won Oscars – Pasolini was not Academy material). Yet in many respects Pasolini is the far more fascinating filmmaker – and not only because of what he achieved,

---

3 *The Conformist* was a key film for the 'New Hollywood' generation. Filmmakers such as Francis Coppola, Paul Schrader, Joel Schumacher, Sydney Pollack and Martin Scorsese cited it as an influence. Cinematographers such as John Bailey and Michael Chapman admired Storaro's work on that film immensely. Bailey (DP on *American Gigolo, Ordinary People, Cat People, The Big Chill* among others) said (in 1984) he'd seen *The Conformist* probably 25 times. 'For me, it's a real treasure chest; it's almost a textbook on filmmaking.

but because of what he hinted at, what he *could* have done.

I wonder if the 'trilogy of life' movies were in part Pier Paolo Pasolini's response to Federico Fellini, and to *Satyricon* (1969) in particular. Maybe Pasolini thought that Fellini was muscling in on his beloved ancient world territory, turning it into a cross between the Venice Carnival, a Roman circus and a night out in Las Vegas (see Appendix).

✦

When Pier Paolo Pasolini wrote the June, 1975 article – "Repudiation of the *Trilogy of Life*" – reversing his position on the 'trilogy of life' movies, and critiquing them with an angry disenchantment (ES, 19), you have to remember that this is how Pasolini was in himself, in his personality. A continual dialogue or dialectic, an argument, a self-analysis. Yet that was one piece of writing. Even if he had written twenty or a hundred essays denouncing his previous three movies, it wouldn't alter anything. To write a 100 articles might take a professional writer a month, two months. To make three movies is at least three years' work – or, in the North American film business, nine years' work. And those three Middle Ages movies were big films, involving 100s of people. In other words, they were a huge effort involving millions of dollars and thousands of hours of work by hundreds of people. So one person denouncing it all, even if it's the director and the co-writer, doesn't wipe away all of that work. (Even if they are an iconoclastic *auteur*, who's regarded as the 'author' of their films – partly, also, because films belong to audiences, too. And once they're out there, in the world, they are not the director's films anymore, anyway).

And Pier Paolo Pasolini was the kind of artist who would alter his views periodically. Had he lived, a year later, in 1976, say, he might've attended a screening of one of the mediæval trilogy movies and found the audience loving it, and changed his mind again (seeing a movie play really well with an audience can be a huge encouragement to a filmmaker[4]).

SCRIPTS AND STRUCTURE.

Structurally, the 'trilogy of life' movies are episodic. There are occasional attempts at inserting structural linkages, such as in *The Decameron*, where Franco Citti pops up from time to time. But it's not very effective. The episodes could be shuffled around in each 'life' movie without changing much. The editing (the pacing, links and structure) of the 'trilogy of movies' is one of their chief faults.[5] How do you structure an episode or anthology movie? (The 1960s produced quite a few episode movies, including *RoGoPaG, The Witches* and *Love and Anger*, to which Pasolini contributed). Well, you open with a very strong item, and you close with a strong piece, with the weaker ones placed in-between. All anthology and episode movies are structured like this, and if there's one episode which audiences will want to see more than any of the others, you put it last.

The Canterbury Tales, for example, opens with a ribald story of ageing lord Sir January taking a young wife who has a lover: it features a join-the-dots narrative, plenty of colour, music and dancing, and the most recognizable actor in *The Canterbury Tales,* Hugh Griffith. But the following stories are somewhat weaker; however, *The Canterbury Tales* closes with the over-the-top scenes of the Devil and his Ten Thousand Sinners.

Another problem with the screenplays for the three mediæval movies is not only that the challenge of an episodic structure is not resolved, but within each episode the scripts are incomplete and incoherent. Many of the episodes have satisfying resolutions, and follow the conventional pattern of scripts – of cause and effect, resolving dangling clauses, paying off foreshadowing, etc. But some are left open and unfinished – though not in the European art film way of being 'ambiguous' or 'open'. Some are simply shabbily brought to a close.

4 However, Pasolini claimed he never dared to see his films with a public audience.
5 Despite having veteran Nino Baragli at the helm

The stories of each of the 'trilogia di vita' movies are simple – as simple as fairy tales or parables. They are shortish episodes revolving chiefly around love and sex, with one or two taking in other topics (such as painting a fresco, or robbing a tomb). However, the way they are presented is confusing and lackadaisical. And some episodes tell simple stories in needlessly complicated ways.

Each 'trilogy of life' movie seems to have run longer in earlier cuts, with scenes hitting the cutting room floor (suggesting that the films were over-written, or at least over-filmed – more so than usual in Pasolini's cinema). These are episodic pictures, comprising self-contained episodes, without a single narrative thread running across the entire movie. One or two episodes are interspersed thru movies, but not in a strong, wrap-around manner. (*The Arabian Nights* tales do have a framing story – of Scheherazade and the Sultan – but this was left aisde).

One important aspect of the 'trilogy of life' movies is humour: after the dour outings like *Medea, Oedipus Rex, Pigsty* and *Theorem*, where there isn't a single laugh and hardly anybody smiles, the 'trilogy of life' films deliver a very welcome burst into comedy and laughter.

The Middle Ages movies find Pier Paolo Pasolini at his happiest – at least in his own cameos as Geoffrey Chaucer and Giotto. Pasolini is also able to send his movies up. He was, as Enzo Siciliano noted, enjoying himself (ES, 348).

The 'trilogy of life' cycle might be regarded as an upbeat, romantic and life-affirming counterpoint to the Ancient Greek tragedies of *Oedipus Rex*, *Medea* and *Oresteia*.

✦

One of the themes of the 'trilogy of life' series is fortune, fate and destiny – how fortune can spin from good to bad instantly. And, as two of the films are set in mediæval Europe, the issue of fortune and well-being is tied to religion (and to the vexed issues of sin, guilt and punishment). Again, that's to be expected of a Pasolini and Grimaldi production, where religion is fore-grounded all the time.

Linked to fortune is the theme of money and early, mercantile capitalism (and also the enshrinement of the peasant class). Being rich, being poor – each of the three 'trilogy of life' movies possesses the simplistic ethics of fairy tales (rich = good, poor = bad). So that stealing (or tricking money out of people) is an important secondary theme. (In the archaic morality of the 'life trilogy' movies, bad deeds are punished, and being righteous is rewarded).

Death is inevitably a major theme, too, as in many tales set in the Middle Ages – there are images of death throughout the 'trilogy of life' movies (from husbands expiring mid-tup to murder, decapitation and the dead carried on biers thru the streets). Underneath the 'trilogy of life' films Enzo Siciliano found a 'tormenting fury', and a feeling of decay underneath the portrayals of bodies (ES, 358).

Tho' the Grim Reaper,[6] the figure of Death, doesn't appear, there are people coming back from the dead, and devils a-plenty. Death has haunted Pier Paolo Pasolini's from his first film as director (*Accattone*) onwards (and he has also used the death of the hero to provide the ending for his movies. That is a formal convention so common (and often so derided), that nobody mentions it. But Pasolini's cinema is full of boring clichés and narrative conventions).

Aligned with the theme of death is fantasy/supernaturalism: nobody would class Pier Paolo Pasolini's cinema as Gothic, but there is a significant proportion of fantasy, of the supernatural, of magic, of spirits (such as ghosts, gods, demons and angels), etc. In the 'trilogy of life' movies, for instance, the Virgin Mary, angels, demons, ghosts, and the Devil appear (and

6 The Grim Reaper is all over the 'trilogia di vita' movies: they are as much a 'trilogy of death' as of 'life'. Pier Paolo Pasolini and the team avoid the classic image of Death as the Ingmar Bergman figure out of *The Seventh Seal*, but they do have a priest in white who mysteriously appears to a trio of *ragazzi* near a church in *The Canterbury Tales*. (And in *Salò o Le 120 Giornate di Sodoma*, the stench of death is every-where).

there's a visit to Hell – but not, inevitably, to Heaven).

Not 'Gothic', then, but one side is certainly pagan, archaic, mythological, and supernatural, and the other is Catholic, religious, dogmatic.

One of the striking aspects of the Middle Ages movies is how prominent religion is, and the trappings and figures of religion – so many monks, friars, nuns and priests. Pier Paolo Pasolini's cinematic mediæval-ism is a close approximation of the famous literature of the period, in which those religious (mainly Catholic) figures are everywhere.

It's also worth pointing out that none of the characters in the 'life' trilogy movies are real people, and probably aren't meant to be real people. They are types, they are embodiments of a point-of-view or an aspect of mediæval society. A monk = religion, Christianity, the law. A peasant = the proletariat or sub-proletariat. A lusty man or woman = sex. A thief = survival. In the films' credits, for example, many actors are not given names but are simply 'Monk', 'Nun', 'Priest', 'Old Man', 'the Cook', etc. Only the main characters have names (importanr actors would of course have agents, and be concerned with exactly how they would be billed).

THE 'TRILOGY OF LIFE' FILMS AS FANTASY AND HISTORY.

Much more useful, I think, is to explore the 'trilogia di vita' movies as a *mediæval* trilogy, or as a *historical* trilogy, or as a *fantasy* trilogy. Because each of three films is based on literature from the Middle Ages. Each movie is recreating the Middle Ages, in Italy, England and the Middle East.

But it's not a historically accurate mediævalism, even though it is plenty scuzzy, lived-in, dusty, ugly, coarse, crude and vulgar. It is as much a 'movie-movie' mediævalism as *Braveheart* (1995) or *Robin Hood* (1992), Hollywood flicks which, like the the historical epics of the 1950s and 1960s, are routinely criticized for their inaccuracies, modernizations, anachronisms, and cheap melodrama and schmaltz. But the mediæval life in Pier Paolo Pasolini's cinema is as ersatz and fake as Hollywood cinema's (and he knew it). And each movie is filled with anachronisms (some of which are fairly bold and crude).

The 'trilogy of life' movies are all based on European narratives (the *1001 Nights* are Middle Eastern, but shifted and transformed into European literature). They come out of the mediæval world; they stand halfway between the ancient world and the modern era (the ancient world of peasants, which Pier Paolo Pasolini idealized, and the modern world of capitalism and economics, which Pasolini found difficult).

The historical and mediæval elements of the 'trilogy of life' movies are fairly easy to discern and evaluate. But these are *fantasy* films, to the same degree that *all* films are fantasies, even the ones that purport to be 'realistic', or documentaries, or 'true to life'. In relation to Pier Paolo Pasolini's cinema, a term like 'realism' is *meaningless*. Because *all* of Pasolini's cinema is fantasy, and fantastical (as the maestro knew well).

So although it's not Alice's Wonderland or Bilbo's Middle-earth or Snow White's Fairyland, the mediæval world in the 'trilogy of life' movies is just as fantastical. The movies celebrate that: they are very conscious of being movies, and of being exaggerated, and of being very theatrical (they all celebrate storytelling, and the artifice of telling stories).

The exuberant theatricality is one of the appeals of the Middle Ages movies. They are vaudeville shows, they are pantomimes, they are street theatre, they are mediæval Mystery plays, they are circus shows. Let's play dressing up, let's goof around in OTT clothes, let's put on silly hats (let's see who can design the silliest hat, the biggest hat – in one scene in *The Decameron*, a woman playing an aristo has nothing less than a very large wicker basket on her head!).[7]

7 Danilo Donati, with each Pier Paolo Pasolini movie, tried to see if he could out-do himself by creating the Silliest Hat.

SEX.

Although the 'trilogy of life-and-death' movies are sex comedies, they are completely unerotic. Intentionally so, probably. Hopefully. No, the filmmakers aren't interested in evoking eroticism, although there are numerous scenes of simulated fucking, and people yearning like crazy for romance, lerrve and sex, and people talking about sex, and planning to have sex.

The 1971-1972-1974 movies are filled with nude bodies, but the filmmakers photograph them like specimens (though not quite as coldly and as scientifically as Peter Greenaway). Somehow, the casting directors (such as Alberto de Stefanis) managed to persuade unknown actors and extras to strip off and perform for the camera. And the nude extras and amateurs do quite a bit more than they standing about as they do in a Peter Greenaway flick.

Not only wholly unerotic, but wholly unemotional. Although these three movies take love, romance, courtship, weddings, marriage, living together and even a little bit of swiving as their chief topic, they are passionless and devoid of feeling. The *filmmaking* is *passionate*, the colours and costumes are *passionate*, the textures and the light and the images and the settings and the luminous smiles of the extras and unknowns are *passionate*, but the emotions within the relationships portrayed in the movies are without feelings. Where is the affection? Where is the embrace, the sweet caress, the loving touch? Not here.

One thing the 'trilogia di vita' movies do is to depict a huge number of romantic and erotic relationships – there are *couples everywhere* in these three pictures. Old couples, young couples, cuckolded husbands and shrewish wives, lusty, old coots and young brides, and plenty of people hopping in and out of beds or tupping in brothels. Yet, for all of the evocations of coupledom, there is very little true romance, true emotion, and true sensuality.

Imagine the 'trilogy of life' movies being filmed on digital video, with all the harshness and unforgiving quality and texture of video. They would be unbearable, and unwatchable. The beauty of celluloid elevates the films.

✦

The 'trilogy of life' movies are very much about pleasure and desire, and about sexual desire. They have a child-like investment in sex as play, in sex as a means to sheer enjoyment. The movies are self-consciously, intentionally indulgent. But in Pier Paolo Pasolini's cinema, sex is not a tease or fulfilment, and it's not eroticism in the conventional sense. Rather, sex breaks the boundaries of norms, of the acceptable – not only the bourgeois limits of what 'taste' and 'decency', or where the bourgeois watchdogs have placed the limits of sexual experience this particular week – but of all sex, all pleasure, all desire. Sex beyond history, beyond art (and cinema), and beyond the social, even.

In Pier Paolo Pasolini's cinema, sex and desire overflow the bounds of the narrative and their form of the European art film. Pasolini's movies happily break the rules – because they have disregarded them in the first place (recall his loathing of the bourgeoisie – despite, of course, being bourgeois himself).[8] His movies have not acknowledged the Law of the Father, or the law of any authority. There *is* no authority in Pasolini's cinema (and certainly not of the director himself).

I see Pier Paolo Pasolini as one of the very few *genuinely* radical filmmakers in cinema (by *genuine* I mean that there are plenty of filmmakers who like to think of themselves as 'radical' or 'rebels', and they are so not!), in that his movies are not only a middle finger raised to authority and government, and to any kind of social hierarchy (as with Jean-Luc Godard's cinema), but almost a rejection of *any* kind of organization of society. All politics. All ideology.

Everything must go was one of the tenets of the

[8] The contradiction wasn't something that Pasolini could resolve. As with many would-be rebellious or revolutionary artists, Pasolini couldn't forget his origins in the bourgeoisie, or that his audience was also bourgeois (and it still is, 50 years later).

Surrealists (Walerian Borowczyk used this mantra in his 1987 movie *Love Rites*). Pier Paolo Pasolini is one of the *very few* filmmakers I can think of who *really would* follow through on that promise. No North American director would, not even Orson Welles or Kenneth Anger. Ingmar Bergman wouldn't. Andrei Tarkovsky wouldn't. Carl Theodor Dreyer wouldn't.

But Jean-Luc Godard probably already has.

CHAMELEON MOVIES.

The 'trilogy of life' movies change with each viewing: they are chameleon movies. It's not that they're so dense and packed with layers that it takes a few viewings to catch everything. It's not that they are so fast-paced you don't absorb everything in one sitting. It's not that they contain so many nuances of performances, so many richly-drawn secondary characters, so many delightful cameos by name actors, so many amusing asides, so many incredible dance numbers or action set-pieces.

No: these movies change with each screening: one time you'll see a marvellous gathering of crazy, wild folk, a screen teeming life and colour, and a sense of place and photography that is grand and magical.

But another time you'll see a shoddy bunch of amateurs being led by a shambolic pied piper of a film director over the edge of the abyss of Dismal Cinema. Sometimes the 'trilogy of life' movies can seem so bad you realize there are better things to do in life than watch this piffle.

Parts of the 'trilogy of life' movies are garbage. Yes, it's tough to say that about a genius film director's work, but it's true. No matter how you defend it, or how many heavyweight academics you wheel to praise it to the skies, sections and scenes from each of the three pictures are simply awful.

Thus, Pasolini's rejection of the 'trilogy of life' series was *intellectualized* by Pasolini, but that was a mask perhaps for Pasolini realizing that the mediæval movies were also terrible too much of the time.

As he was directing these three mediæval movies, did Pier Paolo Pasolini ever ask himself, *what am I doing? Why am I filming this adolescent junk?* Surely some in the crew and the cast must've wondered about the revered æsthete and intellectual Pasolini turning his attention to silly comedy and fumbling doodles that seem far, far below his powers.

There are no conclusions to make, because these movies negate conclusions and resolutions. Try it. There *aren't any*. What are these films *about*? Who knows?! You can wheel in your theoretical apparatus, your Marxism, your materialism, your Freudiansim, your Lacanism, your Kristevanism, your juicy bits of Baudrillard or Jameson or Lyotard or Gramsci or Bataille or Burckhardt or Eliade or La Barre or Spengler or Nietzsche or Barthes or Sartre or Derrida or Cixous or Irigaray or Wittig or Kofman or Williams or Russell or Schopenhauer.

It don't mean a thing.

There is nothing of that in these movies. These flicks are not postmodernist (*Blade Runner*), or psychoanalytic (*Vertigo*), or Marxist (*Battleship Potemkin*), or classical (*Casablanca*), or modernist (*Citizen Kane*), or Jungian (*City of Women*), or Surreal (*L'Age d'Or*), or *avant garde* (*Dog Star Man*), or Nietzschean (*Triumph of the Will*), or voyeuristic (*Rear Window*).

You can apply your Edward Said or Gayatri Chakravorty Spivak and talk about the West's Orientalization, or take up your favourite anthropologists (Roheim, Bachelard), or wax lyrical about post-colonialism, imperialism, territorialism, nationalism, etc. But you'd also have to take in the 'Orientalizing' of thousands and thousands of Western media products. Yes, and even the artiest, trendiest and most politically right-on film directors have taken up Oriental subjects and 'Orientalized' them as glamorously and as simplistically as the cheesiest, Hollywood melodrama.

Besides, the Middle Ages movies aren't especially 'Orientalizing': well, one is about a British, mediæval poem, another is about an Italian, mediæval poem, and only the third one is really, truly, and properly about the Orient: *The Arabian Nights* (or rather, it's about the Middle East, not the Asian Orient, and it's about Arabia as it's been disseminated thru popular Western/ European culture).

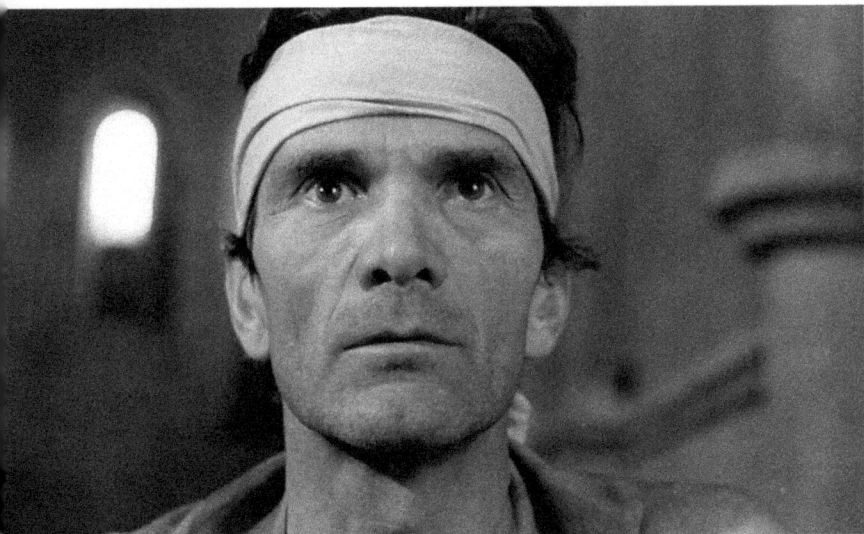

2

IL DECAMERONE

THE DECAMERON

GIOVANNI BOCCACCIO AND *THE DECAMERON*.
Italy has one of the richest and most important histories of fantasy and fairy tale literature in the world. For instance, *Lo Cunto de li cunti* (*The Tale of Tales,* a.k.a. the *Pentamerone,* 1634-36) by Giambattista Basile (1575-1632), is one of the great collections of fairy tales in all Europe. Add to that Giovanni Boccaccio, *Pinocchio,* Carlo Gozzi, Italo Calvino, Luigi Capuana, and the fantastical parts of *The Divine Comedy,* etc.

Il Decamerone (= 'ten days') is one of the great poems of mediæval Italy, alongside Dante Alighieri's *Divine Comedy* and *Vita Nuova* (though far bawdier than anything in Dante's poetry). It is historically linked with *The Canterbury Tales* (which appeared to be influenced by it).

There is a huge amount of material and research on Giovanni Boccaccio (1313-75) and *The Decameron,* if one wants to explore the cultural and historical background of the 1971 movie further (there isn't space here – it would require several books). There have been film versions of *The Decameron* in 1953[1] and 2007 (the

1 The 1953 Hollywood version of Giovanni Boccaccio (*Decameron Nights*) starred Louis Jordan and Joan Fontaine, and was directed by Hugo Fregonese.

latter was produced by Dino de Laurentiis).

Boccaccio '70 (1961) was a precursor of *The Decameron*, produced by Carlo Ponti: four Italian directors took on risqué topics:[2] Federico Fellini, Luchino Visconti, Vittorio de Sica and Mario Monicelli (some of the crew of *Boccaccio '70* later worked for Pasolini).

The Decameron (1349-50) is a central text in Italian culture, like *The Divine Comedy* by Italy's national poet, or the *Rime Sparse* by Francesco Petrarch. As with Petrarch and Dante, Boccaccio straddles the mediæval and early Renaissance eras, the shift from the feudal/ chivalric age and the era of the emerging bourgeoisie, the mercantile class and colonialism. *The Decameron* drew on Classical mythology, *The Divine Comedy*, *chansons de geste*, mediæval *fabliaux, lais*, and other popular tales. The Black Plague (1346-53) was a key event. Geoffrey Chaucer used some of the same sources in *The Canterbury Tales*.

The title *The Decameron* means 'ten-day event' – it takes ten days for the frame story to be told. The sub-title, *Prince Galehaut*, refers to a character in the Arthurian legends, Arthur's enemy, and friend of Lancelot.

An extract from Boccaccio's text (the 'Proem') illustrates the prose style of *The Decameron*:

> Who will deny, that it should be given, for all that
> it may be worth, to gentle ladies much rather than to
> men? Within their soft bosoms, betwixt fear and
> shame, they harbour secret fires of love, and how
> much of strength concealment adds to those fires,
> they know who have proved it. Moreover, restrained
> by the will, the caprice, the commandment of
> fathers, mothers, brothers, and husbands, confined
> most part of their time within the narrow compass
> of their chambers, they live, so to say, a life of
> vacant ease, and, yearning and renouncing in the
> same moment, meditate divers matters which cannot
> all be cheerful.

2 In the end, there was only a minor link to Boccaccio's famous text.

The Decameron has been taken up by authors such as William Shakespeare, John Keats, George Eliot, Edgar Allan Poe, Molière, Jonathan Swift, H.W. Longfellow, Percy B. Shelley, and Thomas Middleton.

It's worth noting the Orientialization of *The Decameron* here: as Jack Zipes remarked in 2012's *The Irresistible Fairy Tale*, and Bartolomeo Rossetti in his 1966 introduction to Giovan Francesco Straparola's *Le Piacevoli notti*,[3] Boccaccio drew heavily upon Oriental fairy tales, especially those that had percolated thru Italy's ports (and Venice in particular). Some of the stories are very old, going back to the ancient world. Pasolini would explore tales of the Orient in the last film in the 'trilogy of life' series, *The Arabian Nights*.

PRODUCTION

The Decameron (*Il Decamerone*, 1971), Pier Paolo Pasolini's take on Giovanni Boccaccio's poem, was produced by Alberto Grimaldi and Franco Rossellini, lit by Tonino Delli Colli, designed by Dante Ferretti, set dressed by Andrea Fantacci, edited by Nino Baragli and Tatiana Casini Morigi, with hair and make-up by Jole Cecchini and Alessandro Jacoponi, costumes by Danilo Donati, casting by Alberto di Stefanis, sound by Gianni D'Amico, Mario Morigi and Pietro Spadoni, the A.D.s were Umberto Angelucci, Paolo Andrea Mettel and Peter Shepherd, with music by Ennio Morricone[4] (who scored all three of the 'life' films).

Released: Dec 12, 1971 (in the U.S.A., by United Artists). Worldwide gross was $6.5 million (over 4 billion Lire in Italy). 106 minutes.[5]

In Italy, *The Decameron* enjoyed 'colossal success' (according to Howard Hughes in his history of Italian

3 Pier Paolo Pasolini would've known Straparola well.
4 The film drew on an album of folk music from Italy (*Italian Folk Music, Volume 5,* Folkways Records). The choral music included *Veni Sancte Spiritus,* and the *Tournai Mass.*
5 In the credits of *The Decameron* there are actors listed who appeared in scenes that were deleted: Patrizia Capparelli as Alibech and Jovan Jovanovic as Rustico. Indeed – the story about Alibech the Tunisian princess (filmed in Tunisia, Yemen and Mt Vesuvius) was cut from the movie before the premiere. Another dropped scene featured a trip to Paris for Girolamo and Salvestra.

film, p. 140), with some 11 million tickets sold (an enormous number), and over 4 billion Lire. A side effect of the success saw other film producers swiftly cashing in with flicks such as *Decameroticus, Hot Nights of Decameron, The Decameron 2, Last Decameron, The Warm Nights of the Decamoeron, Sexy Sinners (Decameron Proibitissimo), Boccaccio caccio mio statti zitto,* and *Decameron's Sexy Kittens* (most appeared in 1972). Pasolini was irked by these rip-off movies (altho' it also proved that his films were hitting the big time. Nobody cashed in on, say, *Mamma Roma*).

In the cast of *The Decameron* were: Franco Citti, Ninetto Davoli, Jovan Jovanovic, Vincenzo Amato, Angela Luce, Giuseppe Zigaina, Maria Gabriella Maione, Vincenzo Ferrigno, Vittorio Vittori, Gianni Rizzo and Monique van Vooren.

The Decameron is a gorgeously *Italian* movie, unapologetic in its *Italianness*, its evocations of Italian institutions, *mœurs* and locales. It *is* a panoply of life, to a degree: you've got sex, marriage, art, family, the Church, Catholicism, crime, politics, work, nature, community, festivals, funerals and other institutions.

The locations in *The Decameron* are unlike any other Italian movie or movie set in Italy in the history of cinema (including Pier Paolo Pasolini's own movies). The poem had been set in Florence, but Pasolini moved the production to Naples,[6] in keeping with his preferences (particularly for Southern Italy, and his love of Napoli and Neapolitan culture). The 1971 movie seeks out marvellous, sun-lit corners and secret, shadowy back alleys of Italy that dazzle and charm the viewer. Catacombs, churches, chapels, squares, back streets, villas, towers, mansions, mills, monasteries, and vineyards (numerous scenes are set in over-grown vineyards).

Locations included: Mount Vesuvius; Naples; Amalfi, Salerno; Ravello, Salerno; Bressanone, and Bolzano, Trentino-Alto Adige; Nepi, Viterbo; Caserta Vecchia, Caserta, Campania; Rome; Safa-Palatino, Rome;

6 And it was played in a Neapolitan accent.

Sorrento; Paris; Sana'a,[7] Yemen; Gafsa, Tunisia; and the Loire Valley.

SOME EPISODES.

The Decameron illustrated a series of bawdy clichés and stereotypes:

• a goofy youth (Andreuccio of Perugia[8] – played of course by Pasolini regular Ninetto Davoli the Hapless) – who's taken for a ride by a woman;

• later, young Andreuccio helps a couple of old coots rob the tomb of a recently-deceased Archbishop in a church;

• the simple-minded, cuckolded husband and his clever, adulterous wife;[9]

• the young lovers, discovered naked in bed on a balcony after a night of sex by their parents (who, instead of scolding their daughter Caterina, congratulate the lovers and persuade them to wed);

• a youth pretending to be deaf and dumb is enrolled as a gardener in a convent, and ends up servicing the inquisitive nuns one by one in an out-house;

• a woman's labourer lover's killed by her jealous brothers; she decapitates the corpse and keeps the head in a plant pot in her bedroom (as you do);

• the pious man whose dead brother appears to tell him that lovemaking isn't a sin after all.

NOTES FOR A FILM OF *THE DECAMERON*.

The Decameron sees Pier Paolo Pasolini the film director in his earthy, bawdy element. *The Decameron* might be seen as a reaction against the seriousness of some of Pasolini's works preceeding it – *Medea, Pigsty, Theorem*, etc. *The Decameron* is a return to the light-hearted approach of *The Hawks and the Sparrows* and *La Ricotta*.

While *The Decameron* is sensuously cinematic,

7 *The Walls of Sana'a* was also made in 1971.
8 Taken from the 'Andreuccio of Perugia' tale, 2.5. (This story goes back to 2nd century Ephesus).
9 From the tale 'Giletta of Nerbona', 3.9.

there are scenes where the direction seems uninspired, and scenes boil down to dull shot-reverse shot patterns, and sections that are just too talky and static (often a sure sign that a director's lacking inspiration, or that the script is over-written and/ or indulgent, or that the editing isn't pacey enough).

The Decameron is a comedy throughout – there are pranks (some with an undercurrent of real aggression), the sex is never sexy, but always interrupted, as in all comedy, and some of the situations come across as an art movie version of a *Carry On* film (except not as funny[10] – as even a *bad Carry On* movie!). It does appear occasionally as if Grimaldi, Pasolini, Rossellini, Delli Colli, Ferretti, Donati and the rest of the team working on *The Decameron* have taken up a mediæval sex comedy script and done it over as an Italian art movie romp.

Sure, the big political themes of Pier Paolo Pasolini's cinema – of Marxism and materialism, of the peasant class, of power relations in societies, of the exploitation of the lower class – are all there in *The Decameron*, if the academic critic in you wants to find them; but just as prominent are silly scenes of wives being interrupted giving blowjobs by husbands getting home too early, or botched robberies, or lusty youths falling into cisterns of doo-doo.

In fact, quite a bit of *The Decameron* comes across as lazy, uninspired and just plain *bad* filmmaking. Can this really be the director who helmed *The Gospel According To Matthew* and *Accattone*? Well, yes, but... They say that no one *deliberately* sets out to make a bad movie (!),[11] but with filmmakers like Pier Paolo Pasolini (and Jean-Luc Godard), sometimes you have to wonder. Because you can't believe that the phenomenally talented and incredibly smart Pasolini could've staged and filmed some of the scenes in *The Decameron* (and ditto with *The Canterbury Tales, The Arabian Nights,*

10 But Raymond Murray noted in *Images In the Dark: An Encyclopedia of Gay and Lesbian Film and Video* that *The Decameron* was 'perhaps Pasolini's funniest film and certainly one of his best' (107).
11 And nobody deliberately pays to see a bad movie.

Pigsty and *The Hawks and the Sparrows*).

✦

Like Jean-Luc Godard, Pier Paolo Pasolini liked to produce notes for films (such as in his *Notes For an African Oresteia* or *Notes For a Film In India*). Not a finished film, but a film essay in which the filmmaker ponders on producing the film. Indeed, some of Uncle Godard's most satisfying works are preparations for movies – as such his *Scenario For Passion, Scenario For Every Man For Himself* and *Petites Notes à propos du film Je vous salue, Marie*. In those short pieces, Godard talks, as only Godard can. Boy, that guy can talk! And so can Pasolini: at the beginning of *Notes For an African Oresteia*, for instance, Pasolini is yakking at length about *Oresteia* and Aeschylus, and it sounds un-scripted, as if Pasolini is simply talking over the images.

Maybe *The Decameron* can be thought of like that – not as a finished, slick 35mm movie, but more as a 16 millimetre, *cinéma vérité* preparation for the movie, much as some filmmakers (like Francis Coppola) have filmed rehearsals on video, and cut them together with production material (part of his concept of 'electronic cinema'), or like filmmakers heavily into visual effects will pre-visualize a movie in storyboard form or in digital, animatic form, adding temp music and sound effects and voices.

THE COMEDY AND THE FLAWS.

Again, the sound and dubbing (by Gianni D'Amico, Mario Morigi and Pietro Spadoni) lets down *The Decameron*, as with too many of the movies that Pier Paolo Pasolini directed. Sometimes it appears as if every movie in Italy after WW2 was dubbed in the same place (often at Cinecittà[12]), and by the same sound team – and they couldn't care less.[13] The sound in too many Italian

---

12 Tho' here it was at the offices of Grimaldi's company.
13 They were probably under-paid, and clocked in and out of work as in a factory. Right after mixing the sound for *The Decameron* they might've done a TV commercial for electric shavers and then the Italian dub for an episode of *Columbo*.

movies is crude and dodgy like the first sound films in Hollywood *circa* 1929 and 1930. And it's such a pity, because we are talking about some truly magnificent masterpieces of cinema here.

In consequence, *The Decameron* loses some of its power to entrance and move an audience. And sometimes it appears as if the film was shot with the same casual, can't-really-be-bothered attitude. There's a point when loose, handheld camerawork becomes grating, and starts to detract not add to the proceedings. However, the camera is on a tripod in the main, dispensing with the irritatingly shaky handheld camera of other Pasolini movies.

And the sound in *The Decameron*, as in many of Pier Paolo Pasolini's other pictures, just appears clumsy and awkward where it should be punchy and convincing. In short, Pasolini's films would not be classed among the great sound movies. In the use of dialogue and sound effects, Pasolini is no Francis Coppola or Orson Welles or Jean-Luc Godard. In terms of *music*, however, Pasolini's films can be astonishing – topped off by the incomparable soundtrack to *Il Vangelo Secondo Matteo*.

It always strikes me as odd – when *so much effort* is put into the costumes or the production design or the casting and dressing of the extras in Pier Paolo Pasolini's cinema, that the soundtrack and looping should be so casually slapped onto the movies (but, once again, it's also due to the way the Italian film industry works. It's also true that after WWII the Italian film industry, as with other European countries, wasn't as well equipped as its North American counterparts). For designs, sets and costumes, weeks might've been spent (and weeks of location scouting); but for sound dubbing and mixing – it looks like a day at most (with a three-hour break for lunch and a siesta).

But that's typical of the film business: crews work incredibly hard on scenes only to have them cut. Sets are built but not used. Costumes are designed and made (sometimes 100s), but the production is cancelled. It goes with the territory. At least many of Pasolini's movies found an audience, so all of that effort wasn't wasted.

(Sets[14] were built for Federico Fellini's grand project *The Journey of G. Mastorna* in the mid-1960s (at Dinocittà outside Roma), but it was abandoned. 22,000 costumes were made for a mid-1990s movie, *Crusade*, starring Arnold Schwarzenegger, but Carolco cancelled it when the budget approached $120 million).[15]

Quite a bit of *The Decameron* appears as if the filmmakers were going thru the motions and couldn't be bothered with it. The luxury of some of the components (the settings, the costumes, the props, the large-scale scenes with extras), are negated by the sorry state of the inept acting, blocking, camerawork, editing, sound and pacing.

And sometimes in *The Decameron* and other Pier Paolo Pasolini movies, like *The Canterbury Tales* or *Arabian Nights*, it appears as if the filmmakers were trying to get by with simply relying on the bizarre faces they'd found from open casting calls in Naples or Rome. The faces *are* extraordinary, and the camera lovingly lingers on them – and, yes, there is nothing so wondrous as the human face. But... sometimes you wish for a little more... In *The Gospel According To Matthew* it worked like gangbusters: the combination of those amazing faces of ordinary folk from Southern Italy and the unusual music, and set within the context of a religious epic, was deeply moving. (This is partly because the narrative framework of the *Gospel* movie – the Christian story – is absolutely enormous, containing a grandeur, a drama, a lyricism that few other stories in the Western world boast).

But in a fundamentally comical/ farce genre, like the 'trilogy of life' movies – which are *comedies*, though heightened and stylized comedies – lingering over faces at length just isn't enough. Close-ups of faces, done like

---

14 Including an airliner, a motel and a Cathedral.

15 The *Crusade* project eventually turned up in 2005, helmed by Ridley Scott. But, oh how woeful was *Kingdom of Heaven*! Sure, the battles and the action were terrific, but Orlando Bloom in the lead role had the charisma of a soggy cardboard box.

this, isn't comedy. A close-up of the wonderful Totò, yes, but not amateur actors. (One has to admit, too, that the film editing by Nino Baragli and Tatiana Casini Morigi is simply not great comedy film editing in the 'trilogy of life' movie series. The finest screen comedies need absolutely ruthless control over the editing. As Woody Allen explained, in working with his editor Ralph Rosenblum, anything that wasn't funny was out, *out*, *out* – anything that didn't get laughs was dropped instantly. *The Decameron* is shoddily edited, in terms of exploiting the humour. However, I haven't seen the movie with an Italian audience in a theatre, and you can bet there are ingredients that go over much better with a home audience (it was Pasolini's biggest hit, remember, selling 11,000,000-plus tickets).16 Comedy is notoriously difficult to carry over cultural and national borders successfully. Also, time is tough on film comedies, isn't it? Somehow, comedy movies have to be much more resilient to stand the test of time, compared with, say, dramas).

One would have to admit that, as with Steven Spielberg, Ridley Scott, James Cameron, Michael Cimino, Bernardo Bertolucci and 1,000s of others, comedy is not one of Pier Paolo Pasolini's strongest points, as a filmmaker. He would like it to be, and there is certainly a smug assurance that the 'trilogy of life' movies *are* funny. But they are not especially amusing. Pasolini is brilliant at irony (sometimes savage, as in *Salò, or 120 Days of Laughing*), and one or two knockabout gags.

Of course, many of the celebrated art movie filmmakers never tried to make comedies – Carl-Theodor Dreyer, Andrei Tarkovsky,17 Stan Brakhage, and Robert Bresson (and some of the ones that did try to do comedies – Ingmar Bergman being the obvious example – were not wholly successful, as 100s of film critics attest). But Pier Paolo Pasolini is definitely trying for broad laughs in his 'mediæval trilogy' films.

16 There is also the novelty factor – films with so much nudity and sex were still relatively new in 1971.
17 An Andrei Tarkovsky comedy?!

And failing.

If a movie fails as a comedy the first place to look – and this applies to any genre, or any type of film – is the script (scripts are worked over and over and *over* in the best comedy films). Unfortunately, in the 'trilogy of life' flicks shaky scripts are further let down by shaky direction and performances and casting.

Take the scene in *The Decameron* where Andreuccio is persuaded by the sly, manipulative robbers to enter the tomb of the recently deceased Archbishop. It's a classic black humour comedy situation of corpses, thieves, nighttime, creeping about a church. Ninetto Davoli isn't a bad comic actor, but the direction, the performances, and the script itself don't exploit the situation. Imagine one of cinema's comedy geniuses tackling the same scene, and you can see how far short Pier Paolo Pasolini and the team fall. However, there's some genuine comedy between the two brothers Meuccio and Tingoccio near the end of the movie.

Let's have a look at some of the stories in *The Decameron*:

CIAPELLETTO.

Franco Citti makes his customary appearance in a Pier Paolo Pasolini movie as an atheistic, violent, morally corrupt heavy, Ciappelletto (i.e., it continues his characterization in *Accattone*), a proto-gangster who'd be quite at home in the world of 20th century Sicily or *The Godfather* (Citti duly appeared in two *Godfather* films). Citti is another of Pasolini's rough-and-ready men of the streets: in an early scene in *The Decameron*, Ciappelletto preys upon a teenage boy, offering him money for sex (touching him near the groin – like the other two 'trilogy of life' movies, actors are often photographed to emphasize the crotch. Pasolini never got tired of filming shots of men's crotches (it began with *Theorem*), and *The Decameron* and the other 'trilogy of life' films contain plenty of them. Once Pasolini realized he was allowed to film crotches, they appear in most of his subsequent films).

Indeed, *The Decameron* opens in a very unusual manner, which seems to come from a different movie: in medium close-up, Franco Citti beats an unseen victim to death (finishing off the task by hefting a large stone). Then Ciappelletto carries the corpse in a sack at dusk up and down steps, and tips it down a slope. This is the first of many, many walking scenes in all three of the mediæval movies. (The scene wrong-foots the audience, but not in a good way).

Only after this sequence does the 1971 movie shift into a more familiar form of narration, with a big, crowd scene in daytime (it's a market, as at the start of *The Canterbury Tales*). It's a mandatory scene in any historical movie, where the production values are shown off[18] (this leads to the start of the first tale).

But why did the filmmakers choose to open *The Decameron* with this very violent scene? It's a murder (killed by death!) in the very first shot! It's played straight, and powerfully. It doesn't fully represent the rest of the movie (tho' there are murders, such as of Lorenzo, Isabella's lover). And there's no build-up, no establishment of dramatic suspense: the film cuts right into the murder as it's happening: we don't meet the victim first, and Ciappelletto stalking him (we only hear some off-screen pleas. After that, the sorry soul is a bundle of meat in a sack).

Is it to put the audience off-balance? To encourage them to expect a particular sort of movie? To understand that this will not solely be a mediæval comedy? (The more obvious opening scene for *The Decameron* would be the following one, depicting Ninetto Davoli as Andreuccio in the big, bustling market scene).

But the scene does establish Ciappelletto's character in broadstrokes, so that when he pops up in the crowd listening to the old storyteller, we already know something of who he is.

The Ciappelletto sub-plot is spread throughout the 1971 film, so that we return to it at several points (thus

18 Look, we hired lots of extras and dressed them and gave them wigs and provided them with props and animals and all!

providing a loose dramatic structure). Sent to collect a debt in Northern Italy,[19] Ciappelletto finds himself out-matched by a pair of wily, old debtors, and ends up dying – or seeming to die (punishment, once again, for 'sins', non-belief, and Doing Bad Things). But not before a *very* lengthy confession scene (yet Ciappelletto barely confesses to anything, telling a bunch of lies instead – his final admission, in keeping with the key themes of a Pier Paolo Pasolini movie, is about his mother, who carried him in her womb for nine months, night and day, and whom he cursed as a youth. It's a continuation, in part, of the characterization of Accarttone).

The priest ministering last rites buys it all, and Ciappelletto is instantly celebrated as a Catholic martyr. In a subsequent scene, which is pure Pasolini, Ciappelletto's corpse is carried into a sepulchre, where a solemn crowd venerates him as a saint (reaching out to touch his body on a raised platform). This is Pasolini the religious anthropologist, fascinated by how (and why) certain individuals are sanctified and worshipped, even if they are thoroughly venal. Even a murderer can become a saint. (This scene ends the first part of *The Decameron*[20]).

ANDREUCCIO.

Back to Ninetto Davoli, playing his usual goofy, well-meaning but simple-minded youth in *The Decameron*, complete with ridiculous frizzy perm (second day – fifth tale in Giovanni Boccaccio's tome) – and the 1971 movie enjoys punishing him for, in this case, simply existing (if you're dumb enough to wander into a Big, Bad City like Napoli without being hard as nails, tough luck!). Davoli's Andreuccio di Pietro is a preening, gullible twerp (when we meet him, he's a vain, strutting guy trying to buy some horses at the Napoli market). He's an easy mark, and the Lady, the Sicilian woman and her whole household connive in fleecing

19 Or is it France?
20 That's your cue to buy ice cream and popcorn in the foyer.

him of his dough (which he foolishly waves about). Yes, Naples was the Babylon of the Middle Ages – when Andreuccio is soundly pranked, everybody is leaning out of their windows, berating Andreuccio loudly, yelling at him to, 'Via! Via!'

This is from Boccaccio in the horse market scene:

> While [Andreuccio] was thus chaffering, and after
> he had shewn his purse, there chanced to come by a
> Sicilian girl, fair as fair could be, but ready to
> pleasure any man for a small consideration. He did
> not see her, but she saw him and his purse, and
> forthwith said to herself: – "Who would be in better
> luck than I if all those florins were mine?" and so
> she passed on. With the girl was an old woman, also
> a Sicilian, who, when she saw Andreuccio, dropped
> behind the girl, and ran towards him, making as if
> she would tenderly embrace him. The girl observing
> this said nothing, but stopped and waited a little
> way off for the old woman to rejoin her. Andreuccio
> turned as the old woman came up, recognised her,
> and greeted her very cordially; but time and place
> not permitting much converse, she left him,
> promising to visit him at his inn; and he resumed
> his chaffering, but bought nothing that morning.

So the Lady invites Andreuccio to her house then robs him, aided by the Sicilian woman (after he's tumbled into a toilet that's been rigged, and climbed out of a window covered in filth).[21] Everybody is in on the jape, and the hapless Andreuccio doesn't stand a chance against these mean locals. The episode introduces the elements of bawdy comedy and farcical (often crude) scenarios which the 'trilogy of life' movies explore at length.

Andreuccio only triumphs in the second episode (the tomb robbing) because there's a second band of looters even more inept than he is: he scares them off (after being trapped in the tomb by the first bunch of thieves), and gets to keep the bishop's shiny, ruby ring from the sepulchre. So Andreuccio dances off into the night out of the chapel – and, yes, Ninetto Davoli really

---

21 The film re-uses this location for part of Petronella's house.

does caper and skip with joy like a Disney bunny rabbit (every Pasolini film from *The Hawks and the Sparrows* onwards had a clause in the film director's contract that a scene of Nino Davoli prancing about must be included: [Clause 21.4.B] *Lo, there will be prancing, and the prancing will be done by Davoli. Amen*).

PERONELLA AND THE CUCKOLD.

The episode (from the seventh day – second tale) featuring the shrewish wife Peronella (Angela Luce)[22] and her gormless, grinning fool of a husband, Giannello (Vincenzo Ferringo), is delightfully (or painfully) idiotic. The script wouldn't survive the first five minutes of any meeting of TV or film writers, but it is obediently acted, dressed, lit and filmed here (when your director is Pier Paolo Pasolini, he is King On The Set, and you just do what he says).

So, after being interrupted mid-tup by the unexpected return home of her useless hubby, Peronella orders the toothy, grinning spouse[23] to climb inside a giant jar to scrub it (it's up for sale, and a shifty guy is hanging around hoping to buy it – she claims), while the lusty wife is taken from the rear by her lover and calls out encouragements to both men – 'higher... lower... that's the spot'.

The Petronella episode is a lame, French farce with some nudity, featuring humour at the level of a saucy newspaper strip. Can this really be the same movie director who made *Oedipus Rex* and *Accattone*? This is Pier Paolo Pasolini the poetical-political firebrand of Italian contemporary culture cutting loose, proving that he's not scarily earnest all of the time, that he can put aside his Communist, anti-capitalist rhetoric and do something different from his rants about the decline of Italian society.

---

22 The most memorable aspect of the Petronella skit in *The Decameron* is the shrill violence with which Angela Luce (or whoever dubbed her voice) attacks her husband.

23 Such a dimwit deserves to be cuckolded.

A GARDENER AND SOME NUNS.

There's an amusing episode in *The Decameron* (third day – first tale) set in a convent by the sea (what a location!),[24] with an attractive youth, Masetto da Lamporecchio (played by Vincenzo Amato) satisfying the itches of a bunch of nuns (the actor spends much of the time wearing only a ragged shirt and nothing else, plus some cute shorts that Danilo Donati has created). Da Lamporecchio pretends to be deaf and dumb (and simple), and offers himself to the convent as a gardener. It's pure male fantasy, right out of adolescent porn, and quite offensive if considered in the light of (second wave) feminism or political correctness (for instance, of course, it's the *nuns* who seduce the gardener, not the other way around. The instigator is a curious nun (Patrizia de Clara) who contemplates in a lengthy dialogue scene the possibilities of communion with her cohort. Meanwhile, da Lamporecchio works up a ladder, in a tree, allowing the sisters to contemplate his groin). At the end of the episode, the Mother Superior opts to sample the gardener's meat and veg too, declaring it a miracle when the guy starts to talk.[25] The scene of the two nuns in the hut with the mute gardener runs thus in Boccaccioi's *Decameron*:

> And then she led him into the hut, where he needed no pressing to do what she desired of him. Which done, she changed places with the other, as loyal comradeship required; and Masetto, still keeping up the pretence of simplicity, did their pleasure. Wherefore before they left, each must needs make another assay of the mute's powers of riding; and afterwards, talking the matter over many times, they agreed that it was in truth not less but even more delightful than they had been given to understand; and so, as they found convenient opportunity, they continued to go and disport themselves with the mute.

The best moment in *Nuns 'R Us* has the Brides of

24 The white-washed walls and tiny cells evoke monasteries in Greece.
25 She disregards the fact that he has violently berated them.

Christ lined up outside their cells, as Mr Weenie works his way from room to room, servicing each one. It might be a Ken Russell or Walerian Borowczyk movie from the Seventies. Except Borowczyk has done this scenario of nuns and sex so much sprightlier and wittier – in *Behind Convent Walls* (1977),[26] for instance, which's a truly wild movie, or the *Thérèse Philosophe* episode from *Immoral Tales* (1974), where God teaches a young woman locked in her room for misbehaving how to masturbate.

Once again, it seems as if this episode, like some others in *The Decameron*, is being treated ironically and cynically by the movie as well as being played straight, *and* for comedy. *The Decameron* seems unsure about how it really feels about the stories and the characters it's presenting, and as if it secretly realizes that this whole movie is total rubbish. But someone's getting paid, someone needs the money on this production, so – what the hell – the filmmakers soldier on.

CATERINA AND RICCARDO.

The lovely Elisabetta Genovese, with her incredible, radiant smile, has her biggest role in a Pier Paolo Pasolini movie as Caterina, the daughter of the merchant Musciatto (Guido Alberti). Clearly not a professional actress,[27] Genovese charms the audience with her performance as a loving young woman who arranges a tryst with her beloved Riccardo on the rooftop of the family home (fifth day – fourth tale). She tells her mom she can't sleep because it's too hot. They make love, of course.

Once again the 'trilogy of life' movies depict young love and first love and virginal love (usually at the same time) – the 1971-1972-1974 films seem to

---

26 *Behind Convent Walls* (1977, a.k.a. *Interieur d'un Convent, Sex Life in a Convent* and *Within a Cloister*) was shot in Italy, and starred Walerian Borowczyk's wife, Ligia Branice and the future star of his later films, Marina Pierro (as Sister Veronica). It was based on Stendhal's *Roman Walks* (I haven't read *Roman Walks*, but somehow I bet Stendhal wouldn't have thought it would be adapted someday into a story with nuns masturbating with dildoes.)
27 She struggles with her dialogue.

promise the possibility of new beginnings and of rebirth. For all the obvious reasons, the 'trilogy of life' pictures keep coming back to new love.

The capper of this episode has Caterina's folks appear on the rooftop in the early morning, discovering the lovers lying naked beside each other (Caterina has her hand possessively on Riccardo's penis – 'this is mine now'). Mom and dad consider the possibilities: death or money. The economic basis of marriage is evoked when the parents decide that the kids' union might increase their wealth.

The Caterina/ Riccardo episode in *The Decameron* is disarmingly simple and charming. It's the closest that Pier Paolo Pasolini's cinema gets to the unapologetic innocence of a Hollywood musical movie, where the entire machinery of film production, which's so expensive, so complicated, and so cynical, is orchestrated by veteran producers to create something as simple and sweet as a teenage love story.

There are no Disney doves optically printed into this episode, there's no cooing, Hollywood choir, and no colourful, lavish M.G.M. sets and props, but the Caterina/ Riccardo segment of *The Decameron* is just as sentimental and cheesy as M.G.M., Disney and Hollywood.

Part of the Caterina/ Riccardo episode is intercut with the Giotto Painting The Church episode – an unusual instance where two of the stories in *The Decameron* are edited in parallel. For example, we see Giotto on the street in the busy marketplace spotting Caterina and her folks (Pasolini as Giotto frames them with his fingers over his eyes, lining up a shot movie director-style). The encounter in the bazaar also suggests how the artist finds his inspiration on the streets, and how a beautiful creature like Caterina might inspire Giotto's version of the Virgin Mary.

✦

Many episodes in the three mediæval movies are actually love poems – poems to love, poems about love, poems made with love. Altho' Pier Paolo Pasolini is portrayed in the media as the super-intelligent, politically radical rebel of Italian cinema, much of the 'trilogy of life' series is actually a straightforward exaltation of love and sex and passion. There are scenes of lovers trysting, of lovers rushing to each other, of lovers mistaking each other, of lovers worshipping each other from afar – all of these are staples of mediæval literature, found in 100s of courtly love poems.

THE DEAD LOVER.

Among the least convincing and shoddiest episodes in *The Decameron* (fourth day – fifth tale) concerned a Sicilian labourer, Lorenzo (Giuseppe Arrigio) who's caught tupping a merchant's daughter, Isabella: her three brothers decide they're going to dispatch Lorenzo (well, this *is* the Middle Ages, and it's Italy, where erasing people who get in the way or who disrupt society is an accepted activity). This was also the source of the famous poem 'Isabella, or The Pot of Basil' by John Keats, and illustrated in Pre-Raphaelite art.

The Isabella episode involved some of the dullest evocations of Italian *braggadocio* and machismo in movies, as the *ragazzi* lure the hapless youth to the family vineyards (but the murder itself occurs off-screen – with a Godardian nonchalance. Just as the brothers hurtle after Lorenzo, with their daggers drawn, the film cuts to Isabella in her chambers).

The episode's reminiscent of the Romeo-Mercutio-Tybalt brawls in William Shakespeare's *Romeo and Juliet*, but crudely and shabbily achieved. Well, at least the episode expressed the corrosive sexism of the period, and portrayed masculinity at its most disagreeable: arrogant, ignorant, stupid, hypocritical,[28] controlling and violent[29] (it portrays the worst aspects of mediæval, European men and patriarchy – but that behaviour and those attitudes can still be found in

28 One of the brothers is seen tupping a woman, but in the double standards of the era, it doesn't matter.
29 One of the other brothers goes scarily apoplectic when he hears their sister is having an affair.

Europe, and Italy).

Only at the end of this episode did something vaguely intriguing occur, when the lover Isabella decides to uncover the grave of her slain boyfriend Lorenzo (he's seen in a dream, visiting Isabella as she sleeps, like the vision of the dead man later on). So Bella goes into the vineyards with her woman-in-waiting, scrabbles in the dirt, finds the corpse, and chops off her beloved's head (as you do).[30] She takes the head home, cleans it and plants it in a pot. Well, that's not something you see everyday in a movie, a young woman decapitating her lover.

The tale of the pot of basil ends thus in *The Decameron* by Boccaccio:

> Whereat the young men, marvelling mightily, resolved to see what the pot might contain; and having removed the earth they espied the cloth, and therein the head, which was not yet so decayed, but that by the curled locks they knew it for Lorenzo's head. Passing strange they found it, and fearing lest it should be bruited abroad, they buried the head, and, with as little said as might be, took order for their privy departure from Messina, and hied them thence to Naples. The girl ceased not to weep and crave her pot, and, so weeping, died. Such was the end of her disastrous love.

GIOTTO AND PAINTING.

The Decameron included a cameo from the director himself as Giotto di Bondone (*c.* 1267-1337), Italy's greatest painter of the 14th century, who, according to Dante Alighieri, out-shone Cimabue. (Sometimes Pier Paolo Pasolini is described in the subtitles as playing a disciple of Giotto). This enabled Pasolini to address directly his passion for painting and for Early Renaissance art and pre-High Renaissance art, with its Renaissance space (the frontal, flattened perspectives of Giotto, Duccio Buoninsegna, Masaccio and Piero della Francesca), and religious subjects. The teeming crowd

---

30 But she simply walks away from the rest of his body! – she doesn't even cover it up.

scenes of Pieter Brueghel were also inspirations. (*Not* Mannerist or Baroque, then, as Italian filmmakers such as Pasolini are often dubbed, along with Bernardo Bertolucci, Luchino Visconti and Federico Fellini).

Playing Giotto (from the sixth day, fifth tale of Giovanni Boccaccio's text) offered a portrait of Pier Paolo Pasolini the *auteur*, surrounded by assistants, the centre of attention, the only one who could add the magic touch and vision of the artist, who can be called 'Master' by his workers (and he played Geoffrey Chaucer, England's great poet, in the next 'trilogy of life' film, *The Canterbury Tales*). Pasolini's Giotto was shown carrying out a major commission in a large Cathedral (evoking Giotto's famous frescoes at Padua, and also Assisi), to paint frescoes on a massive, bare wall in the nave, orchestrating his minions who mixed paint, prepared materials, painted the ground for the frescoes, set up the wooden scaffold, etc (Giotto is visiting from the North, as the film production was).

The painter was depicted as a heroic figure, standing in the centre of the frame while his lackeys pushed the two storey scaffold into place. There were cuts from the frescoes to Pasolini as the painter looking suitably serious and intent in the midst of his work. (Pasolini gave himself very little dialogue, however, as if to preserve the persona of the artist-as-enigma – he yells at his team at one point, hurrying them to work, and apologizes at lunch for leaving early,[31] but not much more[32]).

In the episode, Giotto di Bondone was depicted as an artist so consumed by his work he dreams about it at night (this is where the vision of the Virgin Mary and the angels appears), observes people in the market square outside, and rushes eating his grub so he can get back to work when inspiration strikes him. This is the artist as mirror of life, taking real people as his inspiration (plus some of his visions). It was surprisingly conventional in its view of art and artists,

31 Because he's suddenly inspired.
32 Here, the assistants scurry about with speeded-up film, another silent cinema motif.

perhaps, considering that it came from Pier Paolo Pasolini, a poet who has a highly developed conception of creative issues.

Narratively, the Painting of the Fresco episode amounted to nothing really. It contained no drama, conflicts, goals, resolutions, or propulsion (well, there *are* some ruminations on the relationship between art and life). It was a parable, in essence, a simple story: *And lo, a Painter named Giotto, praised by Boccaccio and Dante, came to a Church in Southern Italy and painted a fresco, and, behold!, it was mighty handsome and good...* So a painter comes to a Cathedral and paints a fresco with a bunch of gnarly, rough-and-ready assistants (plus some Caravaggesque *ragazzi*, of course). That's all there was to this section of 1971's *Il Decamerone*: yes, and at the end of the episode, when the fresco is completed, wine is passed round the workers as they celebrate a job well-done (a kind of wrap party for the movie on screen). Pasolini has the last line in *The Decameron* – looking at his frescoes, he muses if it's better to dream about an artwork rather than making it (maybe it is – but Pasolini didn't take that advice – he never stopped making poetry and art).

However, the Giotto sequence opens Part Two of *The Decameron* (i.e., it's put in a significant place in the movie's structure), and it's intercut with the Caterina/ Riccardo episode, suggesting that Giotto is being inspired by the tale of simple, teenage romance (he uses Caterina as an inspiration for the Madonna). The intercutting (which occurs in the subsequent tales), also gives the Giotto sequence an aspect of a narrative frame, as with the Ciappelletto sequence in Part One of *The Decameron* (which was also intercut at intervals in between the episodes). The Giotto sequence also closes the 1971 picture (another important spot), with the celebration scene in the Cathedral.

I wonder if *Andrei Roublyov* was an influence in this section of *The Decameron*: the 1966 Mosfilm production, directed by Andrei Tarkovsky and co-written with Andrei Mikhalkov-Konchalovsky, is a remarkable recreation of 15th century Russia. Tarkovsky and Mikhalkov-Konchalovsky took up the scenario of an itinerant artist travelling to churches to fulfil commissions to paint frescoes and turned it into a disquisition on the poetry of art and the poetry of cinema. The scene where Giotto, da Rabatta and the boys are caught in a rainstorm in the countryside in *The Decameron* seems to be an *hommage* to the similar scene at the beginning of *Andrei Roublyov*, which, in turn, was likely inspired by Akira Kurosawa and *Rashomon* (1950) and its famous rain scenes. (Meanwhile, Walerian Borowczyk staged a delightful recreation of the Renaissance artists Raphael and Michelangelo Buonarroti painting the Vatican in his amazing 1979 movie *Three Immoral Women*).[33]

THE PRIEST AND THE MARE.

One of the silliest episodes in *The Decameron* (in a film stuffed with dumb tales), concerns a self-important priest/ doctor, Don Giovanni (Vittorio Vittori), who attempts a ridiculous prank on two simple-minded peasants. When Don Giovanni discovers that the wife Gemmatta (Mirella Catanesi) of his attendant Pietro da Tresanti is young and attractive,[34] and as gullible as a two year-old child, he goes along with her request to be turned into a mare. While Gemmatta's gormless spouse da Tresanti looks on, befuddled and spluttering, the priest has Gemmatta undress, then he fondles her and mounts her, all the while gushing over her body which'll make a very fine mare. And pinning on the tail of the mare is the trickiest part of the magical transformation! (It's a saucy version of the kids' party game of being blindfold and pinning the tail on the donkey).

33 *Three Immoral Women* has all of the classic Walerian Borowczyk touches and obsessions: women in lead roles; tons of art on display; plenty of sex scenes and acres of nudity; floaty, white, see-through dresses; historical settings; period music; women bathing; still-lifes; animals; organ music; fabulous costumes and hats; and it's been art directed to perfection.
34 Don't ask how this ugly, unkempt peasant landed himself a lovely, young wife.

The priest and the mare is a farcical riff on authority figures exploiting the peasant class – literally, by taking their women for themselves. Da Tresanti and his wife Gemmatta don't possess strong enough defences against the wiles of a bourgeois, educated priest, who finds them an easy mark. The scenario of power, class and exploitation was reprised later in the 'trilogy of life' films and of course taken to an extreme in *Salò, or The 120 Days of Sodom*.

THE VIRGIN MARY.

In an extraordinary, breathtaking sequence in *The Decameron*, in one of the last tales, the production team recreated an Early Renaissance painting of the Virgin Mary in glory, surrounded by angels, with a Last Judgement acted out underneath (a replay of *Curd Cheese*), as sinners are manhandled by devils into the depths. The scene, which's very brief (and a little clumsily filmed and edited),[35] was accompanied by choral music (*Veni Sancte Spiritus*). It was the nighttime vision of the painter Giotto waking up in bed.

The scene was presented in the flattened space of Renaissance art, against a pale, blue sky and a wall of grey soil (it's taken from a Giotto painting). The Madonna (played by – who else? – Silvana Mangano) sat on a throne, a gold *vesica piscis* enveloping her, with angels (choiring children out of Piero della Francesca) in white robes in rows either side, standing in front of gold, embossed haloes (plus nobles on thrones on either side). The lower half of the scene combined elements from Renaissance depictions of Adam and Eve being expelled from Paradise, the *Crucifixion*, and *The Last Judgment*.[36] (With the curious omission of Christ – the Cross is empty – Jesus is sitting on the Madonna's lap).

Giotto's dream is staged in the fake-theatrical-pictorial manner that seems to be the special province of

35 The dream vision is edited as flash cuts (and some longer pan shots), combined with reaction shots of Giotto in bed, looking slightly off-camera.
36 Some of the bodies hanging are dummies; the Virgin in the wide shot is a dummy, too, to be in scale with Christ on her lap, played by a child.

Italian cinema, a cross between a puppet show at a religious festival, a procession of carnival floats in Venice, and theatrical-cinematic trickery (which became the approach of later Federico Fellini films such as *Casanova* and *City of Women*).

Certainly Pier Paolo Pasolini was at his finest and most overtly romantic as a film director when he and his teams were recreating Italian Renaissance art – in *Curd Cheese, The Canterbury Tales* and *The Decameron,* Pasolini is deliciously self-indulgent. One could happily watch hours of this kind of filmmaking, with its joyous and uniroinic celebration of Italian Renaissance art (but if anybody can render Italian Renaissance art, it's probably best done by a bunch of Italian filmmakers who know it inside-out – it's in their blood[37]).

THE TWO BROTHERS.

In the tale of the two brothers (seventh day – tenth tale), the final story in *The Decameron*, we discover that lovemaking isn't a sin! Yay! *Si si*, we *really* needed to hear that in 1971, didn't we?! Or today!

So here're evocations of sex and repression once again, with sin and guilt as the ever-present moral threat/ punishment hovering over everything in the Catholic/ Christian world. So there's the pious brother (Meuccio) who tries to abstain from sex and the virile brother (Tingoccio) who's out carousing and swiving a lot. Meuccio and Tingoccio are humble merchants who have sweethearts among the stalls near them in the street market (outside the Cathedral, where Giotto is painting inside). Meuccio complains that Tingoccio is at it all the time (two, three, four – nine times a day!). Meuccio is the neurotic one, a 14th century Woody Allen, who worries about getting into Heaven (or, rather, trying to stay out of Hell). Tingoccio has girls as much as he likes, but pays for his actions with death (he's literally killed, it seems, by over-indulgence – the wages of sin).

There is some genuine comedy in the tale of the two brothers in *The Decameron* (both actors are terrific). The

---

37 And who are steeped in it – in Rome.

horny Tinogoccio comes back from the dead at night to let his brother Meuccio know what Hell is like (as they promised each other). When Tinogoccio tells his brother Meuccio that the sin of sex doesn't count in Hell (or Purgatory), what does the pious brother do? He bursts out of bed in joy, rushes gleefully thru the nighttime streets to leap upon his naked beloved in her chamber, crying out, 'it's not a sin!'

The Decameron thus closes with two upbeat episodes: the black comedy of the two brothers, with the message that love isn't a crime, and the completion of the fresco in the Cathedral. The scenes close *The Decameron* with some positive statements: go and make love, folks, because it's not regarded as a sin in Hell... and maybe art is best left in the realm of dreams, where it can swim unfettered.

PASOLINI
LE DECAMERON

The Decameron (1971).
This page and over.

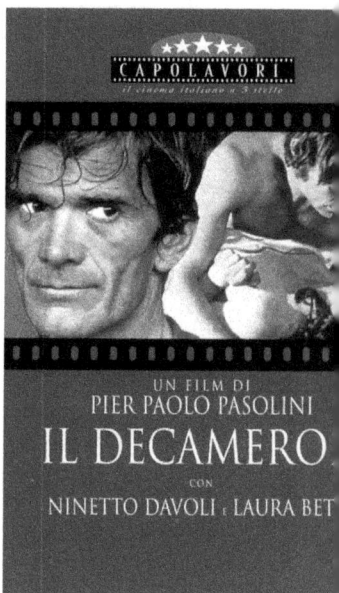

CAPOLAVORI
il cinema italiano a 5 stelle

UN FILM DI
PIER PAOLO PASOLINI
IL DECAMERO
CON
NINETTO DAVOLI E LAURA BET

PASOLINI
le decameron

Pasolini's cameo in The Decameron.

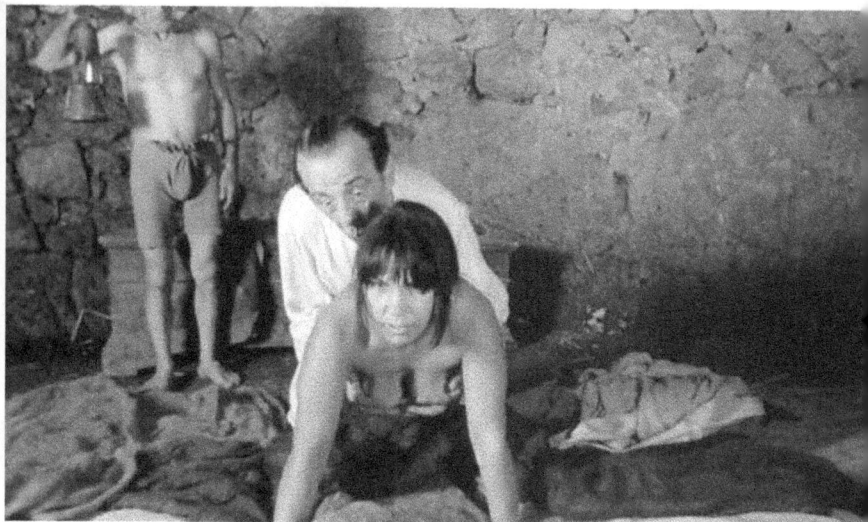
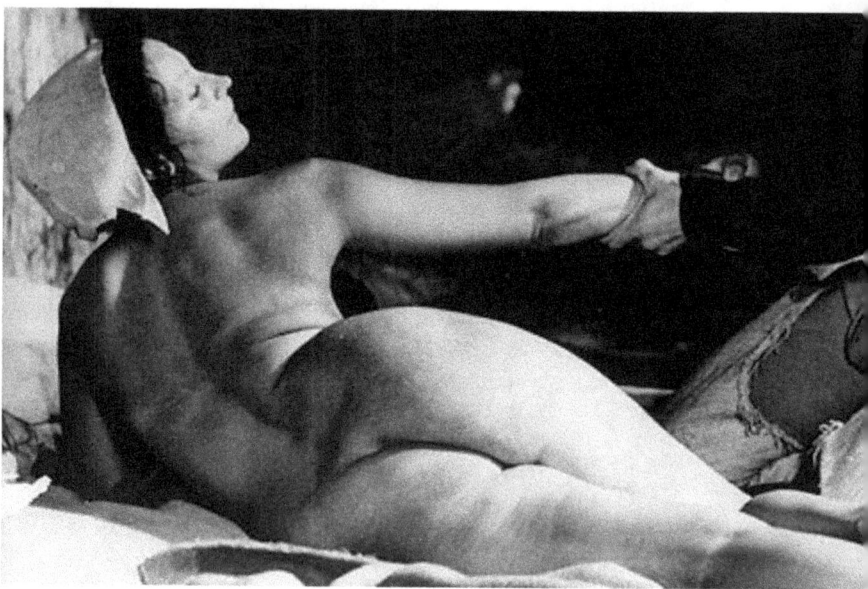

3

I RACCONTI DI CANTERBURY

THE CANTERBURY TALES

This world nis but a thurghfare ful of wo,
And we ben pilgrimes, passinge to and fro;
Death is an ende of every worldly sore.

Geoffrey Chaucer, *The Canterbury Tales*

PRODUCTION.

The Canterbury Tales (*I racconti di Canterbury,* 1972), Alberto Grimaldi's and Pier Paolo Pasolini's 1972 adaptation[1] of Geoffrey Chaucer's famous poem, was the second of the trilogy of mediæval or 'life' films.

Alberto Grimaldi was producer (for Les Productions Artistes Associés and Produzioni Europee Associate); Danilo Donati designed the costumes; Tonino Delli Colli was DP; Dante Ferretti was production designer; Carlo Agati was art director; Ennio Morricone composed the score; Giancarlo De Leonardis was hair stylist; Otello Sisi was make-up artist; the A.D.s were Sergio Citti, Umberto Angelucci and Peter Shepherd;[2] and sound was by Gianni D'Amico and Primimiano

---

1 The script for *The Canterbury Tales* was written in Romania (Pasolini had gone there to scout locales for *Oedipus Rex*).
2 The A.D.s should be admired (or pitied!) for marshalling this huge cast of unruly, ugly Brits.

Muratore.

Released: Sept 2, 1972 (Italy). 122[3] minutes.

European rentals were $2 million (about half of the gross). *The Canterbury Tales* played well in France and Italy (its primary markets), and led to some cash-in movies – *The Lusty Wives of Canterbury, The Other Canterbury Tales, The Forbidden Cantury Tales* and *More Sexy Tales From Canterbury* (all these were produced in 1972. And *The Sexbury Tales* pre-empted Alberto Grimaldi's movie, coming out in 1971). It won the Golden Bear at the Berlin Film Festival.

Just why Alberto Grimaldi took the production to England is a bit of a mystery. Because if Pier Paolo Pasolini and the team can film a Biblical movie in Italy, they can certainly stage a mediæval, European flick from anywhere in Europe back in Italy. And why the maestro selected Geoffrey Chaucer to adapt instead of another mediæval text is curious (*The Romance of the Rose, The Art of Love* and Chrétien de Troyes are obvious candidates, though *I racconti di Canterbury* features the crude humour that Pasolini was looking for).

The Canterbury Tales' cast is non-professionals plus some minor actors almost unknown outside of England, such as Tom Baker, Jenny Runacre, Phil Davis and Robin Askwith; Adrian Street, Alan Webb, Vernon Dobtcheff and Derek Deadman also appear. Some of the British actors're familiar from British TV and movies. Hugh Griffith is probably the biggest name in *The Canterbury Tales* among the Brits (he was in *Ben-Hur* and *Barbarella*), while Italians such as Franco Citti, Laura Betti and Ninetto Davoli make their mandatory appearance in a Pasolini production.

One or two other faces in *The Canterbury Tales* might be recognized by diehard film fans: Charlie Chaplin's daughter Josephine appears; and Jenny Runacre plays the old merchant's wife in one of the middle stories: she was in *Jubilee* (dir. Derek Jarman, 1978; as the Virgin Queen, of course!).

The other two movies in the 'trilogy of life' are

---

3 A cut version runs 110m.

marvellous (tho' with many flaws), but *The Canterbury Tales* is beset with failings. *The Arabian Nights* and *The Decameron* share much of the same production team, and much of the same comic-bawdy-satirical approach as *The Canterbury Tales*, but they are so much more successful. (Maybe I'm just put off by those spotty, freckly, ginger-haired English kids[4] horsing about in *The Canterbury Tales*. Those sideburns! That hair! That acne! Those horrible teeth! Didn't anybody shave or wash in Blighty in 1972? And then there's the curious, somewhat unsettling phenomenon of a bunch of ugly Brits being dubbed by Italians).

Presumably the production team would've advertized for local extras in newspapers and maybe on the radio in England. Along the lines of:

> 'WANTED: Weird-looking old coots required for controversial movie from acclaimed Euro-art director, Mister Danger himself, Pier Paolo Pasolini. Bring your own food if you don't like spaghetti (!). Some nudity and jester-capering required. Pay? Don't expect-a much.'

✦

GEOFFREY CHAUCER.

Many of the elements in Geoffrey Chaucer's (*c.* 1340-1400) poems derive from European sources – the French troubadours, Pierre Ronsard, *The Art of Love,*[5] and the Italian *stil novisti* (Dante Alighieri, Guido Cavalcanti, Guido Guinicelli *et al*). It's all familiar stuff if you know the courtly love poetry tradition: young lovers trysting in secret, separated at dawn... cuckolded older husbands... lusty, old coots hankering for some young flesh... the young lover admiring an unattainable woman from afar (he's a servant, she's a lady)... guys having heart attacks while swiving...

This is a typical verse from the French courtly love poet Arnaut Daniel:

> Del cors li fos, non de l'arma,

---

4 The lads in *The Canterbury Tales* look like they should be on the football terraces of Arsenal and Man U.
5 This is cited in the film.

e cossentis m'a celat dinz sa cambra!
(Would that I might be hers with my body, not with
my soul, and that she might admit me in secret to
her room!) 6

And this is from Beatrice, Countess of Die:

Ben volvia mon cavallier
tener un ser en mos'bratz nut.
(How I'd long to hold him pressed
naked in my arms one night)7

In the mediæval, courtly love tradition, this kind of
fooling around between men and women is given the
full-on, intellectual, philosophical and religious treatment, refined into ever-more exquisite verses composed
for the delectation of highly-educated audiences in
courts (many were composed as songs. These were the
days with no cel phones, television, online games, etc).
But in the earthy, bawdy side of poesie, the primal
instincts and lustful impulses are encouraged to erupt
(with troubadours slyly hiding bodily functions underneath elaborate rhyme schemes, witty puns and over-
cooked symbolism).

The 'trilogy of life' movies are further installments
in the comedy of life genre, thousands of years old,
where sex, love, desire and death are recurring motifs.
It's a style of storytelling that goes back to Ovid and
Catullus in Ancient Rome, and then further back. As
soon as people started telling stories, you can bet that
the earthy, bawdy side of love and romance was a regular
feature.

The Canterbury Tales is one of the treasures of
English literature, endlessly discussed in literary
criticism, and thousands of people study it every year
(to the point where many teenagers probably never want
to hear someone trying to speak mediæval English ever
again). *The Canterbury Tales* has been adapted many

6 G. Toja: *Arnaut Daniel's Canzoni*, Florence, 1960; and in L.T.
Topsfield, *Troubadours and Love*, Cambridge University Press, 1975
214.
7 Quoted in Peter Dronke, *The Medieval Lyric*, Hutchinson, 1968, 106.

times, often for television.

> Love wol nat ben contreyned by maistrye;
> Whan maistrie comth, the god of love anon
> Beteth hise winges, and farewell! he is gon!
> (Geoffrey Chaucer, *The Canterbury Tales*)

Eight of the 24 tales in *The Canterbury Tales* were adapted in the 1972 picture: *The Friar's Tale, The Wife of Bath's Tale, The Cook's Tale, The Merchant's Tale, The Reeve's Tale, The Summoner's Tale, The Pardoner's Tale and The Miller's Tale*. The episodes were not captioned or announced, the film simply moves from one to another. (And there were few attempts at introducing each episode with its own style). There are many study guides published for students for *The Canterbury Tales*, of course – but the Italian movie simply assumes the audience can keep up.

Among the scenes filmed but subsequently deleted from *The Canterbury Tales* were more scenes at the Tabard Inn (including more of Geoffrey Chaucer talking with the guests at the Inn), more of *The Wife of Bath's Tale,* more of *The Summoner's Tale,* and more of *The Pardoner's Tale.* A whole tale was dropped – Sir Thopas (this was filmed at a favourite Pasolini location, Mount Etna). Perhaps the most significant deletion was scenes where characters introduce their tales. The focus thus shifts to Chaucer as the grand architect of the storytelling, rather than each of the travellers at the Tabard Inn telling their tales.

Geoffrey Chaucer's world of lords, ladies, priests, nuns, monks, peasants, millers, prostitutes and farm hands was depicted by Pier Paolo Pasolini and the team with the same irreverence and love of life as the Middle Ages author (of course, Pasolini himself played Chaucer, the lofty artificer of his mediæval fantasies, seen here in scholar's garb (nice cap, Pier Paolo!), dreaming up his stories at a wooden desk (or chuckling over a copy of *The Decameron*), in the short linking passages between the tales. The setting for Chaucer at work was based on

Renaissance depictions of St Jerome, in particular the famous painting *St Jerome In His Study* (1474) by Antonello da Messina, which portrays the scholar at his desk in an ecclesiastical setting).

✦

STYLE, DESIGN, COSTUMES.

The Canterbury Tales was a lavish production, with a very large cast, many extras, props, animals, locations, settings and costumes. Yet it was surprising how casually Pier Paolo Pasolini and the crew approached this production, how expensive crowd scenes would be covered with a shaky handheld camera and barely one or two shots. Pasolini and the team didn't seem bothered with capturing all of that time and effort and expense on screen just for the sake of pleasing people (like the producer (Alberto Grimaldi) and the backers). If the filmmakers caught it on camera, fine; if not, also fine. The loose, informal cinematic approach also applied to the dubbing (*The Canterbury Tales* was very poorly looped. I guess, with the primarily British cast, they acted in English and were dubbed back in Rome by others. Wherever Pasolini made his films, and whatever language the performers spoke, they were always dubbed in the Eternal City, in Italian). As so often with Italian films, at first it's irritating and disorientating, but then it enhances the experience (especially in a film with so many crazy, comical and grotesque things going on).

The attention to detail in *The Canterbury Tales* was startling; rarely has mediæval life been put up on screen in so rounded a fashion. This was Middle Ages existence as a grimy, earth-bound, and practical kind of life, a world away from the glossy, clean castles and palaces of the typical Hollywood, historical movie, with their starchy, ponderous dialogue and starchy, ponderous performances.

The costumes (by Danilo Donati) were beautiful, with some outrageous touches (in particular, as in *The Gospel According To Matthew*, the enormous hats, or the preposterous golden axes sported by Sir January's guards. May's huge white hat at the nuptials is more suited to a fashion show in Paris. Some of Donati's ideas for clothing are absolutely ridiculous, you have to admit, and would be more appropriate for the Venice Carnival. Altho' *The Canterbury Tales* presents an earthy, lived-in mediævalism, the colourful costumes – in scarlet, purple, blue, green – pop out self-consciously).

The Canterbury Tales filmed in Merrie Englande itself,[8] including the counties of Suffolk, Gloucestershire, Essex, Sussex, Kent and Avon. Provincial English towns such as Chipping Campden in Gloucestershire; Lavenham in Suffolk;[9] Cambridge; Bath; Canterbury, St. Thomas a Becket Church, Fairfield and Maidstone in Kent; Rolvenden, Battle Abbey and Rye in Sussex; Layer Marney Tower, Tiptree, Grange Barn, Coggeshall and St Osyth in Essex. Sicily and Italy were also used (Mount Etna, Roma, etc). The cast and crew must've been driving all over the place in cars and buses, as usual for a Pasolini production.

The volume, variety and quality of locations was striking (the location scout, production designer Dante Ferretti and art director Carlo Agati did their jobs very well on *The Canterbury Tales*. The production team was Pasolini's regular one: Grimaldi, Delli Colli, Morricone, Ferretti and Baragli).

One of the odd things about *The Canterbury Tales* (for a British audience) was this: the Pasolini Carnival coming to England.

Because most of *The Canterbury Tales* was shot in locations in England, such as Canterbury, Chipping Camden, Bath, Battle, Maidstone, Rye and Wells. It was curious seeing a cool, radical, European *auteur* like Pier Paolo Pasolini, whose films are full of images of sun-kissed Southern Italy, or the *borgate* in Rome, or the Middle East, winding up in little, English streets under over-cast English skies. (You can see the cinema-

---

8 You can visit the locations for *The Canterbury Tales* on the Pasolini Movie Tour (there are options for tourists to dress up in rags and have terrible teeth fitted).
9 Also used in *Harry Potter and the Deathly Hallows* (2010), *Barry Lyndon* (1975) and *The Witchfinder General* (1968).

tographer Tonino Delli Colli, his gaffer and his camera crew battling against the God-awful light in Britain many times – especially in the outdoor scenes. By the time they'd driven to a new location (down winding, too-narrow lanes), and got everybody in costume, make-up and in place, plus the animals, props and what-not, the light would be going. The light in the other two 'trilogy of life' flicks is far more appealing (of the Mediterranean and the Middle East).)

The English locations, plus the appearances of British TV and film actors (such as Tom Baker, Hugh Griffith and Robin Askwith), plus the bawdy humour, linked *The Canterbury Tales* to movie series of the same period such as the *Carry On* or *Confessions of...* series (camp, British sex comedies).

I challenge you to recall any of the music from the 'trilogy of life' movies. Although the composer is Italian screen legend Ennio Morricone, there isn't a single memorable melody from Morricone in the three Middle Ages flicks. There is plenty of music in the films, though much of it is recreations of Middle Ages music and traditional folk songs.[10] As it plays alongside each movie, it is quite beautiful, but the soundtrack of *Canterbury* is not a masterpiece like *The Gospel According To Matthew* (and *The Gospel* did not use much music specially composed for the movie).

There is an enormous amount of music in *The Canterbury Tales* – and altho' some of it is very fine (there are contemporary folk and 'world music' pieces, as well as recreations of mediæval music – part of the developing fashion for early music), it is mixed into the soundtrack (by Gianni D'Amico) with the customary casual, can't-be-bothered attitude of Italian sound editors of this 1960s/ 1970s period. So what could be really magical scenes fall flat.

Again, it appears as if the filmmakers reconvened at Cinecittà (or the Produzioni Europee Associate studios in Viale Oceano Pacifico) weeks or months after

---

10 Many characters are whistling and singing (the movie opens with a M.C.U. of a guy singing). Perkin winds up in the stocks and sings his defiant, silly song. Curiously, some of the songs seem to be in English.

principal photography wrapped in England, and mixed the music for the movie in half a day, in between lengthy lunches or wine-tasting sessions in the commissary.

+

THE COMEDY OF SEX.

The Canterbury Tales was a panoply of mediæval life, deliberately, self-consciously bawdy, lusty, gross and over-the-top. It was a film of people rutting, cursing, chasing, pissing, farting and dying – life in the Middle Ages as a ship of fools. Copulation seemed to be everywhere: gnarled, fat, old men groaning on top of nubile, young women (tho' only in the missionary position); sexual fantasies out of soft-core pornography (a wedding full of naked women); lovers trysting while the old man's away, etc. And it was all fairly healthy, straightforward stuff (no Marquis de Sade here, no S/M, bondage[11] or role-playing – that came later, in *Salò*. However, you can see the seeds of *Salò* here in the 'trilogy of life' films in the way that bodies are filmed).

+

There's plenty of flesh on display in *The Canterbury Tales* – nude bodies are all over the place, but the movie's anti-erotic (it's about as erotic as a piece of rotting cheese injected with plutonium). The casting director has selected some pretty and unknown actors and actresses for the maestro to use in his movie for the nude scenes, but for all the fooling around, there's a striking lack of sensuality in *The Canterbury Tales*. (Instead, the sensuality is in the textures, the look, the *mise-en-scène*).

If you want earthy eroticism and extraordinary visual style and divine costumes (and maybe some kinky sex) in a mediæval (or Renaissance) setting, the 1970s films of Walerian Borowczyk are far superior to *The Canterbury Tales*: *Immoral Tales, Blanche* and *Behind Convent Walls*.

Instead, *The Canterbury Tales* presents, like all of Pier Paolo Pasolini's movies, the *idea* of sex, sexuality as a discourse to be dissected, and links sexuality to

11 There is a brief scene of a woman whipping a man.

Foucauldian issues like power and ideology (it's sex as 'desire', the term favoured in post-Lacanian theory). It's sex portrayed as one of the key ingredients in relationships between humans. A means to an end, a process by which power and influence are maintained. *The Canterbury Tales* is a series of notes for a possible movie which might be made at some point in the future about sexuality, power, class and relationships in the Middle Ages.

> Tragedie is to seyn a certeyn storie,
> As olde bokes maken us memorie,
> Of him that stood in greet prosperitee
> And is y-fallen out of heigh degree
> Into miserie, and endeth wrecchedly.

Geoffrey Chaucer, *The Canterbury Tales*

SOME SCENES IN *THE CANTERBURY TALES*:

THE FRAMING STORY.

Let's away, then, ladies and gents, let's hie hence – let's put on our curly wigs and rotting teeth and silly hats and shabby rags and undertake a journey through some of the scenes in ye olde filme, *The Canterbury Tales*.

The 1972 movie opens with a messy recreation of a mediæval village, populated by a host of hideous, British extras (plus assorted farmyard animals, hay, wrestlers, priests, musicians, singers, and a market). It's here that Pier Paolo Pasolini makes his entrance as one of England's great poets, Geoffrey Chaucer (sporting a preposterous hat[12]). So it's assumed that Chaucer is there to write all of these stories down.

In the village scene comes the familiar exposition of the pilgrimage to Canterbury and the telling of the tales. The filmmakers hope that everyone knows the

12 In the real England, you'd be lynched for looking like that.

narrative set-up, because the indifferent direction and staging don't deliver it satisfactorily.

In fact, the narrative contract to tell stories isn't set up really – the film simply cuts to the first story, about Sir January the Pompous Knight. Yet this is *one scene* that needed to be delivered fully and properly! It's as if the filmmakers spent so long dressing the set, gathering together the farmyard animals, and costuming (and feeding) the extras, they ran out of time for filming it all fully. (However, the notion of a group of travellers being encouraged to tell stories is announced by a guy on screen; as soon as he introduces the concept, the film shifts to the Sir January tale).

The village and farmyard scenes do, however, offer some clichéd images of life in the Middle Ages, where dogs, ducks, horses and chickens are running around, where kids are playing, where adults are drinking at an Inn, where hicks wrestle for a prize (a goat! a goat for the winner, good folk of Britain!), and where travelling players visit the Inn. (These scenes do have some appeal – that is, if watching a bunch of extras pretending to be mediæval peasants is your thing. *The Canterbury Tales* does come across as the home movie of a third-rate, historical re-enactment society – you know, those guys and gals who pretend to be Napoleonic troops or Civil War soldiers on Summer weekends).

The village sequence in *The Canterbury Tales* also does something that many films do in their opening scenes: it introduces some of the well-known performers early on in the piece (Pier Paolo Pasolini and Laura Betti). After this, they disappear for some time.

SIR JANUARY.

The first story[13] of *The Canterbury Tales* concerns the ageing patriarch Sir January (Hugh Griffith) taking a young wife[14] May (Josephine Chaplin,[15] b. 1949,

13 It was partly filmed in Wells, including the famous mediæval street and houses.
14 May is selected when her buttocks are exposed to Sir January as she kneels in the street. It's an early version of the ass contest in *Salò*.
15 Josephine Chaplin has appeared mainly in French films and TV.

daughter of Charlie Chaplin), while she tries to find ways of meeting her young lover, Damian (Oscar Fochetti, who moons about outside the palace, periodically clutching his crotch in desperation, as you do). The court's a joke, the courtiers ridiculous (Sir January's foppish brothers are satirized), the whole thing's played for laughs but somehow there aren't any laughs to be found anywhere (Griffith seems to recognize that this is a very silly movie, an attempt at a comedy, and based on a comical poem, but somehow not funny at all. With his trademark bulging eyes, grizzled beard and lascivious grin, Griffith[16] evokes Keith Moon in *Tommy* (as Uncle Ernie), but aged up to his sixties. A scary image indeed!).

In Sir January's secret garden[17] (a stand-in for Eden), two gods, Prosperine (Elisabetta Geneovese)[18] and Pluto (Giuseppe Arrigio),[19] wander, naked and garlanded with flowers. Sir January staggers about, now blind, with his sight being lifted by Pluto at the inopportune moment when his wife's in a tree (!) in a clinch with her *inamorato*, just about to do the nasty.

Sir January is a delightfully silly send-up of a lascivious but dim-witted king or lord: the sight of Hugh Griffith tottering about in ridiculously volum-inous scarlet robes[20] (or an equally bulky white night-gown), his eyes rolling in lust, is certainly memorable. For about two minutes. Then you forget this episode entirely.

Again, there's an unfinished, clumsy quality to *The Canterbury Tales*, as with other Pier Paolo Pasolini movies. The maestro defended himself by saying that his films 'asked questions' rather than 'provided

16 Griffith is dubbed by the crustiest, hoarsest voice actor available in Rome.
17 The garden seems made up of several locations, and includes some anachronistic topiary.
18 Elisabetta Geneovese has a spectacular smile which lights up the screen – a close-up of her as Prosperine is used for the Blu-ray and DVD re-releases of *The Canterbury Tales*. Genovese also appeared in *The Decameron*, as the young lover Caterina who sleeps on the balcony in order to meet her beau. She is also in *The Arabian Nights* and *Bawdy Tales*).
19 He wass Lorzenzo in *The Decameron*.
20 The far-too-large clothes enhance the blustering vanity of the knight.

answers' or delivered something 'finished'. But, dear Pier Paolo, what possible 'questions' are being 'asked' in this bodged rendition of a clichéd, simplistic erotic triangle, and of a husband being cuckolded? It's one of the most well-used, oft-known scenarios in all drama, with no philosophy/ spirituality/ ideology/ politics/ morality in it that we haven't already seen a zillion times. *We know all of the answers! And we know all of the questions!* Come on, Pier Paolo, coming from a highly sophisticated, intellectual filmmaker such as yourself, this is puerile claptrap!

THE DEVIL, THE INQUISITOR AND HOMO-SEXUALITY.

Homosexual scenes were depicted in *The Canterbury Tales* – in sequences where people spied on men fucking, hidden behind closed doors and informing on them (the Devil is the ultimate informer, spy, traitor). From this the 1972 movie shifted into witchhunt territory – with a gay man (David Hatton) being burnt to death (an older guy (Athol Coats) manages to bribe his way out of punishment by paying the authorities). Pretty brutal, grotesque stuff, and with all sorts of added resonances because Pier Paolo Pasolini was famously a gay filmmaker, and had been in trouble with the authorities several times for sexual acts, including with minors. (The sequence seems wholly contemporary – 1972 – in ambience).

The execution[21] was portrayed in the same manner as the trials in *Il Vangelo Secondo Matteo* – with a handheld camera from the sidelines, in amongst (and behind) the crowds, as well as in a *tableau*-style drawing on mediæval illuminations. Meanwhile, Satan lurks behind the crowd, selling food from a tray (in this film, even the Devil has to earn a living. It's a classic Italianism, where everybody is on the make).

The execution episode is a huge scene filled with extras, costumes, guards, spectator stands and dignitaries. It was filmed in the cloisters of Canterbury

21 The trial isn't shown.

Cathedral. I bet the clergy in Kent hadn't seen anything like this in their precincts before: a semi-naked man being burnt to death. (Did the authorities of the famous Cathedral know that the crime was for homosexual sex? And that the sequence as a whole featured nudity and gay sex? The administrators of Canterbury Cathedral famously turned down the *Harry Potter* movies which wanted to film there – due, apparently, because they thought that *Harry Potter* promoted paganism or witchcraft).

Voyeurism is a staple of the courtly love poetry tradition (which Geoffrey Chaucer drew on) – lovers are forever being spied on by maids, night watchmen or such like (escaping prying eyes before dawn after a night of intimacy is a popular motif). So in this episode, there were two voyeurs: one's the informer, but the other is no less than Lucifer (only later in this episode does Franco Citti reveal himself as the Devil).

Having Franco Citti as Satan is an attempt at creating a recurring character in *I racconti di Canterbury* (along with Pasolini-as-Geoffrey-Chaucer), but it doesn't really work (*The Decameron* also used Citti as a recurring character – and a vicious one, too). Similarly, the framing device of Chaucer dipping his quill to compose the next scene at his desk or on some parchment during his travels, which duly cuts to the next episode, adds nothing to the piece. (The segment continues with Satan and the Inquisitor (credited as 'O.T') travelling together as tax collectors, to extract payment from an old woman at a remote windmill; she falls to her knees and begs the Inquisitor to send her troubles to the Devil. The Inquisitor makes a Faustian pact with Mr Sulphur).

THE COOK.

Ninetto Davoli makes his mandatory appearance in a Pier Paolo Pasolini movie by playing Perkin the Smirkin' Jerk, a Middle Ages Charlie Chaplin, a simpleton who larks about in the feeblest Chaplin skit you've ever seen. This is one of the low-points in

Pasolini's cinema. The Cook (J.P. Van Dyne) leaves Perkin the Doofus in charge of his egg stall in a bazaar, and silent comedy slapstick ensues. Perkin's a soft-in-the-head thief who, like all of Davoli's characters in Pasolini's movies, goofs around and drifts in and out of the story like a lost child who has had a perpetual cheesy grin nailed onto his face by the curse of an evil witch. Davoli tries hard to make his former lover laugh, singing and skittering about, but it's desperate. (There's a pleasant enough wedding ceremony in *The Cook's Tale* of *The Canterbury Tales*, including a dance and a band of musicians, while the bride's father (Francis De Wolff) becomes irate. Later, Perkin fantasizes about dancing at the wedding, with the guests replaced entirely by nude women, as he shares a threesome in bed with a couple of uncomely Brits).

Charlie Chaplin was a favourite director for Pier Paolo Pasolini, and there are several Chaplinesque touches in *The Cook's Tale*: the father of the bride recalls the burly oaf played by Eric Campbell in Chaplin's movies; Perkin sports the signature bowler hat and cane (several other characters wear bowler hats); hunger, food and poverty[22] is a theme; and of course there are cops to chase Perkin.

THE WIFE OF BATH.

The Wife of Bath episode (which's the most well-known story in Geoffrey Chaucer's *Canterbury Tales*), was one of the more successful segments of the 1972 movie, partly because the concept and story is strong and clear (and Laura Betti's amusing performance as the fierce, domineering Wife of Bath helps).[23] Her new relationship – with the scholar, Jenkin (played by Tom Baker with his usual bug-eyed, Harpo Marxian eccentricity)[24] – is bizarre. It starts[25] off with some voyeurism – and, in an rare reversal of the male voyeur trope, two

22 Perkin queues up with some other hopefuls in a scene out of the musical *Olivier!* (He carries an out-size bowl).
23 Aided by her plump chum Isolde.
24 In this period Tom Baker played Dr Who on TV.
25 Actually, the first shot of the *Wife of Bath* episode is lovemaking between the Wife and Giannozzo.

women watch the scholar bathing nude.

The Wife of Bath episode contains one of the biggest scenes in *The Canterbury Tales*, a festival populated by coachloads of extras (it looks like the Glastonbury Fayre in 1971), as the denizens of dear, old Blighty perform a *Wicker Man*-style ritual burning of a wicker man figure (because when they're at a loose end – when there's nothing on TV and it's raining again and football's cancelled, and there's nothing else to do, the jolly, rosy-cheeked bumpkins of Britain were always burning wicker men in the early Seventies).

In midst of the outdoor jamboree, the Wife of Bath nonchalantly gives the scholar a handjob while he casually reads a book. They discuss marriage. The Wife of Bath soon becomes unenamoured of her new husband, having also worn out the last one, Giannozzo (Reg Stuart), with too much fooling around. Jenkin would rather read a book than do his duty as a husband. (He insults her, they fight, she falls, and asks for a final kiss.; then she bites his nose).

THE YOUNG SCHOLAR.

One of the longer tales[26] in *The Canterbury Tales* is a meandering piece of fluff concerning a scholarly youth's seduction of an older man's wife, Alison (Jenny Runacre). The youth Nicholas (Dan Thomas), who looks like he's wandered in from presenting a groovy, early Seventies kids' TV show, loons and moons about in his rooms, praying (and nursing his weiner). The boy eventually concocts the truly bizarre ruse (with some fire and brimstone religious nonsense) of persuading the old coot John (Michael Balfour) to save himself from the oncoming Biblical Flood and Apocalypse by sheltering in some wooden tubs hanging high up from ropes under the roof.[27] While the old geezer snoozes, the lovers creep out of their tubs and get freaky, as expected. It's one of the strangest sequences in a Pasolini movie.

There's some protracted business with another

26 Filmed in Wells.
27 This scene might be a send-up of *The Bible*, the giant Dino di Laurentiis Italian-American production filmed in Rome.

hapless suitor, Absalom[28] (Peter Cain) calling at night at Alison's home to beg for a kiss, and having Alison stick her ass outside the window in his face and fart. But when the scholar Nicholas does the same a while later, the resourceful Absalom's already run off to a nearby blacksmith to borrow a red-hot poker, which he shoves up the scholar's butt.

Oh boy, they are rolling in the aisles at this nonsense. It's lame. It's comedy in the style of *Tom and Jerry* or Laurel and Hardy but performed by a bunch of tenth grade school kids let loose with a 35mm camera and a canvas sack of Middle Ages costumes.

Meanwhile, back in Rome, someone has edited all of this garbage, someone has organized actors and dubbing stages, actors have looped the dialogue, Ennio Morricone and his team have added music, and it all goes nowhere and does nothing. *The Canterbury Tales* is not a movie that gets better, richer, deeper with each viewing. The opposite, in fact.

THE MILLER.

A windmill[29] and a small holding owned by Miller Simkin (Tiziano Longo) is the location for one of the later stories in *The Canterbury Tales*, in which our heroes (two young, Pasolinian *ragazzi* – Alan (Patrick Duffett) and John (Eamann Howell)), scholars from Cambridge – get the best of him and manage to seduce his wife (Eileen King) and daughter Molly (Heather Johnson). It's played out as broad farce with a nighttime game of can't-see-a-thing switching of beds and partners, complete with the expected misunderstandings (the lads take the women, only to be found out by the Miller when one of them climbs into the wrong bed, and the Miller wakes and explodes. The lads flee after beating the Miller). Again the s-l-o-w cutting and the laborious staging takes the pizzazz out of the potential for humour. This kind of pacing might work in the theatre, but it is too lethargic for comedy.

28 Absalom's chum Martin (Martin Philips) is another goofy youth (and apparently gay).
29 Filmed at Rolvenden in Sussex.

THE BROTHEL.

The section of *The Canterbury Tales* set in a brothel[30] livens up the narrative of the 1972 Italian flick with some sexual *tableaux* (a couple of blowjobs, sex from the rear, and a naked woman whipping a naked man – no historical sex comedy set in Britain is complete without some corporal punishment! Brits love it).

The brothel sequence culminates with Robin Askwith[31] (as Rufus) urinating over everyone in the inn below from a balcony while he rants in mock, Biblical tones (perhaps Askwith's finest hour outside of the *Confessions* sex comedy movies). Would a bunch of peasants sit and laugh while someone pisses on them? And collect the liquid in bowls? In this movie, yes!

DEATH PAYS A VISIT.

The second section of this episode of *The Canterbury Tales* is one of the poorest outings in Pier Paolo Pasolini's cinema – a waste of your time, my time, and everybody else's time. It looks like Pasolini handed it over entirely to a second unit director (but not a *good* second unit director!).[32]

It involves yet another brotherhood of young, Pasolinian, pseudo-Caravaggian *ragazzi*: Dick the Sparrow (Edward Montieth), Jack the Justice (Martin Whelar), and Johnny the Grace (John McLaren). This time the lads are planning to kill Death Himself and steal some shiny loot (the Grim Reaper has cut down one of their number from the bordello in the previous scene – the results of too much whoring, the usual mediæval, Christian moralizing about debauchery). Betrayal, knifing and poisoning swiftly follow (as in the pirate genre), as they squabble over the booty, but the sequence is extraordinarily clumsily staged and shot (and the script is, well, just weedy).

The characters are dull, the scenario is dull, the

30 Filmed in St Osyth in Essex and Chipping Camden.
31 Askwith has dined out on his anecdotes of meeting Pier Paolo Pasolini, filming *The Canterbury Tales*, etc.
32 The location is the outskirts of Rye, one of the haunting, atmospheric parts of England. There's a big market day scene with an English street that's been filled with mud and straw to hide the road markings.

'acting' is dreadful (here is where using amateurs completely backfires), the sound mix is bad, the dubbing comes from another movie, and the sequence contains the barest minimum of camera angles and shots to cover the action (one of several indications that the filmmakers were utterly unengaged with the material).

LET'S GO TO HELL.

Towards the end, like thousands of movies before it and thousands of movies after it, *The Canterbury Tales* throws everything at the viewer, with a truly Out-There sequence set in Hell (which looks suspiciously like the waste ground of Pigneto outside Roma where *La Ricotta* was filmed). A greedy friar (John Francis Lane) is taken there (by an angel, Settimo Castagna) after trying to steal from a dying rich man. Colourful demons in full body make-up (red, blue, green), with bat-wings and fabulous masks torture the sinners (torturing some, and taking others from the rear).[33] Chaos reigns, presided over by a giant, red Satan, who bends over, lifts his tail, and farts out friars. They fly through the air out of a full-size, scarlet butt, accompanied by loud, rasping farts.

Yes, it's truly silly, a *Monty Python*-style skit – but with more money, staged on some waste land. It's a case of filmmakers trying to out-do themselves and everyone else. It's delivered as a mighty joke (except it's not very funny).

This's underlined when the 1972 movie cuts back to Geoffrey Chaucer at his writing desk (wearing another preposterous hat), grinning broadly as he dreams up this schoolboyish, anal-oral nonsense. Maybe Chaucer-Pasolini is simply enjoying the total chaos of filmmaking. Maybe he's thinking, 'hell, someone gave me $2 million to shoot this farce!' Maybe he's chuckling because he knows that this sequence will *really* irritate some sections of the audience (and it did). The 1972 film might just as well have cut to a shot of Pier Paolo Pasolini and the crew standing behind the

33 Being buggered by a demon for years on end would some perv's idea of Heaven!

camera, giggling at the crazy stuff they've cooked up. Oh, what fun and jolly japes it is to be a European art filmmaker in the Seventies![34]

The Canterbury Tales ends swiftly following the visit to Hell: we finally reach Canterbury at the end of Pilgrims' Way. There's the briefest of shots of the Cathedral and a religious ceremony, and then the movie stumbles to a clumsy halt.

It's not a satisfying close to a movie of this kind by any means – *The Canterbury Tales* might have been episodic, like a road movie, but it's not a quest film, or a road movie film in structure. It dispenses with the dramatic structure of a quest and a journey, and focusses on individual episodes. Meanwhile, the sequence in Hell comes from another movie, and jars with the rest of the piece with its outrageous imagery. Nothing can follow that, and the movie seems to acknowledge this, by simply juddering towards a feeble ending. (However, if all of *The Canterbury Tales* had been filmed with the manic intensity and crudity of the Visit To Hell episode, maybe it would have been a much greater work).

HOW BAD IS *THE CANTERBURY TALES*?

You have to see *The Canterbury Tales* for the sheer zaniness of the imagery and scenes. Even if so much of the movie is handled with an amateurish, throwaway quality, as if Pier Paolo Pasolini and the crew are just playing at being filmmakers, as if they're pretending they're not professionals, there is certainly plenty going on. And plenty of it is quite bonkers.

There's enough fumbling around with bawdy comedy and nudity in *Carry On In the Middle Ages* to

34 Indeed, *The Canterbury Tales* closes with a close-up of Mr Pasolini as British poet Geoffrey Chaucer, smiling to himself, all too smugly, at the crazy visions he's just conjured up with a team of artisans (courtesy of Chaucer) back in the final segment of the movie, the Visit To Hell.

keep the viewer amused, if only for the time that elapses as the movie unfolds (after that, after the final, much-longed-for 'FINE', everything is swiftly forgotten, consigned to the oblivion of a billion other movies).

Oh, some of *The Canterbury Tales* is woefully bad.[35] It's bad on the level of direction. It's bad on the level of conception and screenwriting. It's bad on the level of performance. It's bad on the level of camerawork and sound quality. It's bad on the level of casting (so many really grisly, English extras! None of whom can act! They are non-professional actors for a good reason! They stink!).

Sorry to say, but too much of *The Canterbury Tales* comes across as a not very good *Carry On* flick or a *Confessions of* flick or an *Emmanuelle* movie (which were being churned out at the time or not long afterwards). And too often *The Canterbury Tales* is *not* one of those films that are 'so bad they're good'. No. It's just *bad*.

How can this be? This is directed by the man who helmed *Medea* and *Oedipus Rex* and *Il Vangelo Secondo Matteo*! Oh boy. (But did Pier Paolo Pasolini *really* direct *The Canterbury Tales*? Sometimes I wonder if he stayed behind in Rome and let someone else direct this turkey).

Take the humour in *The Canterbury Tales*: it *should* be bawdy, broad and above all it should be *funny*. But it's *not*. At the level of comedy, *The Canterbury Tales* is outrageous and over-the-top, but, darn, it's *not amusing*.

And *The Canterbury Tales* is trying *really hard*. But, let's face it, humour just isn't one of Pier Paolo Pasolini's strengths. Even the grinning, energetic, winsome Ninetto Davoli, playing the foolish Jerkin-Perkin, can't save his section of the piece (instead, he murders it).

When a master of modern European cinema is directing his favourite actor in the guise of an icon of

35 Some scenes are simply thrown away in *The Canterbury Tales* – such as when Satan, skulking thru a Cathedral, stops for a funeral procession (a corpse's carried on a bier with candles flaming above it).

cinema (Charlie Chaplin) in a mediæval romp (in *The Cook's Tale*), you'd expect something better than this. There's some messing about with eggs, some loafing around with games, a gag with an over-size bowl (to receive alms from the Church), and a wedding feast.[36]

Have a look at the first episode of *Everything You Wanted To Know About Sex But Were Too Afraid To Ask*, produced around the same time (1972), to see a really good send-up of the mediæval genre, with all the usual jokes about lusty lovers and royal feasts and courtly life. (Woody Allen's spoof on mediæval courtly lingo has never been done better – and he includes a send-up of arty, would-be cool Italian movies, too![37]).

Woody Allen nails the Middle Ages, and in just a few minutes. *The Simpsons* have also delivered skits on the Middle Ages infinitely superior to *The Canterbury Tales*.

Or have a look at two other films of the same period: *Jabberwocky* (1977) and *Monty Python and the Holy Grail* (1974),[38] which are genuinely amusing, and also depict elements of the mediæval genre beautifully.

FURTHER VIEWINGS.

The notes above were written before I'd seen the movie again: on further viewings, *I racconti di Canterbury* still comes across as bloody awful at times: the direction is often inept, the acting ranges from mediocre to terrible, and the script is really poor.

If *The Canterbury Tales* had been produced for a Hollywood studio (impossible, I know!), the head of production would've ordered Pier Paolo Pasolini to go back and start everything again as soon as they saw the

36 This part of the Chaplin skit was the most successful – particularly in Perkin's night dream of the wedding feast, but populated wholly by young, naked women.
37 In "Why Do Some Women Have Trouble Reaching an Orgasm?", the filmmakers send up modern, European cinema, in particular the more pretentious efforts of directors like Michelangelo Antonioni and Federico Fellini.
38 The Monty Python team spoofed *The Devils* in their King Arthur movie, and also Pier Paolo Pasolini, Ingmar Bergman (*The Seventh Seal*), *Throne of Blood* (Akira Kurosawa), and the films of Walerian Borowczyk (*Goto: Island of Love* and *Blanche*).

first of the rushes.

Put it this way, if *The Canterbury Tales* was the first film directed by Pier Paolo Pasolini you saw, many people would *not* come back for more. And if you knew that this was directed by a guy who's supposed to be one of the great, postwar European *auteurs*, you wouldn't believe it!

Because too much of *The Canterbury Tales* is so amateurish it's not true. Or is it just that the 1972 movie hopes to give the *impression* of a freewheeling, laid-back style, when it's really controlled by a rod of iron by the filmmakers? Is Pier Paolo Pasolini and the team producing a *deliberately* bad movie? No, I don't think so.

The terrible looping doesn't help. This is a film set in England, filmed (mainly) in England, based on an English poem, performed by a mainly English cast, and also acted in English, but dubbed into Italian, and with an Italian crew (at least in the heads of department jobs). And yet the text of Geoffrey Chaucer was updated from mediæval English to modern English, and then an Italian translation would've been used by the filmmakers.

So it's an odd hybrid. It's even odder if you know those locations in Britain very well (as I do), and recognize some of the actors (though I'm sure international audiences wouldn't be familiar with a single actor in *The Canterbury Tales* with the exception of Hugh Griffith, maybe, and Pier Paolo Pasolini's two starring regulars, Ninetto Davoli and Franco Citti).

Part of the time I'm just looking at the beautiful locations in *The Canterbury Tales*, and I'm reminded: isn't England so gorgeous? Aren't there some lovely buildings in Deare Olde Englande?

I wonder what the British extras from towns like Rye and Bath and Wells thought of this Italian production wheeling into town, and what the members of the British crew thought. I wouldn't be surprised if some of the actors and crew reckoned Pier Paolo Pasolini was nuts![39] You only have to look at some of the big scenes, and see what the assistant directors (Sergio Citti, Umberto Angelucci and Peter Shepherd) have got the crowds doing, to see that this was an unusual historical picture.[40] It was no quaint British Broadcasting Corporation TV adaptation aiimed at a family, early evening audience!

Yet *The Canterbury Tales* was so much more effective in evoking the mediæval period than your average television adaptation or movie: the way that Dante Ferretti and Carlo Agati transformed the existing buildings and streets of England was a lesson to all the British TV (British Broadcasting Corporation and Independent Television) and international television historical productions. This was production design as a fine art. And the look and locations are the finest elements in *The Canterbury Tales*.

39 However, some of the actors making *Star Wars* in 1977 thought the movie was just silly sci-fi.
40 They look at the camera with puzzled expressions. The older actors just get on with it and do what they're told.

The Canterbury Tales (1972).
This page and over.

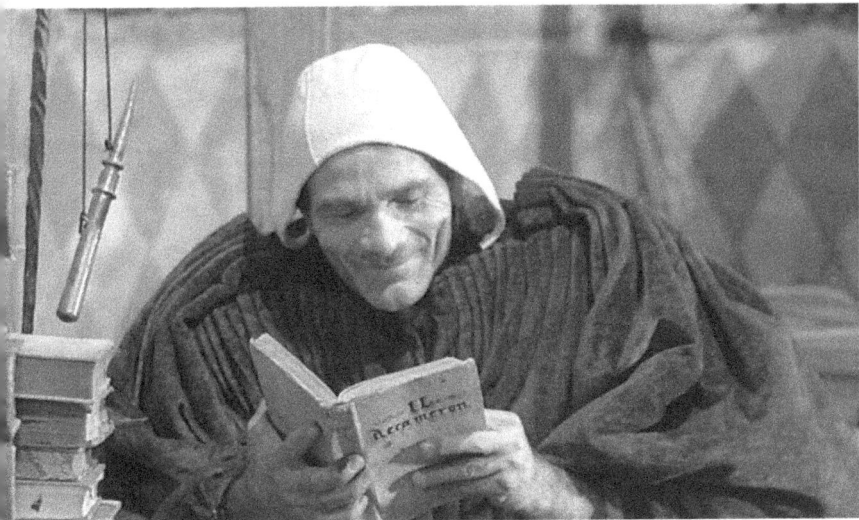

Pasolini's cameo in The Canterbury Tales

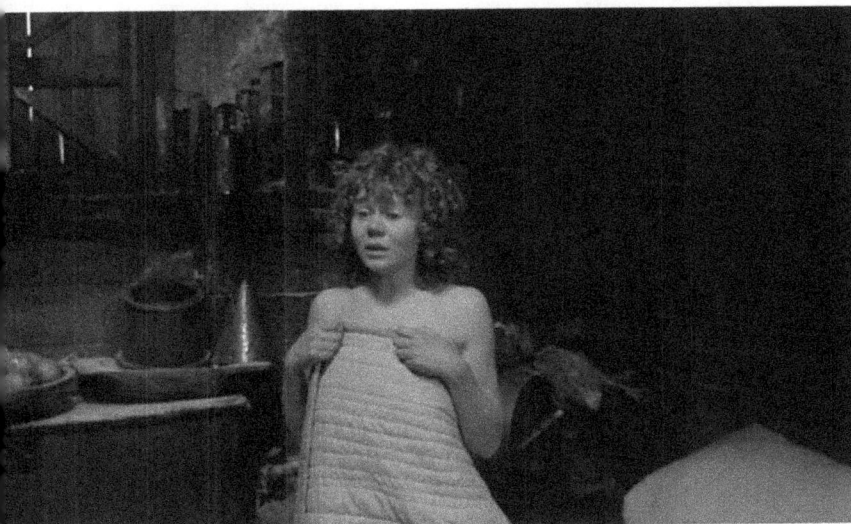

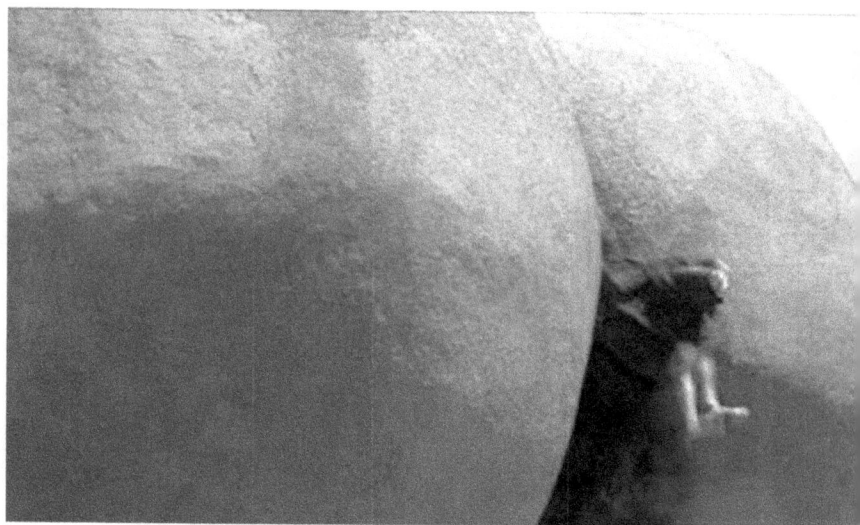

We are going to visit Hell.

4

IL FIORE DELLE MILLE E UNA NOTTE

THE ARABIAN NIGHTS

INTRODUCTION.

Co-written by Dacia Maraini[1] and Pier Paolo Pasolini from *The 1001 Nights*, *The Arabian Nights* (1974, a.k.a. *Il Fiore Delle Mille e Una Notte*), was produced by Alberto Grimaldi, and distributed by United Artists.[2] It won the Grand Prix Special Prize at Cannes in 1974.[3]

Worldwide gross was $4.5 million. Released: June 20, 1974. It is 129[4] minutes long.[5]

The production team working on *Il Fiore Delle Mille e Una Notte* included Pasolini regulars such as Nino Baragli (editor – with Tatiana Casini Morigi), Ennio Morricone (music), Dante Ferretti (production design), Danilo Donati (costumes) and Giuseppe Ruzzolini (camera). Iole Cecchini handled the hair, with

1 The script was written in August, 1973, in Sabaudia.
2 So Leo the Lion roars out of the M.G.M. logo at the start of this most un-American movie!
3 The combination of fantasy, exoticism (Orientalism) and eroticism in *The Arabian Nights* is tailor-made for the arty/ boho sections of the international movie crowd in the South of France in Cannes.
4 An early cut was 155 minutes.
5 There's a couple of deleted scenes on the DVD of *The Arabian Nights*. One involves Zumurrud as the King having a lengthy, badly staged sword fight on some cliffs. Another scene depicts Nuredin quarrelling with his father.

make-up by Massimo Giustini. Fausto Ancillai was sound mixer, and Luciano Wellisch did the sound. Umberto Angelucci, Paolo Andrea Mettel and Peter Shepherd were A.D.s. Once again, Pasolini was working some of the giant talents of the Italian film industry, including Ferretti, Donati and Morricone.

The cast of *The Arabian Nights* included Ninetto Davoli, Franco Citti, Franco Merli, Margareth Clémenti, and Ines Pellegrini, plus a host of unknowns: Tessa Bouché, Zeudi Biasolo, Luigina Rocchi, Alberto Argentino, Salvatore Sapienza, Elisabetta Genovese, Barbara Grandi, Francesco Paolo Governale, Francelise Noel, Ali Abdulla, Jeanne Gauffin Mathieu, Mohamed Ali Zedi, Gioacchino Castellini, Abadit Ghidei, Christian Aligny and Salvatore Verdetti (one or two of these – such as Elisabetta Genovese and Margareth Clémenti – appeared in other Pasolini movies). Notice that altho' *The Arabian Nights* draws on numerous local extras hired in Yemen, Iran and Nepal, most of the key roles are played by Italians (it was the same with other Pasolini productions, whether they were set in Ancient Greece or Ancient Palestine. So the films were not wholly enshrining a poetic vision of the 'Third World').

1001 NIGHTS IN POPULAR CULTURE.

The Thousand and One Nights (*Alf laila wa-laila* in Arabic), a.k.a. *The Arabian Nights*, dates from around the 15th century in its earliest form in manuscripts. There are around 270 core tales, drawing on Persian, Indian and Arabic cultures which stretch back to hundreds of years before the tales were written down between the 9th and 15th centuries.[6] The tales were collated in three important editions: (1) Persian stories with some Indian ingredients which were translated into Arabic by the tenth century; (2) stories collected in Baghdad between the 10th and 12th centuries; and (3) tales collated in Egypt between the 11th and 14th centuries. As Jack Zipes explained in *The Enchanted Screen:*

---

6 See J. Zipes, 2002, 22.

No other work of Oriental literature has had such a profound influence on the western world as *The Thousand and One Nights*. Translated first into French between 1704 and 1717 by Antoine Galland, a gifted Orientalist, the *Nights* spread quickly in French and other translations throughout Europe and then to North America. (84)

In the Western world, key translations included that of 1883-86, by Richard Burton (as *The Book of the Thousand Nights and a Night*).[7] (When I was in Egypt in 1994, people there insisted that *The Arabian Nights* was very much about Cairo, not Baghdad. Certainly, in parts of Cairo you feel like you are in a living *Arabian Nights*).

Pretty much every serious author in Europe attempted a version of *The Arabian Nights*. As *The Oxford Companion To Fairy Tales* put it, 'the magic elements in the *Nights* combined with the explicit and unpretentious representation of sexuality created a powerful inspiration for the European imagination' (372).

James Joyce, Marcel Proust, Jorge Luis Borges, Joseph Addison, Edgar Allan Poe, Samuel Coleridge, Samuel Johnson and Washington Irving are among the many authors who took on the *1001 Nights*.

The Thousand and One Nights has influenced artists and writers (and filmmakers), including Denis Diderot, Voltaire, Thomas De Quincey, George Meredith, Robert Louis Stevenson, Friedrich Schiller, Hermann Melville, John Barth, Robert Southey, Horace Walpole, Charles Dickens, William Thackeray, Alexander Dumas, Stendhal, Walter Scott, Johann Wolfgang von Goethe, Leo Tolstoy, E.T.A. Hoffmann, Alexander Pushkin, etc.

The framing story of *The Thousand and One Nights* concerns clever Scheherazade, daughter of the Grand-Vizier, who placates the murderous Sultan Shahryar (he kills a new woman every morning), by telling him stories (staving off nasty events in the framing story is

7 In Arabic, the key collections were *Calcutta I* (1814-18), a.k.a. *Shirwanee Edition*; *Bulak*, 1835, a.k.a. the *Cairo Edition*; *Calcutta II*, 1839, a.k.a. the *W.H. Macnaughton Edition*; and *Breslau*, 1825-38.

reflected in the tales themselves – the framing story itself begets a series of tales). Some of the aspects of Scheherazade are found in the personality of Zumurrud in the 1974 movie.

In *The Thousand and One Nights*, stories intertwine complexly: stories create further stories, and stories reflect or re-play earlier stories. (The 1974 movie takes up only parts of this concept, tho' it does perform the appealing trick of one story tumbling into another, which helps to give the piece a hypnotic momentum).

The *Thousand and One Nights* tales have provided motifs and characters which've become as well-known as Cinderella or Snow White: Sinbad, Aladdin, Ali Baba, magic lamps and genies, princes, princesses, thieves, merchants, palaces, evil viziers, and so on.

In *The Arabian Nights*, the stories with fairy tale components can be put into categories such as: talisman stories (about magical objects); powerful demon stories; quest stories; transformation stories; and demons under restraint tales.[8] The *Arabian Nights* film uses all of those story types.

The 1974 *Arabian Nights* wasn't the only movie of the *1001 Nights* of the era: Rankin and Bass, for instance, produced a cartoon, *Arabian Nights*, in 1972; plus *The Thousand and One Nights* (Eiichi Yamamoto, 1969), *The Thousand and One Nights* (Karel Zeman, 1974), and a TV series in 1975 (*Arabian Nights*, dir. Fumio Kurokawa and Kunihiko Okazaki). And the *1001 Nights* has been filmed many times since.

Italian cinema had taken up the *1001 Nights* before, of course: there was a mini-cycle in the early 1960s, for instance: *The Conqueror of the Orient* (1960), a Steve Reeves[9] version of *The Thief of Baghdad* (1961), *The Wonder of Aladdin* (1961 – photographed by Pier Paolo Pasolini's chief DP, Tonino Delli Colli), *The Thousand and One Nights* in 1961 (dir. Mario Bava and Henry Levin), *The Golden Arrow* (1962), *Anthar the Invincible* (1964) and *Ali Baba and the Seven Saracens* (1964).

8 See Mia Gerhardt, *The Art of Story-Telling*, 1963.
9 Steve Reeves seems to have starred in everything in the early 1960s, following the huge success of *Hercules*.

Géorges Méliès had pioneered adaptations of *The Arabian Nights* way back in 1905 (just as Méliès got there first with pretty much every famous folk tale, fairy tale and myth).

Films and TV series of the *1001 Nights* appeared in 1920, 1921, 1927, 1940, 1942, 1958, 1959, 1962, 1964, 1968, 1979, 1990, 1991, 1994, 1996, 1999, 2000, etc.

Thus, there are literally 100s of movies based on the *Thousand and One Nights* tales. Many are animated films, and many are made for children and families. Western cinema and TV has taken up *The Arabian Nights* numerous times, from famous Hollywood versions like *The Thief of Bagdad* (1924 and 1940), to many television mini-series (a Tim Burton version for Shelley Duvall's *Faerie Tale Theater*, for ex), and cartoons from Disney (*Aladdin*, 1992) and DreamWorks (*Sinbad*, 2003).

But viewers hoping for a fantasy extravaganza from *The Arabian Nights* like a Disney *Aladdin* or a Ray Harryhausen *Sinbad* will be *very* disappointed! No – the 1974 *Arabian Nights* is *1001 Nights* Euro-art movie style, and this version is definitely *not* for children or families!

THE ARABIAN NIGHTS AS FANTASY.

In *The Arabian Nights*, Pier Paolo Pasolini and his regular cast and crew return to the world of mediæval mythology (for the last time – a pity, because Pasolini could've worked his way thru every classic of Middle Ages literature had he lived longer: Rabelais was discussed in the early 1970s, and *The Divine Comedy* would surely have been high on the list of possible projects, altho' elements of the *Divina Commedia* crop up in many of Pasolini's films).

The Arabian Nights is like no other movie you've seen. On almost every level, it is extraordinary. It is not your conventional movie. Of course, films have been made from the classic, Arabian tales many times – such as the versions of *The Thief of Baghdad*, or Walt Disney's *Aladdin*, or numerous pantomimes and theatre shows (*Aladdin* is a regular Christmas panto). But there's no interpretation of *A Thousand and One Nights* like this 1974 Italian movie. (It's significant that the most successful artistically of the three Middle Ages movies in Pier Paolo Pasolini's cinema should be the non-European one, the Oriental/ Middle Eastern one).

Occasionally, you'll be watching *The Arabian Nights* and wondering what the hell you're looking at. *The Arabian Nights* is so dreamy and hypnotizing, the images and scenes flicker past with a languour and sensuality like a Symbolist painting by Gustave Moreau or a Decadent poem by Paul Verlaine. This is certainly Pasolini's most fantastical movie, a piece which actively pursues fantasy. (The movie opens with a quote about dreams from *1001 Nights* – 'truth lies not in one dream, but in many dreams'[10] – in this movie, dreams beget dreams as stories beget stories. But cinema is, as Pasolini knew well, already poetic and dream-like).

Just to define exactly what is going on in a movie like *Il Fiore Delle Mille e Una Notte* takes some time and effort. Let's start with the *mise-en-scène* of *The Arabian Nights*: it has an extraordinary sense of place, space, texture, colour and light. There is so much going on in Pier Paolo Pasolini's films, that one forgets how visually stunning they are. There are very few film directors with such an acute sense of space and place. Pasolini is up there with Orson Welles, Sergei Paradjanov or Ken Russell[11] in his incredible ability to seek out amazing buildings, squares, walls, doorways, gateways, alleys, covered markets, churches, temples, castles, palaces, arches, fountains and rooms. *The Arabian Nights* contains spaces and places that are so beautiful and unusual – it's a very rare gift in a world smothered with thousands of films and millions of images to find so many sites that can astound the spectator. (However, the *action* that's staged within these amazing spaces is often very boring – a character

10 The line is quoted late in the film.
11 Ken Russell's astonishing *The Devils*, produced a year before *The Canterbury Tales* (and filmed on the backlot at Pinewood Studios), is a textbook example of how to stage a historical piece.

walks or runs thru a square, or leans on a wall, or sits on a stone step. And that's all. Sometimes the staging in Pasolini's cinema is frustratingly static and almost deliberately unengaging and unimaginative).

The look and feel of *The Arabian Nights* is intoxicating in the extreme – simply on the level of *locations* – of the buildings and the towns and the hillsides – *The Arabian Nights* is incredible (I adore Africa and the desert, so I am already converted!). It was filmed in locations such as Ethiopia and Erithrea in Africa, the Red Sea, Shibam, Ta'izz, Seiyun, Wadi Dhar, Zabid and Sana'a in Yemen, Bhaktapur, Kathmandu, and Patan in Nepal, India, and Esfahan in Iran (the Mesjed-e-Imam, Ali Qapu Palace, Masjed-e Jomeh and Chehel Sotoun Palace). Studio scenes were filmed in Rome (at Laparo Film Studios).

Some of the interiors are stupendous in *The Arabian Nights*. Some are real places; the location scout and the location manager deserve every credit (this 1974 production is the result of the team driving hundreds of miles to find those places). If you said, find me the most exotic, richly historical, palatial Islamic interiors possible in Africa or the Middle East, you might come up with something like this. Two interiors are out-standing: the mirrored room in which the crossdressing King Zumurrud has her bedroom (filmed in Chehel Sotoun in Esfahan), and the underground palaces (filmed in Ali Qapu and Chehel Sotoun,[12] not to mention the nearby baths, also filmed in Ali Qapu and Chehel Sotoun). Then there's the whitewashed chamber in the Aziz and Aziza story, with its modernist (anachronistic) stained glass. And bedouin tents. And the strikingly exotic interiors of the Esfahan mosque (Mesjed-e Imam), one of those locations where you can point a camera anywhere and get a great image.

The Islamic architecture, so distinctive and atmospheric, with its abstractions and elegant patterns, and its intense feeling for decoration over flat planes,

12 The scenes where characters descend rope ladders from a beach into underground chambers are wonderful (the narrative device is repeated). And Nuredin is winched up from street level in a basket.

gives *The Arabian Nights* a group of perfect settings. Much of it is built from dusty, crumbly stonework, but even when Pier Paolo Pasolini and the location manager[13] select modern, Islamic buildings, it still works beautifully.[14] (It's startling that *The Arabian Nights* can employ modern apartment blocks in many scenes, and can pan the *macchina fotografica* repeatedly across modern cities in the Near East, and yet it still feels like Middle Ages Arabia (with the judicious use of a few camels, some wicker baskets strewn about, and extras in colourful costumes). There are several scenes on top of the roofs overlooking the town of Sana'a in the Middle East (in the Aziz and Aziza story) which looks completely mediæval (no forests of TV aerials to take down, as some film productions have done in other towns). Maybe it's because the views are carefully selected to include a backdrop of mountains and palm trees, instead of the freeways and cars you might see from the other direction. Maybe it's because modern, Islamic architecture simply looks exotic and different to the Western viewer, or maybe because the beauty of even simple, external decoration in plaster using Islamic designs is so evocative of ancient Arabia, or maybe it's because modern towns in the Maghreb or Middle East have mosques and towers which are built along mediæval lines, or maybe it's because the movie has already persuaded us to buy into it all. But you couldn't do that in a movie made in a Western city, where modern apartment blocks cannot be passed off as mediæval, and filming a wide shot of a city from a roof in the West reveals 100s of modern buildings, with power and telephone cables everywhere, plus jets, helicopters, and ten million lights).

Il Fiore Delle Mille e Una Notte is a magic carpet ride to quite a large degree, and as such the settings are vital in conjuring up the necessary sense of wonder. And then there's the costumes – designed by legend Danilo

13 The production managers were: Giuseppe Banchelli, Mario Di Biase and Alessandro Mattei.
14 The wedding, for instance, was filmed in the Mesjed-e Imam, built in 1638, in Esfahan, Iran.

Donati, a genius among costume designers.

What costumes! The *Arabian Nights milieu* allows the wardrobe dept to indulge itself in gold and embroidered extravagance. Bright red and blue costumes for the nobles, waiters in scarlet Sinbad pants, and extras clad as peasants out of Biblical tales. Oh, and giant, elaborate head-dresses, of course – all of Pier Paolo Pasolini's movies set in the past (which's most of his movies in fact) feature OTT head gear (for instance, the fancy, white felt hats the forty thieves wear, or Nuredin's white and gold turban, or the extraordinary helmet, mask and gold beard combo that crossdressing King Zumurrud sports).

And the props and production design – the incomparable Dante Ferretti creates some jaw-droppingly wonderful settings and props and furniture for this journey into Arabic mythopœia (only a few designers anywhere could've pulled this off (and on this budget), and Ferretti has a look wholly his own). As Ferretti has explained in interviews, sometimes they would dress existing locations quite simply, but sometimes extensively. The mirror room of the Chehel Sotoun Palace in Esfahan, for example, is already an exotic space, but it is still dressed by the art department to stand in for the King's bedchamber.

As a collection of settings, props, locations and architecture within a movie, *The Arabian Nights* has few peers as a Western interpretation of Islamic and Arabic culture and design. Western cinema has been dining out on recreating Middle Eastern culture since the early excursions into Oriental exotica of pioneers like Géorges Méliès, but *The Arabian Nights* has to be one of the finest and most extravagant in film history.

So all of that – the look, the texture, the locations, the costumes, the make-up, the hair, the lighting (by DP Giuseppe Ruzzolini), etcetera – dazzles the viewer in *The Arabian Nights*, and consumes much of their attention. Even before you reach aspects such as performances or narrative or sound or music, the *mise-en-scène* of *The Arabian Nights* is staggering.

CHARACTERS.

The characters in *The Arabian Nights* are types, and they are inter-changeable: the eager, immature lover, the enigmatic, attractive object of his desire, the wily, old pederast or predator, the stern king... You will notice that many character types are *not* represented much at all: older women, grandmothers, wives and queens (the female characters tend to be young women or princesses). Despite the crossdressing and a few role reversals, the *Arabian Nights* movie reflects the very patriarchal, male chauvinist and masculinist slant of the original Arabic tales (most of the sexual relations here are heterosexual, tho' there are depictions of homosexuality – discussed below).

This might be a fantasy version of Pier Paolo Pasolini's beloved ancient world and 'Third World', in which white, bourgeois Europe and the West is superseded and replaced by a dream-cast version of the Middle East, but it is as thoroughly patriarchal as any society in the history of humanity. Women have their place, and they are expected to stay in it. It's men who have agency, who travel, who act (even the kids out on the streets of the Arabia in this film are all boys).

Thus, another reason that Pier Paolo Pasolini later rejected the 'trilogy of life' films might be because the three films valorize societies and cultures which are very regressive, very conservative, very traditional, and very hierarchical. There is no social mobility: every character has their place in the hierarchy of the community and is expected to stay there. Kings and rulers are at the top (i.e., the fascists).

CINEMATIC ASPECTS OF *ARABIAN NIGHTS.*

For some of *The Arabian Nights*, Ennio Morricone provides a dreamy score, which you might not notice on first viewings, because there's so much else going on. However, quite a bit of *The Arabian Nights* is taken up with rather non-descript (European) string quartet (and choral) music (including Wolfgang Mozart's *String Quartet No. 15*). There isn't the dynamic relationship between the images and the music that characterizes the best of Pier Paolo Pasolini's cinematic work. Instead, the music tends to dribble and putter underneath scenes for a long time, without variation, and without much connection to what's happening (so that even Mozart is reduced to the level of muzak, And that is just not right. This is white, bourgeois, European music, too, of the classical era, which jars with the exotic, Middle Eastern *milieu* and characters).

The music in *The Arabian Nights* recalls the tendency in modern, Hollywood movies for filling a film with tons of background music, music which doesn't add much to anything except to be just another sound; music as muzak. (Hollywood producers and studios get uneasy when there isn't any music for some time in a movie, and movies have been re-scored just to fill them out with music. A typical Hollywood movie these days is scored almost throughout its entire running time, adding even more pressure on composers to come up with hours of music).

In *The Arabian Nights*, it looks as if the sound editors (Fausto Ancillai was sound mixer, Luciano Wellisch did the sound, and Nino Baragli was editor), found some temp music of string quartets from a film music library and plastered it underneath the movie in a slipshod manner. After some viewings, you will notice this aspect of the music, and it isn't the finest hour for Pier Paolo Pasolini or Ennio Morricone. You can see what I mean when the movie uses a proper music cue (and properly mixed), and as a result suddenly shifts up a few gears. Similarly, the music that is meant to be played by the actors on screen, but clearly isn't (such as in several of the celebratory scenes), is clumsily incorporated into the flow. (It's a lost opportunity – African and Middle Eastern music is some of the richest and most vibrant in the world. What a pity the sound team didn't record some local musicians while they were on location, or at least buy some audio tapes from local musicians, which anyone can do when travelling in those regions. Stalls selling music cassettes were common in the 1970s).

✦

As to performances – well, the actors and non-professionals are engaging as ever in a Pier Paolo Pasolini picture, but you wouldn't place *The Arabian Nights* in a list of Great Screen Performances. There are the usual Pasolinian faces – such as toothy, curly-haired Ninetto Davoli and suave, dangerous Franco Citti (despite the ginger wig!) – and the film is clearly enamoured of the grinning, fresh-faced teenager Franco Merli, and his *inamorata*, Zumurrud (played by 20 year-old Ines Pellegrini). Merli and Pellegrini are the magical couple at the heart of this wilfully eccentric confection of a movie. Merli is another of the rough *ragazzi* that Pasolini loved to put in his movies – eager and winsome like a puppy, lovelorn and wan like a doll, weepy like an abandoned tot, and so very young. (It's a role that Ninetto Davoli would no doubt have played had he been younger).

The maestro had found 16 year-old Franco Merli (b. 1956) working at a gas station, according to Ninetto Davoli (that does sound like Pier Paolo Pasolini), and decided to cast him as the lead in *The Arabian Nights* (and as one of the principal victims in *Salò* a year later). Merli embodies the spirit of youth, of innocence, of possibility, of yearning – of love – and his Nuredin (Nur-el-Din) character remains uncorrupted throughout the movie (which's remarkable considering his many adventures and trials). The first shot of *The Arabian Nights* is of Nuredin walking through the market where Zumurrud is sold, and the last shot is a close-up of Nuredin, joyful now he's found his long-lost lover Zumurrud.

Like so many actors in Pier Paolo Pasolini's movies, Franco Merli acted in one or two other movies, but not much after that. Indeed, many of the actors in Pasolini's movies only appeared in his films (it's the same with the unknown actors in the films of Walerian Borowczyk or Jean-Luc Godard). In some cases, that's a pity: Ines Pellegrini, for example, is wonderful, but she has only appeared in the 'trilogy of life' movies and *Salò*, and Luigina Rocchi, who played Fatima (Budur) in *The Arabian Nights*, is beautiful, and Merli has a winsome charm.

But there's no *acting* in the usual sense in *Il Fiore Delle Mille e Una Notte*. No. The performances have the naturalistic appearance of just happening in front of the camera, but not in the sense of actors who're professionally trained, and who've rehearsed a lot, to make scenes look as if they were improvized.

Improvization is a much mis-understood and mis-used term. Scenes in *any movie* are *very* rarely improvized in the way that critics and viewers mean. What usually happens is that spectators and critics are fooled into thinking that the stuff that's happening on screen looks as if it just took place spontaneously.

It doesn't (visit a film set and you'll see why instantly). But in *The Arabian Nights*, for once, it does seem as if the actors have been given some rudimentary direction and then been filmed in one or two takes. (The movie encourages the actors not to act, but to be themselves (as the maestro preferred). Impossible perhaps in the very artificial and strange setting of a movie set or a location surrounded by twenty or thirty people in the crew). And besides, the footage of Pier Paolo Pasolini at work filming *Salò, or The 120 Days of Sodom* reveals that he *would* ask for repeated takes, until everyone was satisfied. It also showed that Pasolini was coaxing the actors along with verbal instructions, including throughout shots.

As to acting compared to conventional movies – well, you just can't compare *The Arabian Nights* or the other 'trilogia di vita' pieces to the traditional manner of performance in Western movies. Pier Paolo Pasolini and the team employ a contrived *tableau* approach to some scenes, and many scenes are duly blocked in the static manner of formal/ classical paintings. And in other scenes, actors are given simple directions – run down this path and round the corner – and the scenes are filmed in a loose, casual manner. Quite a bit of *The*

Arabian Nights exhibits the carefree, informal attitude of a home movie – no need for a tripod, the camera is switched on, focussed, framed and the exposure's set quickly, and catches an actor running down an alley. (Much of *The Arabian Nights* has the camera handheld or on a tripod – there are very few tracking shots, and no crane shots). However, there *are* more formal shots, and many duologue scenes are filmed with a tripod and tight close-ups, plus there are some optical/ process shots, and even miniature shots.

✦

The Arabian Nights is another huge undertaking in terms of actors and extras. *The Arabian Nights* marshalls a massive amount of characters on screen, from clusters of running, jeering children to solemn, middle-aged men who sit around palatial feasts, to the usual Pasolinian retinue of crones and old coots. So the assistant directors – Umberto Angelucci, Paolo Andrea Mettel and Peter Shepherd – should take much of the credit here: there are so many big scenes in *The Arabian Nights*, for instance, involving many extras and animals.[15] Just to organize the people and camels and horses in those scenes takes a lot of planning and effort. Some of Pasolini's later movies really are *big films*, on the scale of the Hollywood Biblical epics, though they are usually thought of as a smaller-scale, European art films.

The cast of *Il Fiore Delle Mille e Una Notte* is far from the plastic actors of a Hollywood movie, with their hard, toned, tanned bodies and surgically-enhanced faces. In *The Arabian Nights*, everything is allowed to spill out, and terms such as 'ugly' or 'unshaven' or 'bad teeth' or 'bad hair' don't exist. In a Pier Paolo Pasolini movie, everyone, including the lead actors, looks as if they've walked on set straight from the bus or the hotel. No showers, no make-up trailers, no on-set hair and make-up people fussing around the actors seconds before a take begins. (Of course that's not quite true, and Pasolini's movies, just like most movies, are very

---

15 *The Arabian Nights* is full of animals – doves, horses, chickens, and of course camels. Plus a star role for a chimp!

particular about how the main performers look, and all of the leads are in make-up. And you can't imagine divas like Silvana Mangano or Maria Callas being happy to slum it along with the extras (they'd have hair and make-up artists fussing over them). Hair on *The Arabian Nights* was by Iole Cecchini, and make-up by Massimo Giustini – plus an army of assistants on the Big Scene Days).

And *The Arabian Nights* includes a slew of non-European actors, including many black and African actors. One of the main characters, Zumurrud, is played by a 20 year-old, black woman, Ines Pellegrini (b. 1954). She's terrific, hitting just the right note of naïvety and enthusiasm for a Pier Paolo Pasolini film. Abadit Ghidei and other key actors are also black.

In the scenes in the deep desert, we are far, far away from Cinecittà and anything European – or even anything to do with the usual interpretations of the Arabian tales of the *1001 Nights*. It's a case of Pier Paolo Pasolini wanting to use modern Africa and the Middle East for the ancient or mediæval world, and it's about Pasolini's love for Africa and the 'Third World' (and his insistence on moving away not only from Hollywood, but from the cinema of Rome and Italian cities, too – he preferred to venture into the lesser-known regions of Italy[16]). In the scenes of the poet Sium picking up three guys for sex, for example, towards the beginning of *The Arabian Nights*, everyone appears to be a black, African actor, and the village setting is a place with round huts with straw roofs (this was filmed in Ethiopia).

The Arabian Nights has the appearance, in parts, of a Giant Home Movie – as if Pier Paolo Pasolini had somehow persuaded a bunch of filmmakers (who would *not* be highly paid, one imagines), to trudge to far-flung locations (where decent hotels were thin on the ground, and the food was terrible), and to enact his wildly unusual interpretations of Arabic fairy tales (which nobody else understood, least of all the actors).

16 Yet most of the lead roles in *The Arabian Nights* are played by Italians, as in nearly all of Pasolini's other movies.

Thus, when Orson Welles described Pier Paolo Pasolini as a great leader, he was identifying a key requirement for a film director: leadership. Pasolini was one of those mavericks, one of those unusual and highly talented individuals who could (like Welles) somehow induce film crews and casts to go pretty far – physically, emotionally, psychologically.

✦

As with *Il Decamerone* and the decoration by Giotto di Bondone of a church, there is a painting scene[17] in *The Arabian Nights*: this time it's the decoration of a chamber by the suitor Prince Tagi (Francesco Paolo Governale) to charm the red silk sari off a beautiful, young woman (Princess Dunya ((Abadit Ghidei), the woman who has the disturbing dreams of trapped birds). The art department provides a lavish recreation of mediæval tiles and stained glass, and the two artisans in turn relate (and star in) the later stories of the 1974 movie.

✦

There are visual effects a-plenty in *The Arabian Nights*, too. Now, Pier Paolo Pasolini has always used special effects, which are also known as practical effects, such as effects like fire and smoke, or the special make-up in *Il Vangelo Secondo Matteo*. But in *The Arabian Nights* the filmmakers employ those effects (like models and optical effects) that critics tend to think of when they talk about 'visual' or 'special' effects' (i.e., visual effects created in post-production).

The visual effects in *The Arabian Nights* are ropey – the scene where the Devil takes the Prince for a flying ride, for instance, which combines aerial photography with the actors optically superimposed on top. *Superman* or *Star Wars* this ain't; nor is it anywhere near *The Thief of Baghdad* or one of Ray Harryhausen's marvellous *Sinbad* pictures. But it doesn't matter a jot. (However, the model shots of the boat hitting the cliffs and the sinking of the island are terrible – reminiscent of Ed Wood, but even worse than Wood, if they are

---

17 Also, Aziza paints a scroll for her lover.

meant to be serious).

✦

One of the motifs of *The Arabian Nights* is not
wholly worked-out or quite as satisfying narratively as
it should be: that is the rhyming of visuals, of places, of
rooms, of characters, and of events. There are two upper
chambers, for instance: one where Aziz and Aziza meet,
and one where Princess Dunya's romanced by Prince
Tagi. There are two visits to mysterious underground
palaces. Two scenes where youths lie face-down on beds
with their clothes pulled down. There are two scenes
where Zumurrud in her mirrored bedroom as the King
undresses to reveal she's a woman. These poetic doubles
and rhymes don't quite play out as richly as the material
deserves. (The films of Pasolini tend to avoid really
milking cinematic devices such as visual rhymes).

What *does* work, however, is the interlinking of the
stories, how one story can engender another, how a
meeting with a new character means the relating of a new
story. So the stories form a spiral, a cycle, a flow – of one
story into another – the ending of one story leads
directly into the beginning of another story. And the
tales are dreams-within-dreams, creating an infinity of
dreams, a labyrinth of interconnecting tales. (A good
example occurs when Aziz meets Prince Tagi in the
desert and relates the long story of his courtship of
Fatima and marriage to Aziza, which takes up much of
the middle section of *The Arabian Nights*: when he has
finished his story, Aziz and Tagi venture into another
town, where another story starts up, when they meet the
brothers that Tagi hires to decorate the chamber).

The Arabian Nights is of course a *hommage* to
stories and to storytelling – to the magic of storytelling,
the romance of it, the seduction of it, and the *necessity*
of it. *The Arabian Nights* is one of numerous movies
which remind audiences of the importance and value of
stories and storytelling (good examples would include
The Princess Bride and *Big Fish*).

BAD SOUND.

Where *The Arabian Nights* is let-down, for me, is on the level of sound and dubbing and music. Pier Paolo Pasolini's movies seem to have been staged in a variety of far-flung locations with a large group of people over months. But for the post-production, it appears that they have been dubbed and edited months or even years after the shooting, and the dubbing and cutting would be produced by a small group of people, probably in Rome. And some of those people maybe had nothing to do with the shooting of the movie (i.e., they have no investment in it), so there appears to be a disconnection between the images and the soundtrack. And it seems to have been done too quickly. (Certainly, many of the voice actors are *long ways* from the faces and personalities of the performers on screen).

What I mean is that there's a clumsy, awkward feeling to the sound in a Pier Paolo Pasolini movie, a wilful negligence in the post-production process. As if the voice dubbing was crammed into two days, and the mixing and dubbing into one day.

I don't know the circumstances here – because in the Hollywood system, movies are sometimes taken away from the filmmakers, and very few film directors have *true* final cut (they say they do, but studios still have the *real* final say – not least because studios legally own movies – and they pay for them).

I wouldn't imagine that Pier Paolo Pasolini had movies taken away from him, or that producer Alberto Grimaldi fell out big time and had the films cut in his own way (because, how the hell are you going to re-edit a Pasolini movie without the maestro's input?! Who the hell else can make sense of all that crazy footage?!). It's partly the Italian film industry's standard procedure, of course, of dubbing everything, and not shooting sync sound (there's not much live sound in many of Pasolini's movies, and the maestro wasn't a fan of it anyway). And, clearly, few if any of those extras and actors employed by the production in locations in Africa or Asia were invited to Rome and were present on the dubbing stage (even many of the lead actors, too, are not voicing their own roles – standard practice in the Italian film business even for starring roles). Instead, it's probably the usual bunch of Italian actors who dubbed most every big film that came through Rome. (Ditto with the foley work and the sound effects – in *The Arabian Nights*, they are patchy and inept. Crowd scenes have generic (and inconsistent) 'crowd sounds' (often for the market scenes),[18] music isn't in sync with the performers on-screen (and is clearly nothing like the music being played by the musicians), and the extras are shoddily represented. In short, 70% of the soundtrack of *The Arabian Nights* doesn't fit).

The issue, though, is not live sound vs. looped dialogue, it's that the sound in so many of Pier Paolo Pasolini's movies appears rushed and clunky. Sometimes I wonder that if Pasolini's movies had been dubbed and cut to a much higher standard, along with other technical aspects, Pasolini would now be regarded as a truly major filmmaker like Ingmar Bergman or Akira Kurosawa. For some critics, and for me, he is in that league, but not for many critics and viewers.

WEST MEETS EAST.

When you consider the individual scenes or images in *The Arabian Nights,* there is so much that is striking. Much of the imagery is very beautiful – the *light* of the whole film is absolutely haunting. This is the light of Africa, of North Africa, of Yemen and Iran, and of Asia. I for one *adore* those places, and can watch hours of this kind of footage. *The Arabian Nights*, for instance, is a terrific *desert* film, in the same class as *Lawrence of Arabia* or a John Ford Western.

However, *The Arabian Nights* is plenty more than a mere travelogue of pretty and exotic places. It's got the *A Thousand and One Nights milieu* down to a 'T' – including the princes and nobles in red and blue silk pants at festivals, bustling market scenes (including

18 And the background and atmos sounds (of crowds in the markets, for ex), don't match the scenes, either.

gorgeous, covered *souks*), dusty squares and alleys, elaborate mosques and towers, voyages in creaky, wooden boats, and caravans of camels and merchants moving across the desert. *The Arabian Nights* is unashamed in its evocation of classic movie clichés, and of Westerners' enshrinement of the exotic Middle East. *The Arabian Nights* is 'orientalizing' the East, in Edward Said's term, just as much as *Lawrence of Arabia* or the *Indiana Jones* franchise or *55 Days At Peking*. *The Arabian Nights* is still a European film production taking on the Arabic tales of the mediæval era, and despite Pasolini's (Marxist) politics (always remarked upon in any appraisal of Pasolini's cinema, and, as Pasolini admitted, not that significant in his cinema after all), *The Arabian Nights* is *still* West Meets East, the West exploiting the East, the West using the East for its own ends.[19] (For ex, many European (mostly Italian) actors take the lead roles in each of the stories).

The filmmakers want it both ways (as filmmakers – and all artists – always do): they want to produce a different kind of Middle Eastern movie, a different slant on the usual *1001 Nights*/ fairy tale/ fantasy movie, an *Arabian Nights* using archaic (yet contemporary) Africa instead of the usual 'historical' views of the Levant. But they also want to reproduce the familiar West-meets-East exoticism, and romance, and fantasy. (And they want to have Italians playing most of the lead roles).

SEXUALITY.

And there's sex.

Yes, *The Arabian Nights* contains plenty of tupping and nudity.[20] And men as much as women disrobe in this movie. As erotic as it is (it is probably Pier Paolo Pasolini's most conventionally erotic movie), *The Arabian Nights* departs from your usual picture in its portrayal of sex and nudity. The distanced,

19 I bet, for example, that Alberto Grimaldi's film production team didn't pay the local extras in the Maghreb the going rate they'd get in Cinecittà, and certainly not the union rates for Burbank.
20 For Sam Rohdie, *The Arabian Nights* is a 'myth about eroticism', but it's not 'a film about sexuality which the film converts to myth, but a film about the cinema which presents a myth of a lost sexuality' (54-55).

Brechtian, *tableau* approach to the performances and the narrative in *The Arabian Nights* means that the sex, like the drama or the characters or other narrative elements, is not treated in conventional terms.

In short, *The Arabian Nights* simply does not tell a traditional story in a traditional manner (even tho' it's dealing with probably the greatest set of stories in human history). It does not use the usual elements of dramaturgy – such as rising action, or cause and effect, or motives, or backstory, or goals. Yes, (some of) those elements *are* present, but they are not integrated into the fabric of the movie in the customary way. (But all you need to know in *The Arabian Nights* is that *desire* is all-pervading, and informs everything the characters do: they desire, desire, desire. And the desire is always for romance and love and sex. Which might be another way of pinpointing the desire for fulfilment. Or trans-cendence).

It's one of the aspects of Pier Paolo Pasolini's cinema that takes a little getting used to – the viewer has to shift into a different way of looking at movies. The filmmakers are not going to provide dramaturgy in the usual manner, so don't expect dramatic devices such as rising action, or one scene providing the energy or tension or dialogue cue for the next scene (known as the 'hook'), or for dramatic climaxes (or for dramatic highpoints at the end of scenes). Indeed, the *lack* of narrative climaxes in movies like *The Arabian Nights* is one of the chief characteristics of Pasolini's cinema. A film such as *The Arabian Nights* is certainly telling a story (and is of course a story about stories, about how stories are created, and how one story suggests or gives birth to another, and how stories are dreams which intersect/ multiply), but it *does not* punch home its dramatic highpoints, like a conventional North American or European or Indian or Japanese or Chinese movie.

Oh, there *are* conflicts between characters in *The Arabian Nights*, and scenes where characters argue (with attempts to resolve issues), but the movie is simply not interested in staging conflicts or the resolutions to conflicts in a conventional manner. Consequently, there are no moral messages, no summaries of narrative or theme, no plot devices to update audiences, etc. (The framing story of the *1001 Nights*, for example, is dispensed with – where Scheherazade tries to appease the Sultan Shahryar).

In your typical contemporary, Hollywood flick, relationships and characters and situations are so highly wrought that everything is played at the maximum of emotion and conflict. In those high octane narratives created by M.B.A.s and executives and their writer-slaves in Culver City or Burbank, nobody is happy, everyone has a wise-ass quip about everyone else, and the world is always about to end.

By contrast with contemporary, Hollywood cinema, *The Arabian Nights* is fabulously laid-back and free-wheeling, loose and sensual. However, there *are* some resolutions to conflicts, and some moral outcomes: for instance, some of the villains are punished (like the 'blue-eyed Christian', Barsum, who kidnaps Nuredin's beloved Zumurrud). Aziz is chastized for his abominable treatment of women (with castration). And there *is* a moral pattern established at the end of each episode. (And, yes, some of the characters, such as Nuredin and Aziz, are played at hysterical levels, with their weeping and gnashing of teeth over lost lovers. In many scenes actors've had glycerine applied to simulate tears. Well, hell, this *is* a movie made by Italians! Where weepy men litter the floor! Men weep in three-quarters of Pasolini's movies).

And for some critics, *The Arabian Nights* may come across as self-indulgent and a-political: for the intellectuals and politicos who hanker after Pier Paolo Pasolini-the-Marxist-Revolutionary, *The Arabian Nights* is probably decadent tripe in which a former firebrand of Communist ideology and the left-wing has descended into children's tales of the exotic Levant coupled with travelogue photography and some titillating, soft-core porn sex.

Sure. *The Arabian Nights* is not everyone's cup of champagne. I'd say, tho': how can you *not* enjoy *The Arabian Nights*? It has so much going for it! And it's clear that Pier Paolo Pasolini and the team are exploring the same themes and issues in *The Arabian Nights* that they have always explored. But in *The Arabian Nights*, the trappings and the gift-wrapping are so spectacular and entrancing, it can be very distracting.

And one should always remember with Pier Paolo Pasolini that while his cinema is about poetry and ideology and narrative and ideas and all those elements that critics and intellectuals solemnly discuss and deconstruct, he is also a *filmmaker*, someone who is very concerned with staging and characters and colours and light and music. Pasolini's movies are not essays published in *Diacritics* or *Yale Po-Faced Studies*. They are movies, folks, and even though they are often categorized as European art films, they are also *movies*, just as much as entertainment movies such as *Singin' In the Rain, Grease* or *Avatar*.

✦

Although it is unconventional narratively, and although it contains a lot of nudity and sex, *The Arabian Nights* is totally conservative and even regressive, if you consider it politically in relation to some of Pier Paolo Pasolini's other movies. *The Arabian Nights* enshrines love and sex and romance and the heterosexual couple through and through (just as the original tales did). Even the gender-bending and portrayals of homosexuality are very mild (compared to what we might expect from Pasolini) The crossdressing, for instance, occurs wholly within conventional narrative forms. People having sex and falling in love is always going to be conservative and traditional (tho' the portrayals in art and cinema might not be). Not right-wing and reactionary, or left-wing and Communist or socialist, because love and sex don't have anything to do with that kind of politics in this movie.

Maybe you can find some left-wing or Marxist or right-wing and fascistic politics outside the 1974 movie, or inferred from inside the movie, but if you consider the levels of narrative and characters and themes and images, this is an a-political movie which enshrines love and sex and marriage and the family. (Again, this ardent pursuit of a-politics or non-politics might feed into Pier Paolo Pasolini's artistic reversal about his 'trilogy of life' pictures).

In the Aziz and Aziza story, for instance, there are numerous scenes of Ninetto Davoli running back and forth between his spurned bride Aziza and his beloved Fatima. And that's all it is, for thirty minutes, the sequence goes on and on and on – a man hurrying between two women, with some weedy *Carry On* comedy, and some exotic settings.

Is it bourgeois? Fascist? Totalitarian? Marxist? Communist? Radical? Separatist? Terrorist? It doesn't matter.

And *The Arabian Nights* is episodic in structure, knitted together by the running story of – what? Of a man looking for a woman. Yes folks, the linking narrative in *1001 Nights* is just that: a boy (Nuredin) searching for a girl (Zumurrud), a lover looking for his beloved (which is as conservative and traditional as possible).

HOMOSEXUALITY.

Some critics drew attention to the heterosexual nature of the sexual relations on display in *The Arabian Nights*, but there are many references to (and portrayals of) homosexual identity and gay sex.[21] And there's just as much male nudity as female nudity (all of the actors working for Pier Paolo Pasolini would likely have known by this point in his career that he was a famous gay film director). And not only male nudity, but male bodies filmed with a painter's eye for beauty: if you like young men's butts, there are plenty on show in *The Arabian Nights* (as well, of course, as everything else in the male body).

The Arabian Nights might be P.P. Pasolini's

---

21 There are jokes about some men preferring bananas to figs.

version of the modern art of famous gay artists like Tom of Finland or Robert Mapplethorpe (Mapplethorpe was photographing beautiful, young men in Gotham in a very similar manner as *The Arabian Nights* around this time – the mid-Seventies). And, with the young actors framed in settings such as Byzantine or Early Renaissance chapels, you might be looking at updated versions of the paintings of the two Michelangelos (Buonarroti and Caravaggio).

The scene where a merchant poet (Sium) picks up three youths in a rural (African) village is one of the most obvious (and clichéd) homosexual encounters in Pier Paolo Pasolini's *œuvre* (it's the second sequence in *The Arabian Nights*, so it introduces a homosexual theme early on. It's a scene of full nudity that Pasolini might've filmed in the early 1960s, if the social climate would have allowed it). It's the archaic, stereotypical tale of an old pederast with three pretty boys (a scenario in fiction at least 3,500 years-old): the filmmakers make the gay eroticism of the scene explicit, by having the three black *ragazzi* fully naked, lined up for the fully-clothed poet Sium to inspect and joke with and fondle their genitals. (The scene seems tailor-made for those critics who persist in taking the biographical approach to the cinema of Pasolini – for them, this scene is probably a barely concealed self-portrait of Pasolini the predatory gay man, preying upon comely, young boys).[22]

When Prince Yunan (Salvatore Sapienza) climbs down into the underground palace, late in the movie, there's a frightened youth who's just turned fifteen. Yunan is naked for quite a lot of this episode of *The Arabian Nights* (this is tough acting for Sapienza: he has to swim, clamber over rocks, run around mountains, beaches, climb down rope ladders in the palace, etc, and much of the time fully naked).

The sex acts between Yunan and the 15 year-old kid aren't depicted. Instead, there's a classic evocation of homoerotic bonding – they horse around in a big bath

22 And, yes, some film critics have made that connection.

(in some extraordinary catacombs. You can see a similar scene in the restored *Spartacus*, 1960). There is nudity from both actors, and they sleep in the same bed. (Getting that scene with nude, under-age actors filmed today might be tricky even for a revered *auteur* like Pier Paolo Pasolini.)[23]

The dreamy idyll in the subterranean palace between Prince Yunan and the 15 year-old boy is thoroughly gay-inflected (and the camera dwells lovingly on actor Salvatore Sapienza's form. No one can miss that he also resembles a young Pasolini). When Yunan stabs the boy with a knife (as has been foretold), he pulls down the lad's clothes, for no particular reason, exposing his bare rear (as he lies face-down on the bed). The knife, the blood, the wound, the nudity, the bed, the under-age boy – there are numerous signifiers of sodomy, murder and gay sex (which Pasolini would explore even further in his following film as director, *Saló, or The 120 Days of Sodom*).

There's also a gay theme to the final scene of *The Arabian Nights*, where Nuredin and Zumurrud are re-united, and some of the male guests at the wedding feast quip that they wouldn't mind having Nuredin themselves (it's those big, cute eyes!).

ZUMURRUD AND NUREDIN.

Let's slip on our scarlet, Aladdin pants and rim our eyes with kohl and take a look at some of the episodes in more detail in the 1974 film:

The Arabian Nights opens with a scene designed to turn the tables on the conventions of *1001 Nights* adaptations, with some gender-swopping play: the slave Zumurrud, a woman in amongst a group of men at a slave market, loudly and jokily denounces some of the guys around her, in sexual terms (deriding their manhood). This scene leads to the unlikely formation of the central couple of *The Arabian Nights*, Zumurrud and Nuredin, when Zumurrud announces that she will only be sold to

23 The tabloid press, plus the authorities, would probably seize upon a gay film director with criminal convictions of predation filming under-age actors in sex scenes with relish.

Nuredin, having spotted him in the crowd (and despite some of the buyers coveting her, such as Barsum (Salvatore Verdetti) and his pay master Ali – Ali Abdulla). The seduction by a woman of a man, and a woman who will later become a king (and a black woman, too), sets up the themes of playing around with gender (and race), and a proto-feminism (which isn't really present in the original mediæval *1001 Nights* tales).

Thus, after the customary two minutes of opening credits (in black lettering on white) of a Pier Paolo Pasolini picture, *The Arabian Nights* dives straight into a lively *souk* scene, delivering the cliché of the *Thousand and One Nights* (a bustling, Middle Eastern setting, and Nuredin as the hapless, grinning youth). And, true to form, the 1974 movie also hurries right into a full frontal sex scene, as Zumurrud and Nuredin get freaky (with Zumurrud initiating the virginal and clumsy Nuredin). Thus, the first erotic scene in *The Arabian Nights* is happy, consensual and loving – as if the 'happy ever after' occurs at the top of the movie, and everything disintegrates into disconnection, separation and liminality (or, more bluntly, before it all goes cock-eyed). So the movie begins with consensual love-making, and it ends with our lovers re-united, and the re-affirmation of love – heartfelt, romantic union (it's the sappiest ending to a Pasolini film[24]).

The idyll of love cannot last long, because the insulted men at the slave auction take their revenge: the 'blue-eyed Christian' Barsum kidnaps Zumurrud and has her carried by basket to Ali, who whips her for deriding him in front of everybody in the bazaar.[25] Thus begins the lengthy narrative device of the separation of the lovers, which is sustained throughout *The Arabian Nights*, right up until the reunion of the soulmates in the very final frames (thirty seconds before the caption

24 No death here, then – both characters make it to the end of the show in one piece.
25 There is less rape and abuse than one might expect in this inter-pretation of the *1001 Nights* by Pier Paolo Pasolini and the team – and also in the other 'trilogy of life' movies.

'FINE' comes up).

Barsum and his cohorts (such as the leader of the forty thieves) get their just desserts, with the running gag of guests at the wedding feast taking food without being invited, and being carted off to be crucified[26] (cut to images of crucifixions at sunset outside the city walls. It's a hefty sentence for grabbing a handful of rice, but this is a fairy tale, after all, and it doesn't matter what the taboo is). All of Pasolini's historical movies feature scenes of punishment (sometimes conceived along ritualistic, mythic lines, as in *Medea*).

Poor Nuredin has a pretty tough time of it, wandering thru the whole 1974 movie looking for his lost love Zumurrud (in some scenes he's running like mad, and being chased by a group of yelling kids).

In one of the more bizarre sequences in *The Arabian Nights*, he has an encounter with a magical lion in the desert (who leads him, via the trickery of optical process imagery, to Zumurrud's city).[27] This is where Nuredin is at his lowest point, in the midst of an uninhabited desert: from this lowest ebb, Nuredin's fortunes bounce all the way up the ecstasy (i.e., it's a conventional reversal of fortune, pushing a hero down to the lowest point), when he is led to the city where Zumurrud is King.

However, it's not all bad for Nuredi on his journey: in one scene, he's literally hauled up off the street (in a basket on ropes), and undressed and seduced by three women in an inner courtyard. In another scene, he's bathing naked in a pool surrounded by colourful fruit and flowers with three naked maidens (one of them is Elisabetta Genovese as Munis), where they play the 'Guess the Name For the Genitals' game, teasing Nuredin and kissing him.[28] (Jean-Luc Godard has employed this game in at least three movies – Godard has characters coming up with different words for the buttocks in

26 The actor who plays Barsum (Salvatore Verdetti), with his blue eyes, might be cast as Christ.
27 Both the lion and actor Franco Merli are optically composited into the desert landscapes featuring drifting clouds.
28 The poetic names for genitals are right out of Oriental erotic tales (such as in *The Perfumed Garden* and the *Kama Sutra*).

Masculine Feminine (1966), for example, as they lie in bed, and even has the young Jesus hiding under the Virgin Mary's dress in *Hail Mary* (1985), and talking about her breasts and mound).

Nuredin is the embodiment of love pure and total – he never gives up on Zumurrud,[29] and is seeking her to the end (after the scene with the bathing beauties, Nuredin is soon waking, and hurrying away, crying, 'Zumurrud!', which's his mantra throughout *The Arabian Nights* – 'Zumurrud! Zumurrud!'). Nuredin isn't portrayed as a psychologized (or psychologizing) character – he's no Hamlet or modern, Western character analyzing everything. *The Arabian Nights* seems to draw on (Freudian) psychology, like other Pasolini pictures, but it presents its figures as more archaic, more primitive, and more fundamental than something that modern psychoanalysis can grasp. The characters in *The Arabian Nights* seem anti-psychological, anti-intellectualized – anti-Western. Certainly anti-modern or pre-modern, and anti-capitalist or pre-capitalist.

CARAVAN OF DREAMS.

The caravan of dreams sequence depicts the cliché of Ancient Arabian folk tales, a caravan of camels, horses, kids, animals and merchants in the desert. It's Pier Paolo Pasolini's little piece of *Lawrence of Arabia* – and it's presented, amazingly, without the usual veneers of irony/ politics/ ideology. As if Pasolini, a white, bourgeois, European man really can fly loose of his uptight, intellectual background and stage an Oriental fairy tale with all the trimmings.

Two merchants pick up two fifteen year-old kids, and use them for a quaint, naïve scene exploring the origins of love in the form of a private test. Charm and innocence disguise the elements of exploitation and slavery: Zuedi (Zuedi Biasolo) and Sium the poet watch the teens waking up and making love in a tent from a perch above, like gods. The boy, Berhame (Fessazion

29 Never giving up is one of the hallmarks of a hero.

Gherentiel), wakes,[30] sees the girl, moves over to her bed, and makes love to her, and then vice versa. It's as if love (sex) transcends all.

Maybe Pier Paolo Pasolini disapproved of his 'trilogy of life' films in his famous reversal ("Repudiation of the *Trilogy of Life*", June 1975) because there's too little of the cynicism and irony that seems mandatory in any Euro-art flick. Delivering so many love stories straight, without the usual levels of self-consciousness and self-criticism, was not the done thing. *The Arabian Nights* is certainly a love letter to *love* as well as to the 'Third World', to Africa, and to the Middle East, and to, of course, the past, the ancient world, and the utopia/ paradise that never existed. (It's the world that Pasolini wished Italy still was, which he pined for).

AZIZ AND FATIMA.

Among the most successful episodes in *The Arabian Nights* is the central section, where Aziz (played by Ninetto Davoli) trysts with Fatima (also known as Budur, played by Luigina Rocchi[31]), in one of the story-within-a-story sections (yes, Davoli and his cheesy grin duly turns up in *The Arabian Nights* – 45 minutes into the show. However, this is Davoli's finest role in Pasolini movie).

Aziz and Fatima meet in a beautifully-designed, orange-red fairy tale tent in a desert garden, and make love. This section includes one of the iconic images of Pier Paolo Pasolini's cinema, framed like an illustration from a mediæval manuscript: the nude couple facing each other, Fatima with her legs open, and Aziz brandishing a golden bow and arrow, with a gold cock and balls at the end of it,[32] which he fires into Fatima's holy of holies.

---

30 Prodded awake by the onlookers.

31 Again, the performers in this episode are Italian and French.

32 You can bet that this prop was swiftly stolen from the set. Indeed, if you were turning *The Arabian Nights* into merchandizing for movie fans with money to waste, the golden genitals would be ideal. Pasolini's movies are full of silly props like this which might be sold in a sex toys store.

It's a long episode, filmed in the palm trees and greenery in the desert of Iran, and involves a back-and-forth romantic plot in the manner of *Cyrano de Bergerac*. Aziz is another of Pier Paolo Pasolini's and Ninetto Davoli's dopes, a lusty but very dim youth who falls in love at the drop of a hat with a woman glimpsed for an instant from an upper window, even tho' he's in the midst of marrying Aziza (Teresa Bouché). Poor Aziza becomes the Roxanne for Aziz, feeding the hapless Aziz with lines of romantic verse to say to Fatima, and translating her enigmatic sayings and gestures back for him when he returns. In the end, Aziz betrays both women. (Aziz's mother (Pasolini regular Margareth Clémenti) castigates him for his failings – but not as much as an Italian mother would!).

The Aziz-Fatima episode's strung out for too long and is rather shabbily edited (by Nino Baragli and Tatiana Morigi), but plenty of elements make it one of the more engaging and narratively satisfying sections of the 'trilogy of life' movies (such as the beauty and texture of the imagery, the appeal of the actors (Luigina Rocchi is lovely), the innocence of the lovemaking,[33] and the naïvety of it all, the cuteness,[34] the fact that one could switch Ninetto Davoli and Teresa Bouché and Luigina Rocchi for Disney cartoon animals, and it would still be entertaining[35]).

Indeed, the appeal of *The Arabian Nights* is precisely that the stories themselves are so simple – or, rather, uncomplicated. A man visits a woman, but sees another woman he likes more on the way. That's all it is. The narrative component of *The Arabian Nights* is thus only one ingredient of this shimmering, beautiful movie. It's a little like a Hollywood musical film or a Hong Kong martial arts movie, where the story is often simple[36] and just an excuse for the filmmakers to stage a whole bunch of extravagant set-pieces (thus, insisting

33 There are scenes of Fatima licking wine off Aziz's body, for instance.
34 Wait, did I just say 'cute' about a Pier Paolo Pasolini movie?!
35 Altho' Disney's Bambi and Thumper never got up to this level of naughtiness.
36 Actually, the plots are seldom 'simple', but intricate. The over-arching concept may be 'simple', but the way it is plotted isn't.

on fully developed characters, themes and plots completely misses the point). *The Arabian Nights* might be the closest Pasolini came to making a musical movie (but of all the European New Wave *auteurs*, you just can't imagine Pasolini directing a musical! However, Jean-Luc Godard did – *A Woman Is a Woman* (1961). And other Godard pictures, like *Pierrot le Fou* and *Band of Outsiders,* have musical and dance interludes.[37] And even Ingmar Bergman, for some critics *the* arch miserablist of world cinema, made a few musical and theatrical movies).

But no, no one dances in a Pier Paolo Pasolini movie (except Salomé in *The Gospel According To Matthew*). In the 'trilogy of life' movies, Pasolini got close – he had Ninetto Davoli do a Charlie Chaplin skit, for instance, in *The Canterbury Tales* (though it was awful). And there *are* dances in the 'mediæval trilogy' – but they seem to occur only at weddings – the peasants dance in *The Decameron*, and Perkin dances at a wedding in *The Canterbury Tales*.

The luxuriously staged wedding in *The Arabian Nights*, between Zumurrud and her/ his bride Hayat, cries out for some choreography (but even the music in that scene, which should be as delightful as the colourful costumes and food, is fudged. (If this was a Bollywood musical, the entire ensemble would be dancing across the screen, and Zumurrud would certainly belt out a love song).

Anyway, back to Aziz and Fatima: what happens to Aziz? He is castrated (!) – rather spectacularly, too: he turns up at Princess Fatima's fancy tent in the garden after a year, having married (a third woman) and had a child, and is rightly set upon by a group of harpies at Fatima's behest. That he isn't slaughtered on the spot is amazing – poor Fatima's been waiting a year perched on the same patch of dust outside her tent, without food or water! (Or so she claims). Instead, there's a graphic castration scene, in which Aziz's genitals're tied up with twine in giant close-up. Ouch! (So he becomes a

---

37 Some of these were to please his wife, Anna Karina.

castrated, feminized man. Is this Pasolini's cinematic response to his former lover Davoli getting married? Pasolini was apparently distraught when he heard the news about Davoli, in January, 1973, during the filming of *The Canterbury Tales*. Some observers have thought so. The very long Aziz and Aziza sequence in *The Arabian Nights* is, after all, all about fidelity and infidelity, and for his betrayal of both women, Aziz is severely punished. It looks forward to *Salò*).[38]

DUNYA AND TAGI.

The Arabian Nights also enters dreamland, moving into a character's dreams, though not as often as one might imagine – because the entire movie is so dream-like (and films are already dreams, as Pasolini pointed out). It's Princess Dunya's (Abadit Ghidei) dream of birds, of birds being trapped under nets, and breaking free (it's this dream that becomes the basis of the decoration of the upper chamber by Prince Tagi, in order to woo her. How romantic!). When Dunya sees this, of course she breaks into tears (which's how every lover responds to anything in *The Arabian Nights* – the movie is full of young people weeping from love's cruelty). Tagi and Dunya make love (she kneels down to worship the male organ in the D.H. Lawrencean manner), then they continue on the floor (with Dunya covering up Tagi so he can't look at her as she services him).

There is also a reprise of the caravan of camels and travellers out of Middle Eastern fairy tales in this sequence, when it's attacked by bandits (and the Prince survives by smearing himself with blood and pretending to be dead). The way that the bandits are introduced calls back to the Massacre of the Innocents section of *The Gospel According To Matthew*: a montage of close-ups of the robbers looking off-screen is followed by a sudden burst into movement accompanied by music.

---

38 Pursuing the biographical approach further, Ninetto Davoli is sexually objectified in a striking manner; there are several close-ups of his weiner and buttocks, for instance. And to punish his former lover, Pier Paolo Pasolini has his genitals tied up and tortured on film!

THE ENDING.

Towards the end of *The Arabian Nights*, the film seems to be running out of steam somewhat. It's a long movie – or it *feels* like a long movie (it's two hours and ten minutes long, with a lost, early cut running 2h 35m). But not in a bad way – I for one could watch this kind of movie for hours and hours. But by the one hour and thirty minute mark, the filmmaking team have clearly said pretty much what they wanted to say and staged pretty much what they wanted to stage (here's where really expert editors and screenwriters make their mark, by reviving a flagging audience and revving them up for the last act). When you look at a lot of movies running over two hours, you often find that between 1h 20m and 1h 30m is a danger point (*The Arabian Nights* doesn't have an intermission, as *The Decameron* did, and as very lengthy movies sometimes did in this period).

Although a running time of 2h 10m always means a four-act movie in terms of narrative structure, *The Arabian Nights* is a very rare fiction/ feature film because it isn't composed in act form. Instead, it is fashioned in episode form.

And, no, there isn't going to be a big action climax to this kind of movie. Oh no. But *The Arabian Nights* does reach some interesting places, with sea voyages in old, wooden boats, encounters with magical lions in the desert, islands that collapse into the ocean like mythical Atlantis, and descents into underground palaces.

Franco Citti appears in these scenes in a brief cameo as a demon (a *djinn* = genie): he has a bizarre look, with an orange-red fright wig and Aladdin pants (and he's topless, and also sports a text around his neck).[39] Time for a little bit of Italian horror out of Dario Argento, Mario Bava, and *gialli* cheapies, too, when the demon chops off the hands and feet of Prince Shahzmah's lover, then her head (that she doesn't make a sound, but keeps looking fondly at Yunan is a great touch).

This particular story in *The Arabian Nights* goes further into *ciné fantastique* territory when it has the

39 It's definitely Citti's oddest outfit for a Pasolini movie.

demon turning Prince Shahzmah (Alberto Argentino) into a chimpanzee. Yes, folks, Pier Paolo Pasolini has made a movie where a clever chimp is carried on a litter like a king by slaves, and writes in an elegant, Arabic script! But this isn't a Disney TV special, or *The Jungle Book*, or another re-telling of the Chinese epic *Journey To the West* – it's a tale where the Prince is having A Very Bad Week. As if seeing his beloved having her limbs chopped off, followed by her head, isn't enough, he's turned into a monkey, and is kept as a pet by a laughing sailor.

Filming in India and Nepal paid off in *The Arabian Nights* with some of the most dream-like sequences in the Pier Paolo Pasolini cinematic *œuvre*: as the monkey-king is carried thru a town, bells are rung by onlookers. And then more bells, and more bells – with the sound editors in Rome coming up with something suitably imaginative on the soundtrack (instead of the usual mundane sounds). The staging is uninspired, the acting is low-key, and the action doesn't convince (or move us), but the India and Nepal episode in *The Arabian Nights* is lifted by another set of extraordinary spaces. It's a whole world away from the deserts of Yemen and Iran. (Pasolini might've been the greatest documentary filmmaker of exotic places in recent times had he been inclined. Some filmmakers pride themselves on shooting in remote or dangerous spots – Werner Herzog comes to mind – but Pasolini has a magical ability (a poet's nose) for seeking out the strange and the poetic everywhere he goes. Pasolini could visit a town or city you are very familiar with, where you've lived for years, and he would uncover something you'd never seen before).

The episodic nature of *The Arabian Nights*, and each of the 'trilogy of life-and-death' movies, means that the rising action device and the cause-and-effect mechanisms of the conventional movie aren't going to work. However, the film has employed the running motif of stories-within-stories, which has recurring characters like Zumurrud and Nuredin cropping up: the search for love provides the narrative glue that cements the 1974 movie together at the close (*The Arabian Nights* embodies Pasolini's tenet of art as 'a search for magic').

+

And how about the ending of *The Arabian Nights*? Outside of *The Gospel According To Matthew*, it's the all-out happiest ending in Pier Paolo Pasolini's cinema. What does the ending consist of? The union of the two lovers (Nuredin and Zumurrud) separated in act one, of course. Cue the music! Cue the kissing! Pure fairy tale, pure Hollywood. The most conservative ending possible. Love – sex – romance – it always works.

But even that ending of *The Arabian Nights* has a kinky twist, as Zumurrud, for no particular reason (except maybe she's getting fond of being King), teases poor Nuredin mercilessly by having him massage her feet, then lie on the bed, then turn over, with his pants pulled down over his behind (at this point, the always-innocent Nuredin thinks that the King is a man and he's been summoned to the King's chamber to be his sex slave). Only as she recites poetry does Zumurrud undress and finally reveal herself to Nuredin, who at that point still thinks he's going to be buggered by the man. She takes his hand and puts it between her legs. (The scene shifts from homosexual rape to heterosexual love).

The suggestion of sex games and S/M seems a little out of place, but you can trust Pier Paolo Pasolini and the team not to finish up this far-flung fantasy in wholly expected terms. But when the music swells up and the kissing starts, the world of heterosexual normality is rapidly re-instated (the final image of *The Arabian Nights* is a close-up of Franco Merli, lying on the bed, looking at Zumurrud, happy. Plus the glycerine tears, of course). It is as sappy, as simplistic, as dumb, and as unconvincing as any 'happy ending' in any movie in film history.

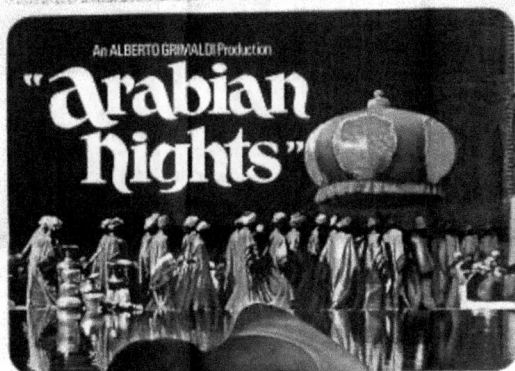

The Arabian Nights (1974).
This page and over.

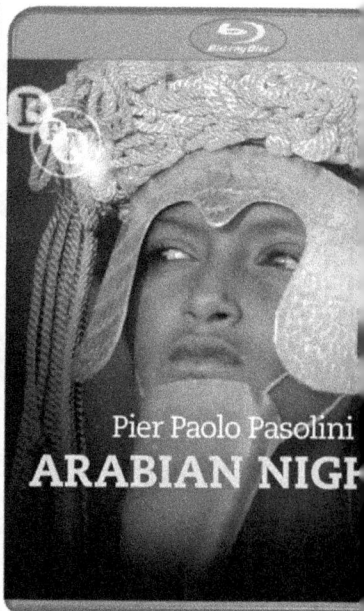

PIER PAOLO PASOLINI

IL FIORE
DELLE
MILLE E
UNA NOTTE

Blu-ray

Pier Paolo Pasolini
ARABIAN NIGH

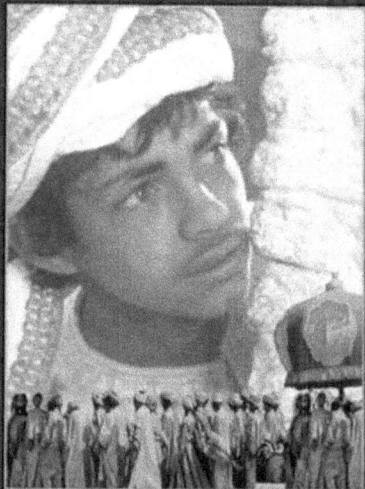

PIER PAOLO PASOLINI

Az ezeregyéjszaka
virágai

DVD

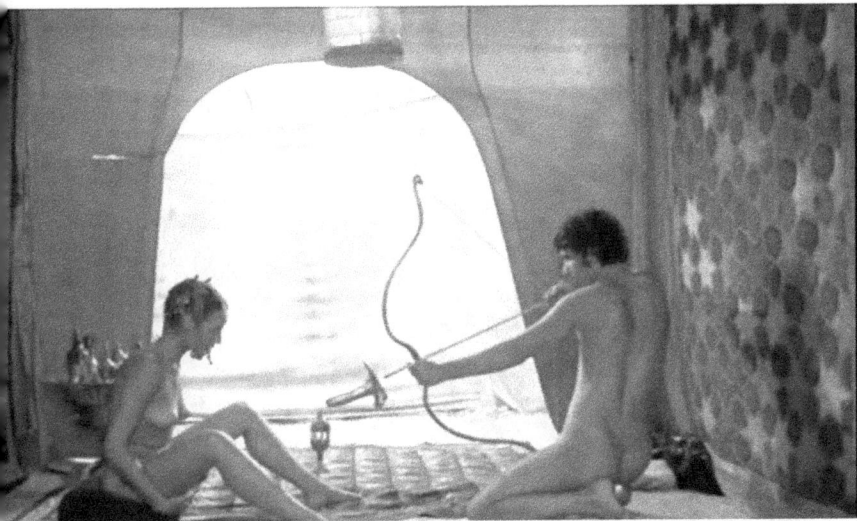

APPENDICES

QUOTES BY
PIER PAOLO PASOLINI

I love life fiercely, desperately. And I believe that this fierceness, this desperation will carry me to the end... Love of life for me has become a more tenacious vice than cocaine. I devour my existence with an insatiable appetite. (1970)

•

...cinema is already a dream

•

...to make films is to be a poet

•

One can cheat in everything except style.

•

Even a sound image, say thunder booming in a clouded sky, is somehow infinitely more mysterious than even the most poetic description a writer could give of it. A writer has to find oniricity through a highly refined linguistic operation, while the cinema is much nearer to sounds physically, it doesn't need any elaboration. All it needs is to produce a clouded sky with thunder and straight away you are close to the mystery and ambiguity of reality.

•

...a tree photographed is poetic, a human face photographed is poetic because physicity is poetic in itself, because it is an apparition, because it is full of mystery, because it is full of ambiguity, because it is full of polyvalent meaning, because even a tree is a sign of a linguistic system. But who talks through a tree? God, or reality itself. Therefore the tree as a sign puts us in communication with a mysterious speaker.

•

When I make a film I'm always in reality, among the trees and among the people; there's no symbolic or conventional filter between me and reality as there's in literature. The cinema is an explosion of my love for reality. I have never conceived of making a film that would be a work of a group, I've always thought of a film as a work of an author, not only the script and the direction but the choices of sets and locations, the characters, even the clothes. I choose everything, not to mention the music. (1971)

•

The cinema is a language which expresses reality with reality. So the question is: what is the difference between the cinema and reality? Practically none.

•

Reality is divine. That is why my films are never naturalistic. The motivation that unites all of my films is to give back to reality its original sacred significance. (1968)

•

I avoid fiction in my films. I do nothing to console, nothing to embellish reality, nothing to sell the goods. (1973)

•

I've never wanted to make a conclusive statement. I've always posed various problems and left them open to consideration. (1971)

NOTES ON
RENAISSANCE ARTISTS

MASACCIO.

Pier Paolo Pasolini responded to the flattened perspectives of Early Renaissance art, to the *tableau* approach to grouping figures, and to the separation of foreground and background. Pasolini didn't need to 'quote' particular painters of the Renaissance, or individual paintings, because his visual approach in cinema is already informed by a frontal perspective, which arranges the action (the figures) at right angles to the camera lens.

Each painter in the Renaissance re-shaped space to his/ her own liking. Art historians dutifully record the development of illusionistic space in a progression of artists – from Cimabue and Giotto di Bondone to Masaccio, Domenico Veneziano and Masolino da Panicale, from Fra Filippo Lippi and Fra Angelico through Sandro Botticelli and Filippino Lippi, Giovanni Bellini and Raphael de Sanzio, finding an apotheosis of depth and *sfumato* in Leonardo da Vinci, but deepening in darkness still further with Michelangelo di Caravaggio, and, later, Rembrandt van Rijn.

In the art of Masaccio (1401-28), space begins to open up from the spaceless, golden backgrounds of Byzantine art. The *Crucifixion* from Masaccio's *Pisa*

Altarpiece (in Naples) depicts four figures (Jesus and the 'three Marys') against a gold background which suggests, as gold always does in Renaissance painting, power and divinity. With the *Trinity* (in Santa Maria Novella, Florence), Masaccio's space deepens. The evocation of the architecture in Masaccio's *Trinity* is very powerful. He creates a barrel vault between two pilasters, seen from a low viewpoint. The architectonics of the *Trinity* are showy, theatrical, like a stage set. Masaccio monumentalizes his subjects, making God the apex of that strongest of all geometric shapes, the triangle or pyramid.

GIOTTO.

Giotto di Bondone (*c.* 1267-1337) was one of the premier artists in Italy of the 14th century, celebrated by Dante Alighieri, and seen today as one of the key architects of the focus in Early Renaissance art on the human figure. Giotto created works in Naples, Assisi, Padua, Florence and Rome; however, only the famous fresco cycle in Padua (in the Arena Chapel) is recognized as definitely authored by Giotto.

In the art of Giotto, the landscape is still very much a *background*, flattened spatially, so the action in the foreground is not connected with it. Early Renaissance landscape is full of marvellous passages of detail and light, but it is flat and relatively undynamic. In the background of Giotto's *Lamentation*, one of the chief works by Giotto, where the weeping angels swarm like crazed birds in the sky, the landscape is hardly painted in: the suggestions of rocks, a tree, and not much more.

In *The Decameron*, Pasolini cast himself as Giotto (as the artist appeared in the fiction of Giovanni Boccaccio). The Giottoan set-piece in *The Decameron* was a quasi-historical representation of the artist painting a fresco commission in a church (alluding to the Paduan fresco cycle).

PIERO DELL A FRANCESCA.

Piero della Francesca (*c.* 1410/ 20-92) has one of the most special and distinctive forms of space in painting. Piero's sense of space stands out from other painters, as with Paul Cézanne, Rembrandt van Rijn and Mark Rothko. The bright, timeless spaces of Piero are instantly recognizable, and critics sometimes evoke Greek sculpture in connection with Piero's paintings.[1] One might also see in Piero's hermetic, ritualized, timeless paintings the art of Chinese landscape painting, with its evocations of emptiness, which hints at the radical void of Eastern mysticism (in Zen Buddhism and Taoism). Piero's hypnotic art coolly melds science with art, space with spirit, the personal with the cosmic, and history, myth and religion with time.

For Piero della Francesca, geometry, proportion, perspective and mathematics had a magical quality. His art exalts, on one level, a *jouissance* of mathematics and measurement, in which the 'science' of Renaissance perspective is joyously explored. Piero seemed to lean towards the cool, impersonal, impassive scientific inquiry of Aristotlean philosophy, rather than the more sensuous, more obviously mystical aspects of Platonic philosophy: he is regarded by Bernhard Berenson as 'impersonal' (1960, 136). Not a few critics have noted the cool, detached, 'impersonal' approach of Piero's art. R. Vischer calls Piero a 'realist': 'above all he wishes to be a realist, to draw in a realist manner'.[2] A. Stokes regards Piero as the first Cubist, a common view of Piero;[3] while for Kenneth Clark, Piero was a fully 'classic artist'.[4] In his *Tratto della Nabilta della Pittura*, Alberti called Piero 'the greatest geometrician of his age.'[5] F.M. Godfrey was equally breathless,

1 Like the art of Ancient Greece, Piero della Francesca's paintings rejoice in eternal brilliance, an architectonic precision, and a 'Classical' sense of proportion and harmony. In Piero's epoch, perspective, proportion and geometry attained a fetishistic quality.

2 R. Vischer: *Luca Signorelli and the Italian Renaissance*, 1879.

3 A. Stokes: *The Stones of Rimini*, 1929.

4 Kenneth Clark: *Piero della Francesca*, Phaidon, 1969.

5 Alberti: *Tratto della Nabilta della Pittura*, 1585.

claiming that '[n]ever before has art blended so nobly with a mathematical purity of space-construction'.[6] Other art critics, though, have not been so convinced of Piero's talents. Lawrence Wright pointed out that 'his geometry is by our standards involved and laborious.[7]

MICHELANGELO MERISI DA CARAVAGGIO.

Of the many Renaissance and post-Renaissance painters, including those of the Baroque and Mannerist eras, the art of Michelangelo Merisi da Caravaggio (1573-1610) stands out as having marked affinities with the æsthetics of Pier Paolo Pasolini. Not, in contrast to the Early Renaissance artists, in the sense of space and visuals, but in subject matter, and in a tragic view of life. And Carvaggio's own life: he was a homosexual with a penchant for the rough trade of the streets (which he famously painted); his career was filled with controversy (and occasional violence); he had a troubled relationship with the authorities; he lived much of the time, like Pasolini, in Roma; and he died, like Pasolini, in mysterious circumstances, way before his time. Caravaggio is a Pasolinian personality, ideal for the subject of a biopic (altho' Pasolini much preferred the Early Italian Renaissance artists, like Masaccio and Giotto, to the Mannerists and Baroque artists).[8]

6 F.M. Godfrey: *A Student's Guide to Italian Paintings 1250-1800*, Alec Tiranti 1965, 88.
7 Lawrence Wright: *Perspective in Perspective*, Routledge 1983, 75.
8 The Pasolinian devotee, Derek Jarman, produced a very disappointing biographical movie about Caravaggio in the 1980s.

Piero, Madonna del Parto

Giotto, The Dream of St Gregory, The Legend of St Francis

Michelangelo da Caravaggio, The Lute Player, Hermitage Museum

FEDERICO FELLINI:

SATYRICON

INTRO.

Satyricon (a.k.a. *Fellini-Satyricon,* 1969) was the maestro's interpretation of Petronius's incomplete account of Ancient Roman life during the reign of the Emperor Nero.[1] Gaius Petronius Arbiter (AD 27-66) wrote the *Satyricon* between 54 and 68 AD. At times, it seems that in *Satyricon,* Fellini is doing his own version of the ancient world movies of Pier Paolo Pasolini. (By 1969, the year of *Satyricon*, Pasolini had already made *Oedipus Rex* and *The Gospel According To Matthew*, and was embarking upon *Medea*). Many in the crew worked on Pasolini's films as well as Fellini's, including *Satyricon.*

THE SCRIPT.

Federico Fellini knew the *Satyricon* from school, and had considered adapting it a number of times. During the war, in 1942, a musical for Aldo Fabrizi was put forward by Marcello Marchesi.[2] In 1966 Fellini planned a *Satyricon* with Claudia Cardinale and Alberto

---

1 I first encountered Federico Fellini's movies at Bournemouth film school – we had 16mm prints shown as part of our film history pro-gramme. We saw *8 1/2* and *Satyricon* (on March 23, 1983). I remember that Chris Fassnidge, our tutor, hired a special anamorphic lens to attach to the 16mm projector for *Satyricon* and the effect was ravishing – a really, *really* wide cinemascope image – far wider than your usual widescreen image. A mind-boggling film
2 J. Baxter, 1993, 239.

Sordi to star, for producer Franco Cristaldi. The script (apparently running to 500 pages) was co-written with Bernardino Zapponi (negating the common view that Fellini worked without scripts!).

Written in Ancient Rome during the era of Emperor Nero, the *Satyricon* is an incomplete text. It allowed Federico Fellini and Bernardino Zapponi the latitude to veer off in all sorts of directions. Which Fellini would've done anyway. For Fellini, the original source material was merely a starting-point for what he and his team really wanted to do (genius film directors such as Orson Welles and Hayao Miyazaki feel exactly the same). But no one has accused Fellini of taking liberties with source material – or, if they have, they've missed the point. For Fellini, as for Welles and Miyazaki, the source work is part of the collaboration, but isn't slavishly adhered to. You begin with a novel or a play or a musical or a *manga*, but you don't end there. You go somewhere. That's part of the point of making the movie in the first place.

So *Satyricon* was never going to be a 'faithful' adaptation of Petronius' *Satyricon.* (Impossible on numerous levels anyway).

THE PRODUCTION.

The spending rose above the agreed budget (as often on a Federico Fellini shoot): United Artists were the backers of *Satyricon*, but the production spent more than the amount agreed, and the budget climbed to $4 million (it would've been far, far more in the U.S.A.). At the time, United Artists was known as one of the more adventurous of the Hollywood studios, and backed some of the more eccentric or left-of-centre productions. U.A. was investing, like other North American studios in the 1960s, in European productions. It was U.A. who persuaded producer Alberto Grimaldi (also Pier Paolo Pasolini's producer), Federico Fellini and the team to consider making *Satyricon* for the youth market (casting young actors in the lead roles was part of that strategy). Although one can imagine segments of a student or intellectual audience embracing *Satyricon* (primarily in metropolitan areas), it would probably be too Out There for the general youth market in the U.S.A. (would cinema-goers in suburban Iowa go for gay marriage scenes in 1969?). Today it seems more niche and eccentric than ever.

Box office in Japan was strongest for *Satyricon*: it stayed in theatres for 4 years (it's easy to see why the Japanese would love it!). In Italy, it grossed about $3m, and about $8m globally.

HISTORY.

There was plenty of historical authenticity in *Satyricon* (Federico Fellini and his team had researched the period of the film meticulously), including a theatrical mime performed by Vernacchio, the museum with its Pompeian frescoes (a fascination with Roman frescoes would resurface in Fellini's later works, such as the scene in *Roma*), storytelling sequences (such as the Widow of Ephesus), many of the costumes and hairstyles, Giton's song (in Pythagorean fourths and fifths), the calf sacrifice, the Carthaginian infanticides, Trimalchio's first beard,[3] the colossal statues, the feast at Trimalchio's villa,[4] and so on. The attention to detail resulted in some memorable sequences, such as the elaborate feast with its dishes of thrush tongues, sow's udders, pheasant brains, Lucanian sausages and chicken, stuffed into a pig's carcass.

For some critics, the filmmakers' attention to detail and historical accuracy was compromised by the more extravagant aspects, such as the acting, the gestures, or the settings. Jon Solomon praised *Satyricon*, remarking in *The Ancient World In the Cinema* that

these details go beyond scholarly authenticity into

3 Bizarrely, Trimalchio at his feast produces the first beard he grew for the delectation of his dinner guests. He waxes lyrical about his youth, when he grew the beard.
4 At the feast, the poet Eumolpo (Salvo Randone) hangs out with Encolpio, and has a loud dispute with host Trimalchio over the authorship of some verses the patriarch recites, which Eumolpo claims are from Lucretius.

visual genius… Some pieces of the film may belong in a classroom, some pieces may belong in an asylum, and some may belong in the bathroom, but the entire creation ultimately results in a revitalized cinematic impression of the spirit of the ancient world. (280)

Federico Fellini explained his approach to the ancient world of *Satyricon* by saying that:

These characters were personalities which seem to have breathed another air, eaten other foods. They behaved differently because they *are* different.

CASTING.

Initially, Federico Fellini wanted to cast big names in his Ancient Roman epic: Danny Kaye, Groucho Marx, Richard Burton, Marlon Brando, Liz Taylor, Jerry Lewis, Lee Marvin, Brigitte Bardot, Peter O'Toole, and the Beatles. (Not so crazy an idea – the 1960s, and especially the late 1960s, were a prime period for all-star movies: *Casino Royale, It's a Mad Mad Mad Mad World, Candy, The Magic Christian* and *Those Daring Young Men In Their Jaunty Jalopies.* Some of which were incredibly *bad*).

Needless to say, Groucho Marx, Mae West, Boris Karloff and Danny Kaye, among others, turned Federico Fellini down, and Fellini's choice for the young leads, Terence Stamp and Pierre Clémenti, proved too expensive.[5] So the maestro and the producers went the other route: a cast of total unknowns. From the production of *Hair* on Broadway the casting directors found Hiram Keller to play Ascylto; British unknown Max Born (then seventeen), a small, pale and androgynous-looking Chelsea hippy, was cast as Giton; Martin Potter (then 24), another Brit, was cast as

5 The unknown actors in the lead roles were certainly cheaper than Stamp or Clémenti: Potter was paid $7,500 and Keller was paid $10,000. Considering the amount of screen time that Potter has, the number of scenes he's in, and the amount of tough, physical acting he has to, that $7,500 is the cheapest fee any actor's been paid in a big movie like this! (Halfway he should've gone to the producers and demanded lots more $$$$).

Encolpio, in some ways the main character of *Satyricon*. A pity – the film could've used some star power among the lead roles.

Casting took place in London, Rome, Paris and New York for the young lead roles, for Encolpio, Giton and Ascylto. It took a while to find them. For a Federico Fellini movie, casting directors would put open calls and receive 100s of actors and wannabes. In September, 1968, 250 actors showed up to a call for beautiful boys. There were always plenty of actors willing to audition for a Fellini movie, but sometimes the maestro, though spoilt for choice, would take a long time selecting his performers.

Roman restaurant owner Mario Romagnoli was cast in the key role of Trimalchio (but Federico Fellini preferred Boris Karloff, Gert Frobe and Aldo Fabrizi). The nymphomaniac and lover of his wife Fortunata (Magali Noël) was Tryphaena (Capucine). Veteran French actor Alain Cuny played the OTT pirate Lidas, complete with false eye. Also in the cast were Salvo Randone, Danika La Loggia, Giuseppe Sanvitale, Genius, Lucia Bosé, Joseph Wheeler, Hylette Adolphe, Gordon Mitchell, George Eastman, Marcello Di Falco, Elisa Mainardi and Fanfulla.

SATYRICON AS AN ANCIENT WORLD MOVIE.

Satyricon is also the response of Federico Fellini and his team to the huge glut of Ancient Roman and Egyptian and Greek and Biblical movies which had flourished from the early 1950s onwards. And many of them were filmed in Italy, of course, including the biggest movie of them all, and one of the largest productions ever mounted, *Cleopatra* (no doubt many of the team at Cinecittà for *Satyricon* had worked on 20th Century Fox's colossal Liz Taylor epic movie. A production of that scale would hire absolutely every-body within 100 miles of Rome).

Satyricon is as if Federico Fellini and his team had decided to out-do all of those Biblical and sword 'n' sandal flicks. As if they had thought, OK, *caro mio,* you want a slave ship scenes *à la Ben-Hur*? We'll give you that – but like you ain't never seen before! (And so there are slaves chained to oars, and wrestling matches, and mutinies, all the rest, but also an amazing wedding scene, where Lichas marries Encolpio.)

OK, you want to see an Ancient Roman feast, just like-a mamma used to make, eh? You got it: and out comes a lengthy, incredibly detailed and extraordinarily over-the-top Ancient Roman feast.

OK, so you want a brothel scene? Federico Fellini and his team give you the longest, the most bizarre and and the most extravagant bordello sequence in cinema.

THE STORY.

The narrative of *Satyricon* follows Giton[7] (Max Born), Encolpio (Martin Potter) and Ascylto (Hiram Keller) on a journey through the Ancient Roman world (note that in this very *Italian* of movies, some of the principal roles were taken by Brits. But dubbed by Italians,[8] of course). Like many of the movies directed by Federico Fellini, *Satyricon* is structured in lengthy self-contained episodes or sequences, rather than the usual movie, which comprises short scenes linked thru cause and effect, with rising action, foreshadowing and pay offs, leading to a climax and resolution. Thus, following the opening scenes in the Baths, there is the episode in the brothel in Suburra, Trimalchio's grand feast, the Lichas pirate ship sequence, and so on.

Satyricon is a romp, a riot of incidents, faces, costumes and bawdy humour. There are many stand-out sequences, each one trying to top the former: Trimalchio's feast, Vernacchio's theatre, the audience

6 The naval scenes were filmed at Fregene and Ponza island.
7 Part-way thru *Fellini-Satyricon*, pretty boy Giton disappears from the story – literally, when he's taken away by the force that captures Lipas's pirate ship (and decapitates the pirate). So in the second half of *Satyricon*, it's Encolpio and Ascylto who take centre stage.
8 Among the voice actors, Gianni Giuliano dubbed Martin Potter, Antonio Casagrande dubbed Hiram Keller, Carlo Croccolo dubbed Fanfulla, Corrado Gaipa dubbed Mario Romagnoli, Aldo Giuffrè dubbed Giuseppe Sanvitale, Oreste Lionello dubbed Genius, Benita Martini dubbed Capucine, Rita Savagnone dubbed Magali Noël and Renato Turi dubbed Salvo Randone.

with the hermaphrodite beside the pool, the brothel in Suburra, Lichas's giant, steel-clad ships, and Encolpio meeting the minotaur in a labyrinth. There is so much going on in *Satyricon*, the screen's often full to bursting with characters and events. All sorts of details strike the viewer, occurring in off-centre areas of the widescreen: two hulks in the whorehouse knocking bricks together, or the passive faces turned towards the camera during the feast,[9] or the odd 'ack-ack' cries of the crowd when Encolpio battles with the minotaur.

Thus, the story and the characters are but one ingredient in this incredibly spectacular movie. You can follow the story and characters in *Satyricon* if you wish, but make sure you don't miss everything else that's going on. *Satyricon* is a movie that demands repeated viewings, because the screen is teaming with incidents and colours. *Satyricon* is not a film to get frustrated by if you can't follow the story and the characters: don't worry, just go along for the ride. Don't worry, either, if you can't follow the dialogue (or the subtitles), it really doesn't matter too much: you can always come back and catch that element of the 1969 movie.

Some critics attacked *Satyricon* for its historical inaccuracies – *completely missing the point*. Did it matter that the pirate Lichas's ships were inaccurate and impractical? No! Did it matter that they seemed much bigger on the inside than on the outside? No! (All ships are like that in movies!) Did it matter that swimming pools didn't exist? No!

This is *Federico Fellini movie*, by Jupiter! This is what Fellini does for a living! If you crave historical accuracy (from a movie? Why? It's a *movie*!), go to a television documentary or a history book (or, even better, make your own movie!). There's no promise from the filmmakers that they're going to deliver a 'historically accurate' movie, and why the hell should they anyway?! Why is historical authenticity so important?

---

9 These images are framed like Renaissance paintings, where one of the crowd faces the viewer and locks them with a steady gaze. It's a brilliant touch.

DESIGN, STYLE AND LOOK.

With *Satyricon*, Federico Fellini and his team seemed to be aiming to make the most extravagant film possible, to out-do the Ancient Roman and Biblical epics of the 1950s and early 1960s, to counter Hollywood's version of Ancient Rome with their own fantastical, overblown vision (and possibly to take on the ancient world films of Pier Paolo Pasolini). In *Satyricon*, Fellini and an army of phenomenally talented filmmakers created a world of grotesques, midgets, giants, prostitutes, pimps, soldiers, slobs, gluttons, actors, and so on. *Satyricon* contains more weird characters, more outlandish sets, more strange make-up, more bizarre gestures, more unusual faces and actors, more masks, and more crazy costumes than most pictures (enough for several carnivals, circuses and festivals – there must've been quite a good trade in selling off costumes and props from Fellini's movies!). You have to go *a long way* find a production as *genuinely* strange and over-the-top and lavish.

In *Satyricon*, Federico Fellini and his collaborators at Cinecittà (Danilo Donati, Giuseppe Rotunno, Nina Rota *et al*) were at their most extreme, really going to town on settings, production design, costumes, make-up, hair, lighting, and the amazing use of primary colours (Donati must take a good deal of the credit, for his fabulous sets, and the inventive combinations of costume and make-up arae outstanding. Donati is one of the co-authors of *Satyricon*).

You can only produce this kind of movie with the entire resources of a fully equipped movie studio and a really dedicated team of filmmakers and workers (as filmmakers discover to their dismay when they leave studios and try to do this kind of thing independently). This sort of movie demands that the production crew go all out, and hold nothing back. It's an exhausting process, and you've got to throw yourself into it whole-heartedly. The shooting schedule of *Satyricon*, for instance, wound on for 26 weeks. And that doesn't include the months of pre-production work and post-production work (and *Casanova* (1976) was even longer).

As a make-up job alone, *Satyricon* is so impressive (Rino Carboni and Luciano Vito were the make-up and hair artists). It is grand opera make-up, high theatre make-up, circus and clown make-up, and no-holds-barred make-up. Blue faces, green faces, hollowed-out eye sockets, kohled eyes, henna on the hands and faces, and partial nudity everywhere. Betsy Langman was an amateur actor from the U.S.A. who was part of the scenes at the lake where Trimalchio brings coterie of guests: she described the make-up process, which began at dawn:

> the make-up was used to extend or exaggerate the features of the actors. The fat were made fatter, the thin thinner, the bald balder, long noses were made longer, big eyes bigger, wide mouths wider. Faces were coloured red, blue, green and yellow, some-times simply to match a dress, sometimes to drama-tise a characterisation – like the sick yellow-grey of the old men or the pale, translucent ivory of the young.[10]

You know those Hollywood film directors which are sometimes thought of as masters of creating weird or unusual cinema? David Lynch, Terry Gilliam, Tim Burton, John Carpenter, Peter Jackson, Tobe Hooper, Clive Barker *et al*? Yeah, maybe. Sorta. But go and look at *Satyricon*. *That's* weird. (It's weirder partly because Federico Fellini *really* doesn't care).

❖

The music (by Nino Rota) was very unusual in *Satyricon*, which's in keeping with the out-thereness of the 1969 movie. Much of the music was existing recorded music, taken from ethnic sources, which Rota and his team adapted and treated in the studio. African and Oriental music was used, and sometimes radically altered. The score for *Satyricon* was thus a world away from the usual ancient world movie score: no trilling

---

10 In J. Baxter, 1993, 249.

choirs here, no sweeps of strings for the good guys or brassy, percussive cues for the villains (but there *were* no heroes vs. heavies in this movie, no good vs. evil, no characters who weren't ambiguous in their allegiances and goals).

A GAY ROMP.

At the heart of *Satyricon* is a trio of male lovers, an erotic triangle that is unabashedly homosexual. Encolpio and Ascylto, two athletic, macho but also sensitive guys in their early twenties fight over the teenage Giton, who's the classic pretty boy of homosexual fantasies.[11] Putting three homosexual youths at the heart of an ancient world epic movie is unusual enough (not even Pier Paolo Pasolini did that), especially one as extravagant and costly as this. Making them play most of the movie semi-naked (and sometimes only in loincloths), is very rare. Having them so physically intimate with each other, and also expressing their love with dialogue and caresses, is even rarer.

And *Satyricon* goes much further in depicting many facets of sexuality than many movies, even those that are promoted as 'daring' or 'edgy' or 'risky'. *Satyricon* doesn't simply illustrate scenes of homosexuality and lesbianism, it also incorporates plenty of the unconventional aspects of sexual practice found in Ancient Rome. And the variety of *bodies* on display is very striking: this is a movie in love with very fat, very tall, very small, very ugly, very old, very young, and very strange people.

This has become a cliché of Federico Fellini's cinema, of course: few filmmakers celebrate humanity in so many of its more unusual varieties, including amputees. For some it's probably a freakshow, a human zoo. Many would find it offensive and exploitative. But it's clear that the filmmakers don't condemn the more unusual people, or laugh at them. Of course Federico Fellini and his team are well aware of the shock value

11 And with his black kohled eyes and short hair, is reminiscent of British pop musician Marc Almond of Soft Cell of 'Tainted Love' fame.

and the entertainment value of bringing on people with no limbs, who have to be carried by others. It's like the Freak Show in the seedier parts of town, or near the boardwalk, where double-headed chickens or the World's Smallest Woman are advertized. It's part of the Fellinian Circus of Life.

Even so, in amongst all of the craziness and pervy goings-on, there are three relatively regular guys at the centre of *Satyricon*, and Enculpio and Asclyto are attractive men, with trim bodies, perpetually covered in sweat (like everyone in *Satyricon* – it does seem to be a mandatory ingredient of ancient world epics, having actors sprayed with water b4 every take).

However, they are not particularly appealing people at times – they are thieves, and criminals, and flawed. Among their worst acts is to kill the old guys guarding the hermaphrodite and steal the demi-god, hoping for a decent ransom. They are not heroes, but anti-heroes (but probably only anti-heroes would work dramatically in a narrative like *Satyricon*).

✧

Few movies are as self-consciously and exaggeratedly camp as *Satyricon* (ultra-camp movies might include *Barbarella,* Kenneth Anger's Crowleyan indie films, and of course the films of John Waters and Ken Russell). But *Satyricon* gives any of the camp classic movies a run for their money. Federico Fellini might've been heterosexual, but that never stopped him (as with Ken Russell) from delivering incredibly heightened, pan-sexual movies.

Rex Reed enthused over *Satyricon*'s

explosion of madness and perversion, designed
like grand opera of the absurd – a homosexual
odyssey in which the creatures of Fellini's mind
writhe like sequined snakes towards some
surrealistic damnation of the soul.

THE BROTHEL SCENE.

The Suburra brothel scene is a masterpiece of cinema on its own. It involves every single weird-looking extra in Rome and for 200 miles (no, 1,500 miles!) in every direction. Pippo Spoletini was the casting director charged with discovering the freakiest extras, and he earned every Lire of his fee.

It is a brothel scene like no other in cinema, utterly beyond belief. It is built in sets comprising sub-terranean tunnels and rooms in Cinecittà's largest sound stages (Cinecittà had among the biggest studios in Europe).

Narratively, Ascylto and Encolpio are wandering around, like Dante and his guide Virgil in the *Divine Comedy*, but the plot is the least significant element in the brothel sequence. Their walking movement as they visit the brothel is the merest excuse for lengthy tracking shots past all of the craziness that the film-makers have assembled in room after room.

The sets, the decor, the colours, the textures, the lighting, the costumes, the make-up, the hair, the props, the compositions, the timing and rhythm of the shots and the editing, the variety of body shapes, the nudity, and the gestures, all combine in one of Federico Fellini's grandest hallucinatory evocations of carnival and madness.

THE SLAVE SHIP.

A send-up of *Ben-Hur, Spartacus, Hercules* and every ancient world movie where the heroes're captured and sold as slaves to a tyrant and put to the oar in a slave ship, the central episode of *Satyricon* is truly bizarre. Lichas the pirate (Alain Cuny) is a predatory homosexual whose hobby is wrestling semi-naked, taking on his slaves, killing them when he wins. The hapless anti-hero Encolpio is of course chosen to fight, and does so; luckily, Lidas falls for him, and decides he's found his future husband.

Then follows the extreme scene of a wedding on the deck of Lidas' pirate vessel in the open sea, with Lidas as the bride, in a veil. Encolpio is his groom, carrying off Lidas (imagine Kirk Douglas or Burt Lancaster playing Encolpio, having a gay marriage with some Hollywood wannabe star!).

Fellini Satyricon (1969).

SERGIO CITTI: TWO FILMS:

OSTIA AND *STORIE SCELLERATE*

OSTIA AND *BAWDY TALES*

OSTIA

Ostia (1970) was produced by Anna Maria Chretien and Alvaro Mancori, written by Sergio Citti and Pier Paolo Pasolini, with music by Francesco De Masi, Mario Mancini was DP, eds.: Nino Baragli and Carlo Reali, prod. des. by Claudio Giambanco, sound by Angelo Spadoni, costumes and set dec. by Mario Ambrosino. The cast included: Laurent Terzieff,[1] Franco Citti, Anita Sanders, Lamberto Maggiorani, Celestino Compagnoni, Nino Davoli, Lily Tirinnanzi, and Settimio Picone. Released Mch 11, 1970. 103 minutes.

Ostia emerges with numerous links to Pier Paolo Pasolini, including many in the crew and the cast, and themes such as the focus on a group of young men, and the suburban, working class, Italian *milieu*. Sergio Citti, tho', steps out from the shadow that Pasolini casts over *Ostia* as a director: despite its many Pasolinian ingredients, *Ostia* is not a Pasolini film. The opening scenes appear Pasolinian at first – the discovery of a young woman (Monica – Anita Sanders) in the

1 He was dubbed by Sergio Citti.

countryside – but soon they become something else. The rhythms and pacing of *Ostia*, for instance, are not Pasolinian, nor is the staging. Much of the movie, too, is filmed in the studio, and focusses on two central characters (it is partly a chamber piece, and a duologue). If Pasolini had taken on *Ostia*, he would've moved his characters out and about much more.

Ostia is one of those movies in which nothing seems to happen, in which characters loaf about, and the narrative seems freewheeling. Like: the trio visits the beach... like: Monica goes for a swim... like: the lads make up a story of their childhood which features venal, drunken parents... like: Monica fascinates Rabbino and Bandiera; she's a ray of light or life in their seemingly humdrum lives...

Ostia is not afraid to contemplate some troubling issues, such as attempted rape and incest (centred around the character of Monica). Homosexuality is evoked numerous times in *Ostia*, from the opening scene, where Rabbino and Bandiera wait downstairs, and get drunk, while Fiorino and the other lads are upstairs fooling around with the foundling, to scenes such as some crossdressing (where Monica puts wigs and make-up on the youths).

The influence of Pier Paolo Pasolini is felt in the final reels of *Ostia*, which move into a more mythological, spiritual realm: the lads visit the beach with Monica for a second time, and there's another trip out in a rowing boat. At night, around an open fire, things get ugly when Bandiera discovers Rabbino attempting to make love with Monica, and lays into him (both have fallen for Monica by now). Rabbino retaliates a little too fiercely with a tree branch, and kills Bandiera.

The ending of *Ostia* is a little too contrived and melodramatic, in terms of what happens amongst the characters. More intriguing is the decision to play all of it without dialogue, and accompanied by religious, choral music (the sort of music that Pier Paolo Pasolini puts in many of his films). The music, plus the images of the calm ocean, and Rabbino staring into the void as he takes Bandiera's corpse out in the boat and dumps it over the side, are haunting.

There is also a curiously effective piece of montage (by editors Baragli and Reali) which features visitors to the beach putting up parasols and tables, preparing for a day at the seaside... and Rabbino is sitting next to the cadaver of Bandiera who might be asleep beside him, so no one notices that he's dead.[2]

BAWDY TALES/ STORIE SCELLERATE

Bawdy Tales (*Storie scellerate*, 1973) is about the closest thing to a Pier Paolo Pasolini movie without being directed by the Master. With Sergio Citti, Pasolini is credited with the story and the script, and the movie was made with many of the same key personnel behind and in front of the camera as Pasolini's movies: Grimaldi (pr.), Ferretti (prod. des.), Donati (cost.), Delli Colli (DP), Baragli (ed.), etc, among the crew, and in the cast: Davoli, Citti, Genovese, Garofolo, etc. Released Oct 12, 1973. 93 mins.

Thus, *Bawdy Tales* is a good example to use as an exploration of just what a director is or does: the conception of *Bawdy Tales,* the way it's filmed, the genre (historical), the technical aspects, the actors and the crew – they're all Pasolinian.

Indeed, Sergio Citti and Pier Paolo Pasolini had worked together so many times, since the mid-1950s, they could've swopped roles (Pasolini working as 1st A.D. for Citti as director, for instance), and directed each other's scripts.

With a script co-written by Pier Paolo Pasolini, *Bawdy Tales* displays all of the familiar Pasolinian touches. One of the most obvious ones is the structure of *Bawdy Tales:* it's based around storytelling, with

2 A death at Ostia has sad links to Pasolini's own demise.

Ninetto Davoli and Franco Citti as two small-time crooks who tell each other stories (the 'bawdy tales' of the title).[3]

Bawdy Tales has many affinities with the 'trilogy of life' movies, including a similar sort of approach, and some of the same cast (Franco Citti, Ninetto Davoli, Elisabetta Genovese, etc).

Bawdy Tales presents a colourful world of lovers, cuckolded husbands, horny priests and greedy thieves. Indeed, the title may be *Bawdy Tales*,[4] but there is as much here about ruffians and crime. Indeed, the frame story, of Davoli and Citti, has them murdering a guy on their travels (for his loot), and finding themselves caught and imprisoned. Even in jail, they continue to tell tales, and are laughing about their latest yarn on the scaffold, as they're hung.

Bawdy Tales displays the high art aspects of Pier Paolo Pasolini's cinema – the historical settings, the costumes, the Church, the clergy, religion, etc, as well as the crudity, the nudity, the erotica, the groups of virile youths, etc.

Costume designer Danilo Donati makes perhaps his worst selection in *Bawdy Tales* when he puts all of the guys in flares. All movies are about and reflect the time of their production, but the early 1970s sees flared pants, big collars, long hair and other aspects of clothing which would look great in a disco in Rome (but haven't aged well).

In the first story of *Bawdy Tales,* we are in Rome *circa* 1800, with a clichéd yarn about cuckolded husbands and their lusty wives. So Caterina di Ronciglione (Nicoletta Machiavelli) has a weak, submissive, older, spoilt husband, Duca di Ronciglione (Silvano Gatti), and fancies something younger and more energetic. While he sleeps, she slips away for nighttime dalliances. In a later sequence, she takes on a

---

3 The thieves meet in a classic, Pasolinian manner – as they hurry away to find somewhere to shit.

4 The relationships are heterosexual in *Bawdy Tales*, but Citti and Pasolini manage to squeeze in a river full of naked boys bathing (completely gratuitous).

whole bunch of *ragazzi* (one of whom is played by Ettore Garofolo, the son in *Mamma Roma*). Fellatio leads to group sex (for an erotic comedy, *Bawdy Tales* is very coy, and cuts away from the deeds).

The alluring Elisabetta Genovese (with her kilowatt smile, seen in *The Arabian Nights* and *The Canterbury Tales*) plays Bertolina, another bored wife in the first story; she has an affair with the local priest, much to her husband Nicolino's (Enzo Petriglia) dismay.

Other stories in *Bawdy Tales* include a thief who frames a priest with the promise of a woman, who then robs him; a long tale (which we return to) of the clergy; another yarn about a betrayed husband, etc.

Bawdy Tales features one of the silliest things that Pier Paolo Pasolini and Sergio Citti cooked up together as scriptwriters: the Chopping Of The Weiner. Yes, the first bawdy tale in *Bawdy Tales* has both wives receiving their punishment. The husband and his pal, armed with knives, burst in upon Bertolina and the priest: Bertolina is stabbed, and dies; then the youths force the priest to cut off his penis. Meanwhile, the furious Duca di Ronciglione commands his wife to undress at home, then drags her down to the basement, hurling her into a room and locking it. And then, before a window overlooking the cell, he slices off his own member in front of his wife, collapsing to the ground in agony.

It's remarkable, perhaps, how unremarkable *Bawdy Tales* is (despite scenes such as weiner removal). The concept and the narrative is wholly clichéd (tho' still sort of new in 1973, in the degree of sexual explicitness). And the story progresses exactly how you'd expect. The comedy, sadly, is rather routine and again suffers from its difficulty in traversing national/ cultural borders.[5]

---

5 Consider how funny Woody Allen's movies were of this time, which also took on historical genres: *Love and Death* and the first skit in *Everything You Wanted To Know About Sex*. An unfair comparison, of course – because Allen is a comic genius, and the pacing is about 2 million miles-an-hour faster than *Bawdy Tales*.

Ostia (1970).

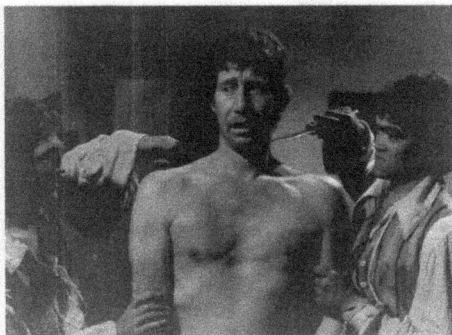

Bawdy Tales (1973)

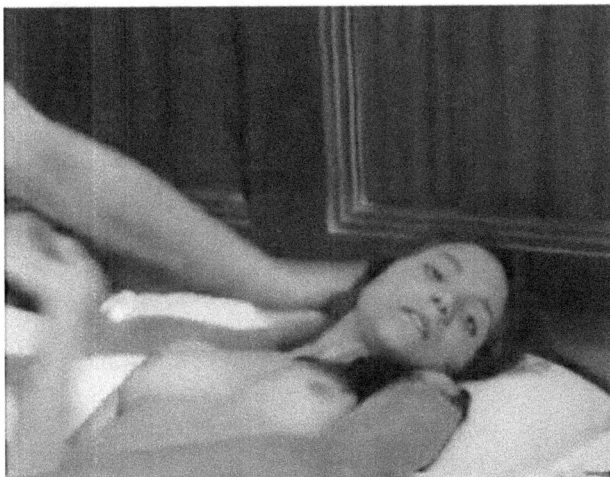

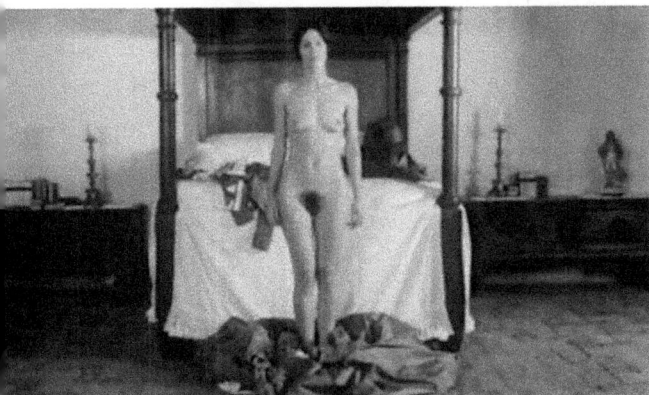

FILMOGRAPHY

IL DECAMERONE

THE DECAMERON

Released: Dec 12, 1971. 106 mins.

CAST

Franco Citti – Ciappelletto
Ninetto Davoli – Andreuccio of Perugia
Jovan Jovanovic – Rustico
Vincenzo Amato – Masetto of Lamporecchio
Angela Luce – Peronella
Giuseppe Zigaina – Monk
Pier Paolo Pasolini – Allievo di Giotto
Vincenzo Ferrigno – Giannello
Guido Alberti – Musciatto, wealthy merchant
Vittorio Vittori – Don Giovanni
Gianni Rizzo – Father Superior
Patrizia De Clara – Nun
Monique van Vooren – Queen of Skulls
Enzo Spitaleri – Monk
Luciano Telli – Monk
Maria Gabriella Maione
Vincenzo Cristo
Giorgio Iovine
Salvatore Bilardo
Luigi Seraponte
Antonio Diddio
Mirella Catanesi
Vincenzo De Luca

Erminio Nazzaro
Giovanni Filidoro
Lino Crispo
Alfredo Sivoli
Giacomo Rizzo
E. Jannotta Carrino
Adriana Donnorso
E. Maria De Juliis
Guido Mannari
Michele Di Matteo
Giani Esposito
Giovanni Scagliola
Giovanni Davoli
Annie Marguerite Latroye
Gerhard Exel
Wolfgang Hillinger
Franco Marletta
Vittorio Fanfoni
Detlef Uhle
Elisabetta Genovese – Caterina
Silvana Mangano – the Madonna
Patrizia Capparelli – Alibech
Giuseppe Arrigio – Lorenzo
Lucio Amatelli
Giuliano Fratello

CREW

Produced – Alberto Grimaldi
Franco Rossellini – executive producer
Directed – Pier Paolo Pasolini
Script – Pier Paolo Pasolini
Original Music – Ennio Morricone
Cinematography – Tonino Delli Colli
Film Editing – Nino Baragli, Tatiana Casini Morigi
Casting – Alberto De Stefanis
Art Direction – Dante Ferretti
Set Decoration – Andrea Fantacci
Costume Design – Danilo Donati
Iole Cecchini – hair stylist
Alessandro Jacoponi – makeup artist
Mario Di Biase – production manager
Sergio Galiano – production supervisor
Umberto Angelucci – assistant director
Sergio Citti – assistant director
Paolo Andrea Mettel – assistant director
Carlo Agate – assistant art director
Italo Tomassi – set designer
Mario Morigi – sound mixer
Pietro Spadoni – sound
Gianni D'Amico – assistant sound mixer
Giovanni Ciarlo – camera operator

Giuseppe Fornari – assistant camera
Alessio Gelsini Torresi – assistant camera
Carlo Tafani – assistant camera
Mario Tursi – still photographer
Piero Cicoletti – wardrobe assistant
Anita Cacciolati – assistant editor
Enzo Ocone – supervising editor
Beatrice Banfi – continuity
Vittorio Bucci – production assistant
Giuseppe Anatrelli – voice dubbing
Eugene Rizzo – unit publicist

I RACCONTI DI CANTERBURY

THE CANTERBURY TALES

Released: Sept 2, 1972 (Italy). 122 mins.

CAST

Hugh Griffith – Sir January
Laura Betti – the Wife from Bath
Ninetto Davoli – Perkin
Franco Citti – the Devil
Josephine Chaplin – May
Alan Webb – Old Man
Pier Paolo Pasolini – Geoffrey Chaucer
J.P. Van Dyne – the Cook
Vernon Dobtcheff – the Franklin
Adrian Street – Fighter
O.T. – Chief Witch-Hunter
Derek Deadman – he Pardoner
Nicholas Smith – Friar
George Bethell Datch – Host of the Tabard
Dan Thomas – Nicholas
Michael Balfour – John the carpenter
Jenny Runacre – Alison
Peter Cain – Absalom
Daniele Buckler – Witch Hunter (as Daniel Buckler)
John Francis Lane – Greedy friar
Settimo Castagna – Angel
Judy Stewart-Murray – Alice
Tom Baker – Jenkin
Oscar Fochetti – Damian
Willoughby Goddard – Placebo
Peter Stephens – Justinus
Giuseppe Arrigio – Pluto
Elisabetta Genovese – Prosperine
Gordon King – Chancellor
Patrick Duffett – Alan
Eamann Howell – John

Tiziano Longo – Simkin the Miller
Eileen King – Simkin's wife
Heather Johnson – Molly
Robin Askwith – Rufus
Martin Whelar – Jack the Justice
John McLaren – Johnny the Grace
Edward Monteith – Dick the Sparrow
Kervin Breen
Franca Sciutto
Vittorio Fanfoni
Leonard S. Brooks – Businessman
Stephen Calcutt – the Groom
Charles De la Tour – Inn-keeper
Francis De Wolff – the Bride's father
Michael Derrek – Robin
Andrew Dymock – Bill
V. Edwards – the Old Woman
Dorothy Everall – Perkin's mother
Diana Fisher – the Bride
Chris Greener – Sir Elephant
Judo Al Hayes – Fighter
Terry Hooper – L'allodoliere
Robert Brook Howard – Vicar of the Monastery
Karl Howman – 1st homosexual lover
Philip Davis – 2nd homosexual lover
Athol Coats – Rich homosexual
Richard Hughes – Administrator
Laurie Inch – Mary
Charlotte Kell – the Prioress
Pinky Martin – the Nun
Alan McConnell – Master Gervaso
Norman McGlen – Perkin's father
Peter McGregor – the Merchant
Hugh McKenzie-Bailey – Thomas
Roderick McLeod – Knight's Attendant
Anthony Moore – the Spy
Ken Muggleston – Doctor
Patrick Newell – Prior
Ray Parks – Sergeant
Martin Philips – Martin
Selwyn Roberts – the Knight
Anita Sanders – Thomas' wife
Mary Stuart – Priest
Reg Stuart – 4th Husband
Steve Whitton – Youth Without Name

CREW

Produced – Alberto Grimaldi
Directed and written – Pier Paolo Pasolini
Original Music – Ennio Morricone
Cinematography – Tonino Delli Colli

Film Editing – Nino Baragli
Production Design – Dante Ferretti
Costume Design – Danilo Donati
Giancarlo De Leonardis – key hair stylist and wig maker
Otello Sisi – makeup artist
Ennio Onorati – production manager
Alessandro von Norman – production manager
Umberto Angelucci – assistant director
Sergio Citti – assistant director
Carlo Agati – assistant designer
Gianni D'Amico – sound mixer
Primimiano Muratore – sound
Luciano Anzellotti – special effects
Mimmo Cattarinich – still photographer
Maurizio Lucchini – assistant camera
Claudio Sabatini – assistant camera
Carlo Tafani – camera operator
Vanni Castellani – assistant costume designer
Stephen Bearman – colorist
Anita Cacciolati – assistant editor
Ugo De Rossi – assistant editor
Ennio Morricone – music advisor
Pier Paolo Pasolini – music supervisor
Beatrice Banfi – secretary
Adriano Magistretti – English production coordinator
Anthony Moore – production coordinator
Ken Muggleston – interior designer
Peter Shepherd – assistant to director
Franca Tasso – production secretary
Marco Bellocchio – voice dubbing: John Francis Lane
Eduardo De Filippo – voice dubbing: Alan Webb
Francesco Leonetti – voice dubbing: George Bethell Datch

IL FIORE DELLE MILLE E UNA NOTTE

THE ARABIAN NIGHTS

Released: June 20, 1974. 129 mins.

CAST

Ninetto Davoli – Aziz
Franco Citti – the Demon
Franco Merli – Nuredin
Tessa Bouché – Aziza
Ines Pellegrini – Zumurrud
Margareth Clémenti – Aziz's mother
Luigina Rocchi – Fatima
Alberto Argentino – Prince Shahzmah
Francesco Paolo Governale – Prince Tagi
Salvatore Sapienza – Prince Yunan
Zeudi Biasolo – Zeudi
Elisabetta Genovese – Munis
Abadit Ghidei – Princess Dunya
Salvatore Verdetti – Barsum
Fessazion Gherentiel – Berhane
Giana Idris – Giana
Barbara Grandi
Gioacchino Castellini
Christian Aligny
Jocelyne Munchenbach
Luigi Antonio Guerra
Jeanne Gauffin Mathieu
Francelise Noel
Franca Sciutto
Ali Abdulla
Mohamed Ali Zedi

CREW

Produced – Alberto Grimaldi
Directed and written – Pier Paolo Pasolini
Script – Dacia Maraini
Music – Ennio Morricone
Cinematography – Giuseppe Ruzzolini
Film Editing – Nino Baragli and Tatiana Casini Morigi
Production Design – Dante Ferretti
Costume Design – Danilo Donati
Iole Cecchini – hair stylist
Massimo Giustini – makeup artist
Giuseppe Banchelli – production supervisor
Mario Di Biase – production manager
Alessandro Mattei – production supervisor
Umberto Angelucci – assistant director
Peter Shepherd – assistant director
Fausto Ancillai – sound mixer
Luciano Welisch – sound
Angelo Pennoni – still photographer
Alessandro Ruzzolini – camera operator
Marcello Mastrogirolamo – assistant to camera operator
Claudio Sabatini – assistant camera
Stephen Bearman – colorist
Ugo De Rossi – assistant editor
Alfredo Menchini – assistant editor
Enzo Ocone – supervising editor
Beatrice Banfi – continuity
Carla Crovato – production secretary
Maurizio Forti – administrator
Daniele Tiberi – administrator
Nico Naldini – press

PIER PAOLO PASOLINI

FILMOGRAPHY
AND BIBLIOGRAPHY

FEATURE FILMS

Beggar (*Accattone*, 1961)
Mother Rome (*Mamma Roma*, 1962)
Love Meetings (a.k.a. *Lessons In Love*, *Comizi d'Amore*, 1964)
The Gospel According To Matthew (*Il Vangelo Secondo Matteo*, 1964)
The Hawks and the Sparrows (*Uccellacci e Uccellini*, 1966)
Oedipus Rex (*Edipo Re*, 1967)
Theorem (*Teorma*, 1968)
Pigsty (*Porcile*, 1969)
Medea (*Medea*, 1969)
The Decameron (*Il Decamerone*, 1971)
The Canterbury Tales (*I Racconti di Canterbury*, 1972)
The Arabian Nights (*Il Fiore Delle Mille e Una Notte*, 1974)
Salò, or The 120 Days of Sodom (*Salò, o le Centoventi Giornate di Sodoma*, 1975)

SHORT FILMS

The Anger (*La Rabbia*, 1963)
Curd Cheese (*La Ricotta*, episode in *RoGoPaG*, 1963)
The Earth Seen From the Moon (*La Terra Vista Dalla Luna*, episode in *The Witches = Le Streghe*, 1967)
What Are the Clouds? (*Che Cosa Sono le Nuvole?*, episode in *Caprice Italian Style = Capriccio all'Italiana*, 1968)
The Sequence of the Flower Field (*La Sequenza del Fiore di Carta*, episode in *Love and Anger = Vangelo '70/ Amore e Rabbia*, 1969)

DOCUMENTARIES

Location Hunting In Palestine (*Sopralluoghi in Palestina Per Il Vangelo secondo Matteo*, 1965)

Notes For a Film In India (*Appunti Per un Film Sull'India,* 1969)

Notes For a Garbage Novel (*Appunti Per un romanzo dell'immondizia,* 1970)

Notes Towards an African Oresteia (*Appunti Per un'Orestiade Africana,* 1970)

The Walls of Sana'a (*Le Mura di Sana'a,* 1971)

12 December 1972 (*12 Dicembre 1972,* 1972)

Pasolini and the Shape of the City (*Pasolini e la forma della città,* 1975)

SCRIPTS

The River Girl (1954)
Il Prigioniero della montagna (1955)
Manon: Finestra 2 (1956)
Nights of Cabiria (1956)
A Farewell To Arms (1957)
Marisa la Civetta (1957)
Giovani Mariti (1958)
Grigio (1958)
La Notte Brava (1959)
Marte di un Amico (1960)
From a Roman Balcony (1960)
Il Carro armato dell'8 settembre (1960)
I Bell'Antonio (1960)
La Lunga Notte del '43 (1960)
Accattone, F.M., Rome, 1960
La Ragazza In Vetrina (1961)
La Commare Secca (1962)
Mamma Roma, Rizzoli, Milan, 1962
Il Vangelo secondo Matteo, Garzanti, Milan, 1964
Uccellacci e uccellini, Garzanti, Milan, 1966
Oedipus Rex, Garzanti, Milan, 1967/ Lorrimer Publishing, 1984
Requiescant (1967, uncredited)
Il Ragazzo-motore (1967)
Theorem, Garzanti, Milan, 1968
Medea, Garzanti, Milan, 1970
Ostia, Garzanti, Milan, 1970
Storie Scellerate (1973)
Trilogia della vita, Cappelli, Bologna, 1975
San Paolo, Einaudi, Turin, 1977

WORKS AFTER PASOLINI'S DEATH

Laboratorio teatrale di Luca Ronconi (1977)
Mulheres... Mulheres (1981)
Calderon (1981)

Die Leiche murde nie gefunden (1985)
L'Altro enigma (1988)
Who Killed Pasolini? (1995)
Complicity (1995)
Il Pratone del casilino (1996)
Le Bassin de J.W. (1997)
Una Disperata vitalità (1999)
Orgia (2002)
Salò: Yesterday and Today (2002)
Pasolini prossimo nostro (2006)
'Na specie de cadavere lunghissimo (2006)
La Rabbia di Pasolini (2008)
Pilades (2016)

POETRY

Poesie e Casarsa, Libreroa Antiqua Mario Landi, Bologna, 1942
Poesie, Stamperia Primon, 1945
Diarii, 1945
I Pianti, Publicazioni dell-Academiuta, Casarsa, 1946
Dove la mia patria, Publicazioni dell-Academiuta, Casarsa, 1949
Poesia dialettale del Novecento, Guanda, Parma, 1952
Tal cour di un frut, Editizioni Friuli, Tricesimo, 1953/ 1974
Dal Diario, Salvatore Sciascia, Caltanisetta, 1954
Il Canto popolare, La Meridiana, Milan, 1954
La Meglio gioventu, Sansoni, Florence, 1954
Le Ceneri di Gramsci, Garzanti, Milan, 1957
L'Usignolo della Chiesa Cattolica, Loganesi, Milan, 1958/ Turin, 1976
Roma 1950, Milan, 1960
Sonetto primaverile, Milan, 1960
La Religione del mio tempo, Garzanti, Milan, 1961
Poesia in forma di rosa, Garzanti, Milan, 1964
Poesie dimenticate, Società Filologica Friulana, Udine, 1965
Potentissima Signora, Longanesi, Milan, 1965
Poesie, Garzanti, Milan, 1970/ 1999
Transumanar e organizzar, Garzanti, Milan, 1971
Le Poesie, Garzanti, Milan, 1975
La Nuova giovento, Einaudi, Turin, 1975
Poesie e pagine ritrovate, 1980
Poems, New York, 1982
Sette Poesie e due lettere, 1984
Roman Poems, City Lights, 1986
Poems, 1996
Poems Scelte, 1997
Poesie rifiutate, 2000
La Nuova gioventu, 2002
Tutte le poesie, 2003
Meditazione orale, 2005
Poeta delle ceneri, 2010

FICTION

Ragazzi di Vita, Garzanti, Milan, 1955/ London, 1989
Una Vita Violenta, Garzanti, Milan, 1959
Donne di Roma, Il Saggiatore, Milan, 1960
A Dream of Something, 1962
Roman Nights and Other Stories, 1965
La Divina Mimesis, 1975
Amado mio, Aitti impuri, 1982
Petrolio, 1992/ 2005
Stories From the City of God, 1995
Romanzi e racconti, 1998
Il re dei giapponesi, 2003

BIBLIOGRAPHY

PIER PAOLO PASOLINI

Pasolini On Pasolini, ed. Oswald Stack, Thames & Hudson, London, 1969

Entretiens avec Pier Paolo Pasolini, Belfond, Paris, 1970

Interview, *Lui*, no. 1, June, 1970

Empirismo eretico, Garzanti, Milan, 1972

Interview, *The Guardian*, Aug 13, 1973

Con Pier Paolo Pasolini, ed. E. Magrelli, Bulzoni, Rome, 1977

Il dialogo, il potere, la morte: la critica e Pasolini, ed. L. Martellini, Cappelli, Bologna, 1979

"Sopralluoghi o la ricerca dei luoghi perduti" (1973), in M. Mancini & G. Perella, 1982

Lutheran Letters, tr. S. Hood, Carcanet Press, 1987

A Future Life, Rome, 1989

"The Lost Pasolini Interview", *Celluloid Liberation Front*, 2012

OTHERS

G. Aichele. "Translation as De-canonization: Matthew's *Gospel* According to Pasolini", *Cross Currents*, 2002

T. Aitken. "The Greatest Story – Never Told", *The Tablet*, Dec 23, 1995

H. Alpert. *Fellini: A Life*, Paragon House, New York, N.Y., 1988

R. Altman, ed. *Sound Theory, Sound Practice*, Routledge, London, 1992

—. *Film/ Genre*, British Film Institute, London, 1999

D. Andrew. *The Major Film Theories*, Oxford University Press, Oxford, 1976

—. *Concepts In Film Theory*, Oxford University Press, Oxford, 1984

—. ed. *Breathless*, Rutgers University Press, New Brunswick, N.J., 1987

G. Andrew. *The Film Handbook*, Longman, London, 1989

G. Annovi. *Pier Paolo Pasolini*, Columbia University Press, 2017

S. Arecco *Pier Paolo Pasolini*, Partisan, Rome, 1972

G. Austin. *Contemporary French Cinema*, Manchester University Press, Manchester, 1996

B. Babington. *Biblical Epic and Sacred Narrative In the Hollywood*, Manchester University Press, Manchester, 1993

G. Bachmann. "Pasolini on de Sade", *Film Quarterly*, vol. 29, no. 2, 1975-76

—. "The 220 Days of Sodom", *Film Comment*, vol. 12, no. 2, Mch-Apl, 1976 (and in *Scraps From the Loft*, June 7, 2018)

M. Barker, ed. *The Video Nasties: Freedom and Censorship In the Media*, Pluto Press, London, 1984

—. & J. Petley, eds. *Ill Effects: The Media/ Violence Debate*, Routledge, London, 1997

R. Barthes. *S/Z*, Hill and Wang, New York, N.Y., 1974

—. *The Pleasure of the Text*, Hill and Wang, New York, N.Y., 1975

—. *Image, Music, Text*, tr. S. Heath, Fontana, London, 1984

G. Bataille. *Literature and Evil*, Calder & Boyars, London, 1973

—. *The Story of the Eye*, Penguin, London, 1982

L. Bawden, ed. *The Oxford Companion To Film*, Oxford University Press, Oxford, 1976

J. Baxter. *An Appalling Talent: Ken Russell*, M. Joseph, London, 1973

—. *Fellini*, St Martin's Press, New York, 1993

A. Bazin. *What Is Cinema?*, University of California Press, Berkeley, C.A., 1960, 2 vols

—. "Cinema and Theology", *South Atlantic Quarterly*, 91, 2, 1992

M. Beja. *Film and Literature: An Introduction*, Longman, London, 1979

—. ed. *Perspectives On Orson Welles*, G.K. Hall, Boston, M.A., 1995

D. Bellezza. *Morte di Pasolini*, Milan, 1981

R. Bellour & M. Bandy, eds. *Jean-Luc Godard*, Museum of Modern Art, N.Y., 1992

Maurizio De Benedictis. *Sergio Citti. Lo "straniero" del cinema italiano*, Lithos, 2008

Bernard Berenson: *The Italian Painters of the Renaissance*, Phaidon 1952/ Fontana 1960

A. Bergala & J. Narboni, eds. *Pasolini Cinéaste*, Paris, 1981

R. Bergan & R. Karney. *Bloomsbury Foreign Film Guide*, Bloomsbury, London, 1988

D. Bergman. *Gaiety Transfigured*, Madison, 1991

I. Bergman. *Bergman On Bergman, Interviews with Ingmar Bergman*, eds. S. Björkman *et al*, tr. P. B. Austin, Touchstone, New York, N.Y., 1986

—. *The Magic Lantern: An Autobiography*, London, 1988

—. *Images: My Life In Film*, Faber, London, 1994

A. Bertini. *Teoria e tecnica del film in Pasolini*, Rome, 1979

B. Bertolucci. *Bertolucci By Bertolucci*, with E. Ungari and D. Ranvard, Plexus, London, 1987

P. Biskind. *Easy Riders, Raging Bulls: How the Sex 'n' Drugs 'n' Rock 'n' Roll Generation Saved Hollywood*, Bloomsbury, London, 1998

V. Boarini. *Da Accattone a Salo*, Bologna, 1982

P. Bogdanovitch. *This Is Orson Welles*, Da Capo, New York, 1998

L. Bolton & C.S. Manson, eds. *Italy On Screen: National Identity and Italian Imaginary*, New Studies in European Cinema Series, Peter Lang, 2010

J. Boorman, ed. *Projections 4*, Faber, London, 1995

—. *Projections 4 1/2*, Positif Editions/ Faber, London, 1995

D. Bordwell & K. Thompson. *Film Art: An Introduction*, McGraw-Hill Publishing Company, New York, N.Y., 1979

—. *The Films of Carl-Theodor Dreyer*, University of California, Berkeley, 1981

—. *et al. The Classical Hollywood Cinema: Film Style and Mode of Production To 1960*, Routledge, London, 1985

—. *Narration In the Fiction Film*, Routledge, London, 1988

—. *Ozu and the Poetics of Cinema*, British Film Institute, London, 1988

—. *Making Meaning*, Harvard University Press, Cambridge, M.A., 1989

—. & N. Caroll, eds. *Post-Theory: Reconstructing Film Studies*, University of Wisconsin Press, Madison, W.I., 1996

—. *The Way Hollywood Tells It*, University of California Press, Berkeley, C.A., 2006

—. & K. Thompson. *Film History*, McGraw-Hill, 2010

F. Brady. *Citizen Welles*, Scribner's, New York, 1989

P. Braunberger. *Pierre Braunberger*, Centre National de la Cinématographie, Paris, 1987

D. Breskin. *Inner Voices: Filmmakers In Conversation*, Da Capo, New York, 1997

R. Bresson, *Notes On the Cinematographer*, Quartet, London, 1986

F. Brevini, ed. *Pasolini*, Mondadori, Milan, 1981

R. Brody. *Everything Is Cinema: The Working Life of Jean-Luc Godard*, Faber, London, 2008

R. Brown, ed. *Focus On Godard*, Prentice-Hall, N.J., 1972

Gian Piero Brunetta. *The History of Italian Cinema*, Princeton University Press, 2009

S. Bukatman. *Terminal Identity: The Virtual Subject In Postmodern Science Fiction*, Duke University Press, Durham, N.C., 1993

P.J. Burgard, ed. *Nietzsche and the Feminine*, University Press of Virginia, Charlottesville, 1994

R. Burgoyne. *Bertolucci's 1900*, Wayne State University Press, Detroit, M.I., 1991

F. Burke and M. Waller, eds. *Federico Fellini: Contemporary Perspectives*, University of Toronto Press, 2002

I. Butler. *Religion In the Cinema*, A.S. Barnes, New York, N.Y., 1969

J. Butler. *Gender Trouble: Feminism and the Subversion of Identity*, Routledge, London, 1990

R. Butter *et al*, eds. *Displacing Homophobia: Gay Male Perspectives In Literature and Culture*, London, 1989

I. Cameron, ed. *The Films of Jean-Luc Godard*, Praeger, N.Y., 1969

A. Carotenuto. *L'Autunno della Conscienza*, Turin, 1985

N. Carroll. *Mystifying Movies: Fads and Fallacies of Contemporary Film Theory*, Columbia University Press, New York, N.Y., 1988

S. Casi. *Desiderio di Pasolini*, La Sonda, Turin, 1990

J. Caughie, ed. *Theories of Authorship: A Reader*, Routledge, London, 1988

—. & A. Kuhn, eds. *The Sexual Subject: A* Screen *Reader In Sexuality*, Routledge, London, 1992

Centro Studi sul Cinema e sulle Communicazioni di Massa. *La Giovani generazioni e il cinema di Pier Paolo Pasolini, La Scene e lo schermo*, Dec, 1989

G. Chester & J. Dickey, eds. *Feminism and Censorship: The Current Debate*, Prism Press, Bridport, Dorset, 1988

M. Ciment. *Projections 9: French Filmmakers On Filmmaking*, Faber, London, 1999

H. Cixous. *The Newly Born Woman*, tr. B. Wing, Minnesota University Press, Minneapolis, 1986

—. *The Hélène Cixous Reader*, ed. Susan Sellers, Blackwell, Oxford, 1994

D.A. Cook. *A History of Narrative Film*, W.W. Norton, New York, N.Y., 1981, 1990, 1996

P. Cook & M. Bernink, eds. *The Cinema Book*, 2nd ed., British Film Institute, London, 1999

T. Corrigan. *A Cinema Without Walls: Movies and Culture After Vietnam*, Rutgers University Press, N.J., 1991

P. Cowie. *The Cinema of Orson Welles*, Da Capo, New York, N.Y., 1973

—. *Ingmar Bergman*, Secker & Warburg, London, 1982

R. Crittenden, ed. *Fine Cuts: The Art of European Film Editing*, C.R.C., Press, 2012

M. Crosland, ed. *The Marquis de Sade Reader*, Peter Owen, 2000

J. Davidson. *The Greeks and Greek Love*, Weidenfeld & Nicholson, London, 2007

G. Day & C. Bloch, eds. *Perspectives On Pornography: Sexuality In Film and Literature*, Macmillan, London, 1988

L. De Giusti. *I Film di Pier Paolo Pasolini*, Gremese, Rome, 1990

T. de Lauretis & S. Heath, eds. *The Cinematic Apparatus*, St Martin's Press, New York, N.Y., 1980

—. *Alice Doesn't: Feminism, Semiotics, Cinema*, Indiana University Press, Bloomington, I.N., 1984

—. *Technologies of Gender*, Macmillan, London, 1987

G. Deleuze & F. Guattari. *Cinema 1: The Movement Image*, Athlone Press, London, 1989

—. *Cinema 2: The Time Image*, Athlone Press, London, 1989

—. *What Is Philosophy?*, Verso, London, 1994

J. Derrida: *Of Grammatology*, Johns Hopkins University Press, Baltimore, M.D., 1976

—. *Spurs: Nietzsche's Styles,* University of Chicago Press, Chicago, I.L., 1979

—. *Writing and Difference,* University of Chicago Press, Chicago, I.L., 1987

—. *Archive Fever,* University of Chicago Press, Chicago, I.L., 1999

G. DeSanti *et al. Perchè Pasolini*, Guaraldi, Florence, 1978

J. Distefano. "Picturing Pasolini", *Art Journal,* 1997

W.W. Dixon. *The Films of Jean-Luc Godard*, State University of New York Press, Albany, N.Y., 1997

J. Dollimore. *Sexual Dissidence*, Oxford, 1991

J. Duflot. *Entretiens avec Pier Paolo Pasolini*, Pierre Belfond, Paris, 1970

R. Durgnat. *Films and Feelings*, Faber, London, 1967

A. Dworkin. *Pornography: Men Possessing Women*, Women's Press, London, 1984

—. *Intercourse*, Arrow, London, 1988

—. *Letters From a War Zone: Writings, 1976-1987*, Secker & Warburg, London, 1988

A. Easthope, ed. *Contemporary Film Theory*, Longman, London, 1993

M. Eliade. *Ordeal by Labyrinth*, University of Chicago Press, Chicago, I.L., 1984

—. *Symbolism, the Sacred and the Arts*, Crossroad, New York, N.Y., 1985

A. Eliot. "*Oedipus Rex* by Pier Paolo Pasolini", *Literature Film Quarterly*, 2004

T. Elsaesser. *European Cinema*, Amsterdam University Press, Amsterdam, 2005

P. Ettedgui. *Production Design & Art Direction*, RotoVision, 1999

Etudes cinématographiques, special Pasolini number, 109-111, 1976

D. Fairservice. *Film Editing*, Manchester University Press, Manchester, 2001

M. Farber. *Negative Space*, Studio Vista, London, 1971

C. Fava & Aldo Vigano. *The Films of Federico Fellini*, Citadel, New York, N.Y., 1990

F. Fellini. *Fellini On Fellini*, Delacorte, New York, N.Y., 1976

—. *Fellini On Fellini*, ed. C. Constantin, Faber, 1995

—. *I'm a Born Liar: A Fellini Lexicon*, ed. D. Pettigrew, Abrams, New York, 2003

A. Ferrero. *Il Cinema di Pier Paolo Pasolini*, Marsilio, Venice, 1977

J. Finler. *The Movie Directors Story*, Octopus Books, London, 1985

—. *The Hollywood Story*, Wallflower Press, London, 2003

John Fletcher & Andrew Benjamin, ed. *Abjection, Melancholia and Love: The Work of Julia Kristeva*, Routledge, London, 1990

K. Forni. "A "cinema of poetry": What Pasolini Did To Chaucer's *Canterbury Tales*", *Literature Film Quarterly*, 2002

G.E. Forshey. *American Religious and Biblical Spectaculars*, Praeger, Westport, C.T., 1992

M. Foucault. *The History of Sexuality*, Penguin, London, 1981

—. *The Use of Pleasure: The History of Sexuality*, vol. 2, Penguin, London, 1987

—. *Politics, Philosophy, Culture: Interviews and Other Writings, 1977-1984*, ed. L.D. Kritzmon, Routledge, New York, N.Y., 1990

J. Franklin. *New German Cinema*, Columbus Books, 1986

K. French, ed. *Screen Violence*, Bloomsbury, London, 1996

P. French *et al. The Films of Jean-Luc Godard*, Blue Star House, 1967

A. Frisch. "Francesco Vezzolini: Pasolini Reloaded", interview, Rutgers University Alexander Library, New Brunswick, N.J.

Diana Fuss. *Essentially Speaking*, Routledge, New York, 1989

—. ed. *Inside/ Out: Lesbian Theories, Gay Theories*, Routledge, London, 1991

F. Gado. *The Passion of Ingmar Bergman*, Durham, N.C., 1986

J. Gallagher. *Film Directors On Directing*, Praeger, New York, N.Y., 1989

H. Geduld, ed. *Filmmakers On Filmmaking*, Indiana University Press, Bloomington, I.N., 1967

J. Geiger & R. Rutsky, eds. *Film Analysis*, Norton & Company, New York, N.Y., 2005

J. Gelmis. *The Film Director As Superstar*, Penguin, London, 1974

D. Georgakas & L. Rubenstein, eds. *Art Politics Cinema: The Cineaste Interviews*, Pluto Press, London, 1985

F. Gérard. *Pier Paolo Pasolini*, Seghers, Paris, 1973

—. *Pasolini ou le mythe de la barbarie*, Université de Bruxelles, 1981

J. Gerber. *Anatole Dauman: Pictures of a Producer*, British Film Institute, London, 1992

M. Gervais. *Pier Paolo Pasolini*, Paris, 1973

L. Gianetti. *Godard and Others*, Tantivy, 1975

—. *Understanding Movies*, Prentice-Hall, N.J., 1982

P.C. Gibson & R. Gibson, eds. *Dirty Looks: Women, Pornography, Power*, British Film Institute, London, 1993

Jean-Luc Godard. *Godard On Godard*, ed. A. Bergala, Cahiers du Cinéma, Paris, 1985

—. *Godard On Godard*, eds. J. Narobi & T. Milne, Da Capo, New York, N.Y., 1986

—. *Interviews*, ed. D. Sterritt, University of Mississippi Press, Jackson, 1998

—. *Godard On Godard 2*, ed. A. Bergala, Cahiers du Cinéma, Paris, 1998

—. *Histoire(s) du cinéma*, Gallimard-Gaumont, Paris, 1998

—. "An Audience With Uncle Jean-Luc", *The Guardian*, Feb 11, 2000

J. Gomez. *Ken Russell*, Muller, 1976

R. Gottesman, ed. *Focus On Orson Welles*, Prentice-Hall, Englewood Cliffs, N.J., 1976

P. Grace. *The Religious Film: Christianity and the Hagiopic*, Wiley-Blackwell, Sussex, 2009

D. Graham, ed. *Film and Religion*, St Mungo Press, 1997

B.K. Grant, ed. *Film Genre*, Scarecrow Press, Metuchen, N.J., 1977

—. ed. *Crisis Cinema: The Apocalyptic Idea In Postmodern Narrative Film*, Maisonneuve Press, 1993

—. *Film Genre Reader II*, University of Texas Press, Austin, T.X., 1995

J. Green. *The Encyclopedia of Censorship*, Facts on File, New York, N.Y., 1990

N. Greene. *Pier Paolo Pasolini: Cinema As Heresy*, Princeton University Press, N.J., 1990

Elizabeth Grosz. "Philosophy, Subjectivity and the Body", in C.

Pateman, 1986

—. "Desire, the body and recent French feminism", *Intervention*, 21-2, 1988

—. *Sexual Subversions*, Allen & Unwin, London, 1989

—. "The Body of Signification", in J. Fletcher, 1990

—. "Fetishization", in E. Wright, 1992

—. *Volatile Bodies,* Indiana University Press, Bloomington, I.N., 1994

—. *Space, Time and Perversion*, Routledge, London, 1995

B. Groult: "Les portiers de nuit", in *Ainsi soit-elle*, Grasset, Paris, 1975, and in E. Marks, 1981

L. Hanlon. *Fragments: Bresson's Film Style*, Farleigh Dickinson University Press, Rutherford, 1986

S. Harwood. *French National Cinema,* Routledge, London, 1993

P. Hartnoll, ed. *The Oxford Companion To the Theatre,* Oxford University Press, Oxford, 1985

S. Hayward & G. Vincendeau, eds. *French Film*, Routledge, London, 1990

S. Heath. *Questions of Cinema*, Macmillan, London, 1981

—. *Cinema and Language*, University Presses of America, 1983

W. Herzog. *Herzog On Herzog*, ed. P. Cronin, Faber & Faber, London, 2002

G. Hickenlooper. *Reel Conversations: Candid Interviews With Film's Foremost Directors and Critics*, Citadel, New York, N.Y., 1991

C. Higham. *Orson Welles,* St Martin's Press, New York, N.Y., 1985

J. Hill & P.C. Gibson, eds. *The Oxford Guide To Film Studies*, Oxford University Press, Oxford, 1998

J. Hillier, ed. *Cahiers du Cinéma: The 1950s, New-Realism, Hollywood, New Wave*, Harvard University Press, Cambridge, M.A., 1985

—. *The New Hollywood*, Studio Vista, London, 1992

L.C. Hillstrom, ed. *International Dictionary of Films and Filmmakers: Directors*, St James Press, London, 1997

D. Holmes & A. Smith, eds. *100 Years of European Cinema*, Manchester University Press, Manchester, 2000

H. Hughes. *Cinema Italiano*, I.B. Tauris, London, 2011

G. Indiana. *Salò*, British Film Institute, London, 2000

—. "Pasolini, *Mamma Roma,* and *La Ricotta"*, Criterion, 2004

A. Insdorf. *Indelible Shadows: Film and the Holocaust*, Cambridge University Press, Cambridge, 1989

L. Irigaray. *The Irigaray Reader,* ed. M. Whitford, Blackwell, Oxford, 1991

F. Jameson. *Signatures of the Visible*, Routledge, New York, N.Y., 1990

—. *Postmodernism, or the Cultural Logic of Late Capitalism*, Verso, London, 1991

D. Jarman. *Modern Nature*, Century, London, 1991

P. Kael. *Kiss Kiss Bang Bang*, Bantam, New York, N.Y., 1969

—. *Going Steady*, Bantam, New York, 1971

—. *Taking It All In*, Marion Boyars, 1986

—. *State of the Art*, Marion Boyars, London, 1987

—. *Movie Love*, Marion Boyars, London, 1992

A. Kaes. *From Hitler To Heimat: The Return of History As Film*, Harvard University Press, Cambridge, M.A., 1989

E. Ann Kaplan, ed. *Psychoanalysis and Cinema*, Routledge, London, 1990

B.F. Kawin. *Mindscreen: Bergman, Godard and First-Person Film*, Princeton University Press, Princeton, N.J., 1978

—. *How Movies Work*, Macmillan, New York, N.Y., 1987

P. Keough, ed. *Flesh and Blood: The National Society of Film Critics On Sex, Violence, and Censorship*, Mercury House, San Francisco, C.A., 1995

T. Kezich. *Fellini: His Life and Work*, Faber and Faber, New York, N.Y., 2006

G. Kindem. *The International Movie Industry*, Southern Illinois University Press, Carbondale, I.L., 2000

R. Kinnard & T. Davis. *Divine Images: A History of Jesus On the Screen,* Citadel Press, New York, N.Y., 1992

C. Klimke. *Kraft der Vergangenheit: Zu Motiven der Filme von Pier Paolo Pasolini,* Frankfurt, 1988

T. Jefferson Kline. *Bertolucci's Dream Loom: A Psychoanalytic Study of Cinema*, University of Massachusetts Press, Amherst, 1987

P. Kolker. *The Altering Eye: Contemporary International Cinema*, Oxford University Press, New York, N.Y., 1983

—. *Bernardo Bertolucci*, British Film Institute, London, 1985

—. *A Cinema of Loneliness: Penn, Stone, Kubrick, Scorsese, Spielberg, Altman*, Oxford University Press, New York, N.Y., 1988/ 2000

S. Kracauer. *Theory of Film*, Princeton University Press, Princeton, N.J., 1997

L. Kreitzer. *The New Testament In Fiction and Film*, J.S.O.T., 1993

—. *The Old Testament In Fiction and Film*, Sheffield Academic Press, Sheffield, 1994

J. Kristeva. *Powers of Horror: An Essay On Abjection*, tr. L.S. Roudiez, Columbia University Press, New York, 1982

—. *Desire In Language: A Semiotic Approach To Literature and Art*, ed. L.S. Roudiez, tr. Thomas Gora, Alice Jardine & L.S. Roudiez, Blackwell, Oxford, 1982

—. *Revolution In Poetic Language*, tr. Margaret Walker, Columbia University Press, New York, 1984

—. Article in *Art Press*, 4, 1984-85

—. *The Kristeva Reader*, ed. T. Moi, Blackwell, Oxford, 1986

—. *Tales of Love*, tr. L.S. Roudiez, Columbia University Press, New York, N.Y., 1987

—. *Black Sun: Depression and Melancholy,* tr. L.S. Roudiez, Columbia University Press, New York, N.Y., 1989

—. *Strangers To Ourselves*, tr. L.S. Roudiez, Harvester Wheatsheaf, Hemel Hempstead, 1991

A. Kuhn. *Women's Pictures: Feminism and the Cinema*, Routledge & Kegan Paul, London, 1982

A. Kurosawa. *Something Like an Autobiography*, Vintage, New York, N.Y., 1983

J. Lacan. *Écrits: A Selection*, tr. Alan Sheridan, Tavistock, 1977

—. and the École Freudienne. *Feminine Sexuality*, eds. J. Mitchell and J. Rose, Macmillan, London, 1988

R. Lapsley & M. Westlake, eds. *Film Theory: An Introduction*, Manchester University Press, Manchester, 1988

A. Lawton. *The Red Screen: Politics, Society, Art In Soviet Cinema*, Routledge, London, 1992

B. Leaming. *Orson Welles*, Viking, New York, 1985

V. Lebeau. *Psychoanalysis and Cinema*, Wallflower, London, 2001

P. Leprohan. *The Italian Cinema*, tr. R. Greaves & O. Stallybrass, Secker & Warburg, London, 1972

E. Levy. *Cinema of Outsiders: The Rise of American Independent Film*, New York University Press, New York, N.Y., 1999

J. Lewis. *Whom God Wishes To Destroy: Francis Coppola and the New Hollywood*, Duke University Press, Durham, N.C., 1995

—. ed. *New American Cinema*, Duke University Press, Durham, N.C., 1998

—. *Hollywood v. Hard Core: How the Struggle Over Censorship Created the Modern Film Industry*, New York University Press, New York, N.Y., 2000

—. ed. *The End of Cinema As We Know It: American Film In the Nineties*, New York University Press, New York, N.Y., 2002

J. Leyda, ed. *Filmmakers Speak*, Da Capo, New York, 1977/ 84

—. *Kino: A History of the Russian and Soviet Cinema*, 3rd edition, Allen & Unwin, London, 1983

M. Litch. *Philosophy Through Film*, Routledge, London, 2002

P. Livington. *Ingmar Bergman and the Rituals of Art*, Cornell University Press, Ithaca, N.Y., 1982

V. LoBrutto. *Sound-On-Film*, Praeger, New York, N.Y., 1994

—. *Stanley Kubrick*, Faber, London, 1997

Y. Loshitzky. *The Radical Faces of Godard and Bertolucci*, Wayne State University Press, Detroit, M.I., 1995

L. Lourdeaux. *Italian and Irish Filmmakers In America: Ford, Capra, Coppola and Scorsese*, Temple University Press, Philadelphia, P.A., 1990

L. Lucignani & C. Molfese, eds. *Per Conoscere Pasolini*, Bulzoni, Rome, 1978

C. MacCabe. *Godard, Images, Sound, Politics*, Macmillan/ British Film Institute, London, 1980

—. *Godard: A Portrait of the Artist At 70*, Faber, London, 2003

—. *"The Decameron"*, Criterion, 2012

M. Macciocchi, ed. *Pasolini*, Grasset, Paris, 1980

A. Maggi. *The Resurrection of the Body: Pier Paolo Pasolini From St Paul To Sade*, University of Chicago Press, 2009

P. Malone. *Movie Christs and Antichrists*, Crossroad, 1990

R. Maltby. *Harmless Entertainment: Hollywood and the Ideology of Consensus*, Scarecrow Press, Metuchen, N.J., 1983

—. *Hollywood Cinema*, 2nd ed., Blackwell, Oxford, 2003

M. Mancini & G. Perella. *Pier Paolo Pasolini: corpi e luoghi*, Theorema, Bologna, 1982

Mao Tse-tung. *The Little Red Book (Quotations From Chairman Mao Tse-tung)*, Foreign Language Press, Peking, 1967

E. Marks & I. de Courtivron, eds. *New French Feminisms: an anthology*, Harvester Wheatsheaf, Hemel Hempstead, 1981

T. Martin. *Images and the Imageless: A Study In Religious Consciousness and Film*, Bucknell University Press, 1981

G. Mast *et al*, eds. *Film Theory and Criticism: Introductory Readings*, Oxford University Press, New York, N.Y., 1992a

—. & B Kawin, *A Short History of the Movies*, Macmillan, New York, N.Y., 1992b

T.D. Matthews. *Censored*, Chatto & Windus, London, 1994

J.R. May & M. Bird, eds. *Religion In Film*, University of Tennessee Press, Knoxville, 1982

—. *Image and Likeness: Religious Vision In American Film Classics*, Paulist, 1992

—. *New Image of Religious Film*, Sheed & Ward, London, 1996

J. Mayne. *The Woman At the Keyhole: Feminism and Women's Cinema*, Indiana University Press, Bloomington, I.N., 1990

M. Medved. *Hollywood vs. America*, HarperCollins, London, 1992

P. Mellencamp & P. Rosen, eds. *Cinema Histories, Cinema Practices*, University Publications of America, Frederick, M.D., 1984

—. *A Fine Romance: Five Ages of Film Feminism*, Temple University Press, Philadelphia, P.A., 1995

M. Miles. *Seeing and Believing: Religion and Values In the Movies*, Beacon, Boston, M.A., 1996

M.C. Miller. ed. *Seeing Through Movies*, Pantheon, New York, N.Y., 1990

Wu Ming. "The Police vs. Pasolini, Pasolini vs. the Police", Verso Books, 2016

T. Modleski, ed. *Studies In Entertainment*, Indiana University Press, Bloomington, I.N., 1987

—. *The Women Who Knew Too Much: Hitchcock and Feminist Theory*, Methuen, London, 1988

—. *Feminism Without Women: Culture and Criticism In a 'Postfeminist' Age*, Routledge, London, 1991

T. Moi. *Sexual/ Textual Politics: Feminist Literary Theory*, Methuen, London, 1983

J. Monaco. *The New Wave: Truffaut, Godard, Chabrol, Rohmer, Rivette*, Oxford University Press, New York, N.Y., 1977

I. Moscati. *Pasolini e il teorema del sesso*, Milan, 1995

P. Mosley. *Ingmar Bergman*, Marion Boyars, London, 1981

R. Murphy, ed. *The British Cinema Book*, Palgrave/ Macmillan, London, 2nd edition, 2009

R. Murray. *Images In the Dark: An Encyclopedia of Gay and Lesbian Film and Video*, Titan Books, London, 1998

S. Murri. *Pier Paolo Pasolini*, Rome, 1984

N. Naldini. *Nei camp dei Friuli: La giovanezza di Pasolini*, Pesce d'Oro, Milan, 1984

—. *Pasolini, una vita*, Einaudi, Turin, 1989

J. Naremore. *The Magic World of Orson Welles*, Southern Methodist University Press, Dallas, T.X., 1989

J. Natoli. *Hauntings: Popular Film and American Culture 1990-92*, State University of New York Press, Albany, N.Y., 1994

—. *Speeding To the Millennium: Film and Culture 1993-1995*, State University of New York Press, Albany, N.Y., 1998

—. *Postmodern Journeys: Film and Culture, 1996-1998*, State University of New York Press, Albany, N.Y., 2001

S. Neale. *Cinema and Technology*, Macmillan, London, 1985

—. & B. Neve. *Film and Politics In America*, Routledge, London, 1992

J. Nelmes, ed. *An Introduction To Film Studies*, Routledge, London, 1996

R. Neupert. *The End: Narration and Closure In the Cinema*, Wayne State University Press, Detroit, M.I., 1995

K. Newman & J. Marriott. *Horror! The Definitive Companion To the Most Terrifying Movies Ever Made*, Carlton Books, London, 2013

G. Nowell-Smith. *Visconti*, British Film Institute, London, 1973

—. ed. *The Oxford History of World Cinema*, Oxford University Press, Oxford, 1996

—. & S. Ricci, eds. *Hollywood and Europe*, British Film Institute, London, 1998

—. *Making Waves: New Cinemas of the 1960s*, Bloomsbury, 2013

J. Orr & C. Nicholson, eds. *Cinema and Fiction*, Edinburgh University Press, Edinburgh, 1992

—. *Cinema and Modernity*, Polity Press, Cambridge, 1993

—. *Contemporary Cinema*, Edinburgh University Press, Edinburgh, 1998

C. Ostwalt. "Religion & Popular Movies", *Journal of Religion and Film*, 2, 3, 1998

R. Palmer, ed. *The Cinematic Text*, A.M.S., New York, N.Y., 1989

A. Panicali & S. Sestini, eds. *Pier Paolo Pasolini*, Nuovo Salani, Florence, 1982

E. Passannanti. *Il Corpo & Il Potere*, Joker, 2004

—. *La Ricotta*, Mask Press, 2007

—. *Il Cristo dell'Eresia*, Joker, 2009

—. *La Nudita del Sacro nei Film di Pier Paolo Pasolini*, Brindin Press, 2019

Carole Pateman & Elizabeth Grosz, eds. *Feminist Challenges*, Allen & Unwin, Sydney, 1986

A. Pavelin. *Fifty Religious Films*, A.P. Pavelin, Chiselhurst, Kent, 1990

C. Penley, ed. *Feminism and Film Theory*, Routledge, London, 1988

—. *et al*, eds. *Close Encounters: Film, Feminism and Science Fiction*, University of Minnesota Press, Minneapolis, 1991

V.F. Perkins. *Film As Film: Understanding and Judging Movies*, Penguin, London, 1972

T. Peterson. *The Paraphrase of an Imaginary Dialogue: The Poetics and Poetry of Pier Paolo Pasolini*, New York, 1994

S. Petraglia. *Pier Paolo Pasolini*, Nuova Italia, Florence, 1974

D. Petrie. *Screening Europe: Image and Identity In Contemporary European Cinema*, British Film Institute, London, 1992

G. Phelps. *Film Censorship*, Gollancz, London, 1975

K. Phillips. *New German Filmmakers*, Ungar, New York, N.Y.,

1984

L. Polezzi & C. Ross, eds. *In Corpore: Bodies In Post-Unification Italy*, Fairleigh Dickinson University Press, 2007

C. Potter. *Image, Sound and Story: The Art of Telling In Film*, Secker & Warburg, London, 1990

N. Power & G. Nowell-Smith. "Subversive Pasolini", 2012-13, ninapower.net, 2017

P. Powrie, ed. *French Cinema In the 1990s*, Oxford University Press, Oxford, 1999

R. Prendergast. *Film Music*, W.W. Norton, New York, N.Y., 1992

S. Prince. *Savage Cinema: Sam Peckinpah and the Rise of Ultraviolent Movies*, University of Texas Press, Austin, T.X., 1998

—. ed. *Screening Violence*, Athlone Press, London, 2000

—. *A New Pot of Gold: Hollywood Under the Electronic Rainbow*, Scribners, New York, N.Y., 2000

S. Projansky. *Watching Rape: Film and Television In Post-feminism Culture*, New York University Press, New York, N.Y., 2001

T. Pugh. "Chaucerian Fabliaux, Cinematic Fabliau: Pier Paolo Pasolini's *I racconti di Canterbury*", *Literature Film Quarterly,* 2004

M. Pye & Lynda Myles. *The Movie Brats: How the Film Generation Took Over Hollywood*, Faber, London, 1979

T. Rayns, ed. *Fassbinder*, British Film Institute, London, 1979

K. Reader. *Robert Bresson,* Manchester University Press, Manchester, 2000

A. Reinhartz. "Jesus in Film: Hollywood Perspectives on the Jewishness of Jesus", *Journal of Religion and Film,* 2, 2, 1998

A. Restivo. *The Cinema of Economic Miracles: Visuality and Modernization In the Italian Art Film*, Duke University Press, 2002

La Revue d'estgétique, special Pasolini number, 3, 1982

J. Rhodes. *Stupendous, Miserable City: Pasolini's Rome*, University of Minnesota Press, 2007

P. Rice & P. Waugh, eds. *Modern Literary Theory: A Reader*, Arnold, London, 1992

J. Richards, ed. *Films and British National Identity*, Manchester University Press, Manchester, 1997

M. Richardson. *Surrealism and Cinema*, Berg, New York, N.Y., 2006

D. Richie. *The Films of Akira Kurosawa*, University of California Press, Berkeley, C.A., 1965

R. Rinaldi. *Pier Paolo Pasolini*, Mursia, Milan, 1982

D. Robinson. *World Cinema*, Methuen, London, 1981

G. Rodgerson & E. Wilson, eds. *Pornography and Censorship*, Lawrence & Wishart, London, 1991

S. Rohdie. *Antonioni*, British Film Institute, London, 1990

—. *The Passion of Pier Paolo Pasolini*, British Film Institute, London, 1995

J. Romney & A. Wootton, eds. *Celluloid Jukebox: Popular Music and the Movies Since the 50s*, British Film Institute, London,

1995

P. Rosen, ed. *Narrative, Apparatus, Ideology: A Film Theory Reader*, Columbia University Press, New York, N.Y., 1986

A. Rosenstone, ed. *Revisioning History: Film and the Construction of a New Past*, Princeton University Press, Princeton, N.J., 1995

R. Roud. *Jean-Luc Godard*, Thames & Hudson, London, 1970

R. Ruiz. *The Poetics of Cinema*, Dis Voir, Paris, 1995

P. Rumble & B. Testa, eds. *Pier Paolo Pasolini*, University of Toronto Press, Toronto, 1994

—. *Allegories of Contamination: Pier Paolo Pasolini's Trilogy of Life*, University of Toronto Press, Toronto, 1996

K. Russell. *A British Picture: An Autobiography*, Heinemann, London, 1989

M. Russell & J. Young. *Film Music,* RotoVision, 2000

V. Russo. *The Celluloid Closet: Homosexuality In the Movies*, Harper & Row, New York, N.Y., 1981

M. de Sade. *The 120 Days of Sodom*, tr. A. Wainhouse & R. Seaver, Arrow, London, 1996

J. Sanford. *The New German Cinema*, Da Capo Press, New York, N.Y., 1982

A. Sarris, ed., *Interviews With Film Directors*, Avon, New York, N.Y., 1969

T. Schatz. *Hollywood Genres,* Random House, New York, N.Y., 1981

—. *Old Hollywood/ New Hollywood*, U.M.I. Research Press, Ann Arbor, M.I., 1983

—. *The Genius of the System: Hollywood Filmmaking In the Studio Era*, Pantheon, New York, N.Y. 1988

Naomi Schor. *Breaking the Chain: Women, Theory and French Realist Fiction*, New York, 1985

—. & Elizabeth Weed, eds. *Differences: More Gender Trouble: Feminism Meets Queer Theory*, 6, 2-3, Indiana University Press, Summer, 1994

P. Schrader. *Transcendental Style In Film: Ozu, Bresson, Dreyer*, Da Capo Press, 1972

M. Schumacher. *Francis Ford Coppola*, Bloomsbury, London, 2000

B. Schwartz. *Pasolini Requiem*, Vintage Books, New York, 1995

P. Schwenger. *Phallic Critiques: Masculinity and 20th Century Literature*, London, 1984

O. Schweitzer. *Pier Paolo Pasolini*, Hamburg, 1986

Bernhart Schwenk & Michael Semff, eds. *Pier Paolo Pasolini and Death*, Ostfildern 2005

M. Scorsese. *Scorsese On Scorsese*, ed. D. Thompson & I. Christie, Faber, London, 1989, 1995

Screen Reader I: Cinema/ Ideology/ Politics, Society for Education in Film & TV, 1977

Screen Reader II: Cinema and Semiotics, British Film Institute, London, 1982

C. Sharrett, ed. *Crisis Cinema*, Maisonneuve Press, Washington, D.C., 1993

D. Shipman. *The Story of Cinema*, Hodder & Stoughton, London,

1984

—. *Caught In the Act: Sex and Eroticism In the Movies*, Hamish Hamilton, London, 1986

T. Shone. *Blockbuster: How the Jaws and Jedi Generation Turned Hollywood Into a Boom-Town*, Scribner, London, 2005

E. Showalter, ed. *The New Feminist Criticism,* Virago, London, 1986

Enzo Siciliano. *Pasolini: A Biography*, tr. John Shepley, Random House, New York, 1982

L. Sider *et al*, eds. *Soundscapes: The School of Sound Lectures 1998-2001*, Wallflower Press, London, 2003

M. Silberman. *German Cinema,* Wayne State University Press, Detroit, M.I., 1995

K. Silverman. *The Subject of Semiotics*, Oxford University Press, New York, N.Y., 1983

—. *The Acoustic Mirror: The Female Voice In Psychoanalysis and Cinema*, Indiana University Press, Bloomington, I.N., 1988

—. *Male Subjectivity At the Margins*, Routledge, London, 1992

—. & H. Farocki. *Speaking About Godard,* New York University Press, New York, N.Y., 1998

P. Adams Sitney, ed. *The Film Culture Reader*, Praeger, New York, N.Y., 1970

—. *Vital Crises In Italian Cinema*, University of Texas Press, Austin, T.X., 1995

S. Snyder. *Pier Paolo Pasolini*, Twayne, 1980

V. Sobchack, ed. *The Persistence of History: Cinema, Television, and the Modern Event*, Routledge, London, 1995

A. Solomon. *20th Century-Fox: A Corporate and Financial History*, Scarecrow Press, Metuchen, N.J., 1988

J. Solomon. *The Ancient World In the Cinema*, London, 1978

—. *The Ancient World In the Cinema*, Yale University Press, New Haven, C.T., 2001

P. Sorlin. *The Film In History: Restaging the Past*, Blackwell, Oxford, 1980

S. Spignesi. *The Woody Allen Companion*, Plexus, London, 1994

George Stambolian & Elaine Marks, eds. *Homosexuality and French Literature: Cultural Contexts/ Critical Texts,* Cornell University Press, Ithaca, 1979

B. Steene. *Ingmar Bergman*, Twayne, Boston, M.A., 1968

—. *Ingmar Bergman: A Guide To References and Resources*, Boston, M.A., 1987

N. Steimatsky. "Pasolini on Terra Sancta: Towards a Theology of Film", *Yale Journal of Criticism*, 11, 1, 1998

L. Stern. *The Scorsese Connection*, British Film Institute, London, 1995

D. Sterritt. *The Films of Jean-Luc Godard*, Cambridge University Press, Cambridge, 1999

P. Steven, ed. *Jump Cut: Hollywood, Politics and Counter Cinema*, Between the Lines, Toronto, 1985

G. Stewart. *Between Film and Screen: Modernism's Photo Synthesis*, University of Chicago Press, Chicago, I.L., 1999

C. Sylvester, ed. *The Penguin Book of Hollywood*, Penguin,

London, 1999

Y. Tasker. *Spectacular Bodies: Gender, Genre and the Action Cinema*, Routledge, London, 1993

M. Temple & J. Williams, eds. *The Cinema Alone: Essays On the Work of Jean-Luc Godard, 1985-2000*, Amsterdam University Press, Amsterdam, 2000

—. *et al*, eds. *Godard For Ever*, Black Dog Publishing, London, 2004

S. Teo. *Hong Kong Cinema*, British Film Institute, London, 1997

N. Thomas, ed. *International Dictionary of Films and Filmmakers: Films*, St James Press, London, 1990

K. Thompson. *Breaking the Glass Armor: Neoformalist Film Analysis*, Princeton University Press, Princeton, N.J., 1988

—. & D. Bordwell. *Film History: An Introduction*, McGraw-Hill, New York, N.Y., 1994

—. *Storytelling In the New Hollywood*, Harvard University Press, Cambridge, M.A., 1999

D. Thomson. *A Biographical Dictionary of Film*, Deutsch, London, 1995

C. Tohill & P. Tombs. *Immoral Tales: Sex and Horror Cinema In Europe 1956-1984*, Titan Books, London, 1995

Sergio Toffetti. *La Terra vista dalla luna: il cinema di Sergio Citti*, Lindau, 1993

C. Tonetti. *Luchino Visconti*, Columbus Books, 1985

—. *Bernardo Bertolucci*, Twayne, Boston, M.A., 1994

E. Törnqvist. *Between Stage and Screen: Ingmar Bergman Directs*, Amsterdam University Press, Amsterdam, 1995

J. Trevelyan. *What the Censor Saw*, Michael Joseph, London, 1973

H. Trosman. *Contemporary Psychoanalysis and Masterworks of Art and Film*, New York University Press, New York, N.Y., 2000

F. Truffaut. *The Films In My Life*, tr. L. Mayhew, Penguin, London, 1982

P. Tyler. *Sex Psyche Etcetera In the Film*, Horizon, New York, N.Y., 1969

—. *Screening the Sexes: Homosexuality In the Movies*, Doubleday, New York, N.Y., 1973

M. Valck & M. Hagener, eds. *Cinephilia: Movies, Love and Memory*, Amsterdam University Press, Amsterdam, 2005

K. Van Gunden. *Fantasy Films*, McFarland, Jefferson, NC 1989

M. Viano. *A Certain Realism: Making Use of Pasolini's Film Theory and Practice*, University of California Press, Berkeley, 1993.

G. Vincendeau, ed. *Encyclopedia of European Cinema*, British Film Institute, London, 1995

—. ed. *Film/ Literature/ Heritage: A Sight & Sound Reader*, British Film Institute, London, 2001

P. Virilio & S. Lotringer. *The Aesthetics of Disappearance*, tr. P. Beitchman, Semiotext(e), New York, N.Y., 1991

—. *The Vision Machine*, tr. J. Rose, Indiana University Press, Bloomington, I.N., 1994

J. Vizzard. *See No Evil: Life Inside a Hollywood Censor*, Simon &

Schuster, New York, N.Y., 1970

A. Vogel. *Film As a Subversive Art*, Weidenfeld & Nicolson, London, 1974

A. Walker. *Sex In the Movies*, Penguin, London, 1968

—. *Hollywood, England: The British Film Industry In the Sixties*, Harrap, London, 1986

J. Wasko. *Movies and Money*, Ablex, N.J., 1982

—. *Hollywood In the Information Age*, Polity Press, Cambridge, 1994

P. Webb. *The Erotic Arts*, Secker & Warburg, London, 1975

E. Weiss. & J. Belton, eds. *Film Sound: Theory and Practice*, Columbia University Press, New York, N.Y., 1989

O. Welles. *This Is Orson Welles*, HarperCollins, London, 1992

—. *Orson Welles: Interviews,* ed. M. Estrin, University of Mississippi Press, Jackson, 2002

Helen Wilcox *et al*, eds. *The Body and the Text: Hélène Cixous, Reading and Teaching,* Harvester Wheatsheaf, Hemel Hempstead, Herts., 1990

P. Willemen, ed. *Pier Paolo Pasolini*, British Film Institute, London, 1977

L. Williams, ed. *Viewing Positions: Ways of Seeing Film*, Rutgers University Press, New Brunswick, N.J., 1995

L.R. Williams. *Critical Desire: Psychoanalysis and the Literary Subject*, Arnold, London, 1995

—. *Sex In the Head*, Harvester Wheatsheaf, Hemel Hempstead, 1995

W. Willimon. "Faithful to the Script", *Christian Century,* 2004

S. Willis. *High Contrast: Race and Gender In Contemporary Hollywood Film*, Duke University Press, Durham, N.C., 1997

R. Wilson & W. Dissanayake, eds. *Global/ Local: Cultural Production and the Transnational Imaginary*, Duke University Press, Durham, N.C., 1996

E. Wistrich. *'I Don't Mind the Sex It's the Violence': Film Censorship Explored*, Marion Boyars, London, 1978

M. Wolf. *The Entertainment Economy,* Penguin, London, 1999

P. Wollen: *Signs and Meaning In the Cinema*, Secker & Warburg, London, 1972

B. Wood. *Orson Welles*, Greenwood Press, Westport, C.T., 1990

P. Wood, ed. *Scorsese: A Journey Through the American Psyche*, Plexus, London, 2005

R. Wood. *Ingmar Bergman*, Praeger, New York, N.Y., 1969

—. *Hollywood From Vietnam To Reagan... and Beyond*, Columbia University Press, New York, N.Y., 2003

T. Woods. *Beginning Postmodernism,* Manchester University Press, Manchester, 1999

Elizabeth Wright, ed. *Feminism and Psychoanalysis: A Critical Dictionary*, Blackwell, Oxford, 1992

J. Wyatt. *High Concept: Movies and Marketing In Hollywood*, University of Texas Press, Austin, T.X., 1994

E.C.M. Yau, ed. *At Full Speed: Hong Kong Cinema In a Borderless World,* University of Minnesota Press, Minneapolis, MN, 1998

J. Young, ed. *The Art of Memory: Holocaust Memorials In*

History, Prestel, New York, N.Y., 1994

G. Zigaini. *Pasolini e la morte*, Marsilio, Venice, 1987

J. Zipes, ed. *The Oxford Companion To Fairy Tales*, Oxford University Press, 2000

—. *Sticks and Stones: The Troublesome Success of Children's Literature From Slovenly Peter To Harry Potter*, Routledge, London, 2002

—. *The Enchanted Screen: The Unknown History of Fairy-tale Films*, Routledge, New York, N.Y., 2011

—. *The Irresistible Fairy Tale*, Prince University Press, Princeton, N.J., 2012

S. Zizek. *Looking Awry*, Verso, London, 1991

—. *Enjoy Your Symptom: Jacques Lacan In Hollywood and Out*, Routledge, New York, N.Y., 1992

—. ed. *Everything You Always Wanted To Know About Lacan (But Were Too Afraid To Ask Hitchcock)*, Verso, London, 1992

—. *The Metastases of Enjoyment*, Verso, London, 1994

—. *The Indivisible Remainder*, Verso, London, 1996

—. *The Fright of Real Tears: The Uses and Misuses of Lacan In Film Theory*, British Film Institute, London, 1999

Websites for Pasolini-related material include:

pierpaolopasolini.com
pasoliniroma.com
jclarkmedia.com
bernardobertolucci.org

JEREMY ROBINSON has published poetry, fiction, and studies of J.R.R. Tolkien, Samuel Beckett, Thomas Hardy, André Gide and D.H. Lawrence. Robinson has edited poetry books by Novalis, Ursula Le Guin, Friedrich Hölderlin, Francesco Petrarch, Dante Alighieri, Arseny Tarkovsky, and Rainer Maria Rilke.

Books on film and animation include: *The Akira Book* • *The Art of Katsuhiro Otomo* • *The Art of Masamune Shirow* • *The Ghost In the Shell Book* • *Fullmetal Alchemist* • *Cowboy Bebop: The Anime and Movie* • *The Cinema of Hayao Miyazaki* • *Hayao Miyazaki: Pocket Guide* • *Princess Mononoke: Pocket Movie Guide* • *Spirited Away: Pocket Movie Guide* • *Blade Runner and the Cinema of Philip K. Dick* • *Blade Runner: Pocket Movie Guide* • *The Cinema of Donald Cammell* • *Performance: Donald Cammell: Nic Roeg: Pocket Movie Guide* • *Pasolini: Il Cinema di Poesia/ The Cinema of Poetry* • *Salo: Pocket Movie Guide* • *The Trilogy of Life Movies: Pocket Movie Guide* • *The Gospel According To Matthew: Pocket Movie Guide* • *The Ecstatic Cinema of Tony Ching Siu-tung* • *Tsui Hark: The Dragon Master of Chinese Cinema* • *The Swordsman: Pocket Movie Guide* • *A Chinese Ghost Story: Pocket Movie Guide* • *Ken Russell: England's Great Visionary Film Director and Music Lover* • *Tommy: Ken Russell: The Who: Pocket Movie Guide* • *Women In Love: Ken Russell: D.H. Lawrence: Pocket Movie Guide* • *The Devils: Ken Russell: Pocket Movie Guide* • *Walerian Borowczyk: Cinema of Erotic Dreams* • *The Beast: Pocket Movie Guide* • *The Lord of the Rings Movies* • *The Fellowship of the Ring: Pocket Movie Guide* • *The Two Towers: Pocket Movie Guide* • *The Return of the King: Pocket Movie Guide* • *Jean-Luc Godard: The Passion of Cinema* • *The Sacred Cinema of Andrei Tarkovsky* • *Andrei Tarkovsky: Pocket Guide.*

'It's amazing for me to see my work treated with such passion and respect. There is nothing resembling it in the U.S. in relation to my work.'
(Andrea Dworkin)

'This model monograph – it is an exemplary job, and I'm very proud that he has accorded me a couple of mentions… The subject matter of his book is beautifully organised and dead on beam.'
(Lawrence Durrell, on *The Light Eternal: A Study of J.M.W. Turner*)

'Jeremy Robinson's poetry is certainly jammed with ideas, and I find it very interesting for that reason. It's certainly a strong imprint of his personality.'
(Colin Wilson)

'*Sex-Magic-Poetry-Cornwall* is a very rich essay... It is a very good piece… vastly stimulating and insightful.'
(Peter Redgrove)

ARTS, PAINTING, SCULPTURE

web: www.crmoon.com • e-mail: cresmopub@yahoo.co.uk

The Art of Andy Goldsworthy
Andy Goldsworthy: Touching Nature
Andy Goldsworthy in Close-Up
Andy Goldsworthy: Pocket Guide
Andy Goldsworthy In America
Land Art: A Complete Guide
The Art of Richard Long
Richard Long: Pocket Guide
Land Art In Great Britain
Land Art in Close-Up
Land Art In the U.S.A.
Land Art: Pocket Guide
Installation Art in Close-Up
Minimal Art and Artists In the 1960s and After
Colourfield Painting
Land Art DVD, TV documentary
Andy Goldsworthy DVD, TV documentary
The Erotic Object: Sexuality in Sculpture From Prehistory to the Present Day
Sex in Art: Pornography and Pleasure in Painting and Sculpture
Postwar Art
Sacred Gardens: The Garden in Myth, Religion and Art
Glorification: Religious Abstraction in Renaissance and 20th Century Art
Early Netherlandish Painting
Jasper Johns
Brice MardenLeonardo da Vinci
Piero della Francesca
Giovanni Bellini
Fra Angelico: Art and Religion in the Renaissance
Mark Rothko: The Art of Transcendence
Frank Stella: American Abstract Artist
Alison Wilding: The Embrace of Sculpture
Vincent van Gogh: Visionary Landscapes
Eric Gill: Nuptials of God
Constantin Brancusi: Sculpting the Essence of Things
Max Beckmann
Gustave Moreau
Caravaggio
Egon Schiele: Sex and Death In Purple Stockings
Delizioso Fotografico Fervore: Works In Process I
Sacro Cuore: Works In Process 2
The Light Eternal: J.M.W. Turner
The Madonna Glorified: Karen Arthurs

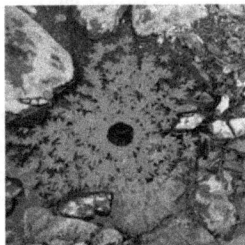

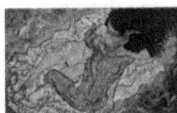

POETRY

Ursula Le Guin: *Walking In Cornwall*
Peter Redgrove: Here Comes The Flood
Peter Redgrove: Sex-Magic-Poetry-Cornwall
Dante: Selections From the *Vita Nuova*
Petrarch, Dante and the Troubadours
William Shakespeare: *The Sonnets*
William Shakespeare: Complete Poems
Blinded By Her Light: The Love-Poetry of Robert Graves
Emily Dickinson: Selected Poems
Emily Brontë: Poems
Thomas Hardy: Selected Poems
Percy Bysshe Shelley: Poems
John Keats: Selected Poems
John Keats: Poems of 1820
D.H. Lawrence: Selected Poems
Edmund Spenser: Poems
Edmund Spenser: *Amoretti*
John Donne: Poems
Henry Vaughan: Poems
Sir Thomas Wyatt: Poems
Robert Herrick: Selected Poems
Rilke: Space, Essence and Angels in the Poetry of Rainer Maria Rilke
Rainer Maria Rilke: Selected Poems
Friedrich Hölderlin: Selected Poems
Arseny Tarkovsky: Selected Poems
Paul Verlaine: Selected Poems
Novalis: *Hymns To the Night*
Arthur Rimbaud: Selected Poems
Arthur Rimbaud: *A Season in Hell*
Arthur Rimbaud and the Magic of Poetry
D.J. Enright: By-Blows
Jeremy Reed: *Brigitte's Blue Heart*
Jeremy Reed: *Claudia Schiffer's Red Shoes*
Gorgeous Little Orpheus
Radiance: New Poems
Crescent Moon Book of Nature Poetry
Crescent Moon Book of Love Poetry
Crescent Moon Book of Mystical Poetry
Crescent Moon Book of Elizabethan Love Poetry
Crescent Moon Book of Metaphysical Poetry
Crescent Moon Book of Romantic Poetry
Pagan America: New American Poetry

MEDIA, CINEMA, FEMINISM and CULTURAL STUDIES

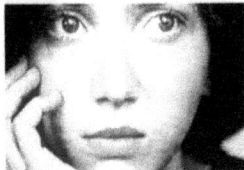

The Light Eternal is a model monograph, an exemplary job. The subject matter of the book is beautifully organised and dead on beam. (Lawrence Durrell)
It is amazing for me to see my work treated with such passion and respect. (Andrea Dworkin)
ex-Magic-Poetry-Cornwall is a very rich essay... It is like a brightly-lighted box. (Peter Redgrove)

CRESCENT MOON PUBLISHING P.O. Box 1312, Maidstone, Kent, ME14 5XU, Great Britain
0044-1622-729593 cresmopub@yahoo.co.uk www.crmoon.com

www.ingramcontent.com/pod-product-compliance
Lightning Source LLC
Chambersburg PA
CBHW070328100426
42812CB00005B/1290